Film

$21^{95}

$10^{50}

DREAMING IN THE RAIN

DREAMING
How Vancouver Became

IN THE RAIN

Hollywood North by Northwest

David Spaner

ARSENAL
PULP PRESS
VANCOUVER

ARSENAL PULP PRESS
103-1014 Homer Street
Vancouver, B.C.
Canada v6b 2w9
arsenalpulp.com

The publisher gratefully acknowledges the support of the Canada Council for the Arts and the
British Columbia Arts Council for its publishing program, and the Government of Canada
through the Book Publishing Industry Development Program for its publishing activities.

Design by Solo Corps
Cover photo courtesy Luke Carroll
Back cover photos courtesy Lynne Stopkewich, Mina Shum, Bruce Sweeney,
    John Pozer, Jason Weir, Luke Carroll
Title page photo courtesy Luke Carroll
Printed and bound in Canada

Efforts have been made to locate copyright holders of source material wherever possible.
The publisher welcomes hearing from any copyright holders of material used in this book
who have not been contacted.

NATIONAL LIBRARY OF CANADA
CATALOGUING IN PUBLICATION DATA:
    Spaner, David
    Dreaming in the rain : how Vancouver became Hollywood North by Northwest /
    David Spaner.

    Includes index.
    ISBN 1-55152-129-6

    1.Motion picture industry – British Columbia –
    Vancouver Metropolitan Area--History. I. Title.
    PN1993.5.C32V35 2003   384'.8'0971133   C2003-910738-8

For Anne Feldman Spaner,
who's always said the
movies are something to love.

CONTENTS

"Cloud so swift
the rain falling in,
Going to see a movie
called *Gunga Din*"

– Bob Dylan

FOREWORD

February 16, 2003: Director Larry Kent and actor Tom Scholte sit in a small room in the basement of the Emily Carr School of Art watching a black-and-white television screen.

Kent, Vancouver's first independent filmmaker, clicks the remote and the old images freeze. Turning to Scholte, a mainstay of the city's current indie scene, Kent says: "So, you'll have a run at the bloody thing."

While in town for a retrospective of his films, Kent, who lives in Montreal now, is putting the finishing touches to his first film, the half-hour *Hastings Street* (originally called *The Street*), never finished because of sound difficulties when it was shot in the prehistory, cinematically speaking, of 1963 Vancouver.

Kent presses the clicker again and, on screen, Alan Scarfe enters a pool hall to confront another young actor, Scott Douglas (who later changed his last name to Hylands). Kent is dubbing his actors of forty years earlier, with the younger voices of Scholte as Douglas, and actor Jonathan Scarfe, who earlier recorded his father Alan's lines.

Scholte pulls the sweater over his head, tosses it aside. "I ain't got it, Charlie," he says, body moving to the junkie dialogue. "If I have one bad day I start shaking and I get sick, real sick. Then I can't play pool."

Kent looks up at his actor, smiles. "You got it," he says, slapping Scholte on the back. "You nailed him."

While this piece of Vancouver film history is being completed forty years after it began, another shoot is taking place across town, on a rainy rooftop of a cheap Hastings Street hotel. Shot in the same neighbourhood as *Hastings Street*, this new production, a CTV movie tentatively titled *The Life* (it's also had more than one working name, including *The Street*, *The Squad*, *The Odd Squad*, and *Skid Road*), involves some of the city's heavyweight talents, including actor Bruce Greenwood (*Double Jeopardy*), director Lynne Stopkewich (*Kissed*), and writer-producer Chris Haddock (*Da Vinci's Inquest*).

§

The creative forces at work on these two Hastings Street stories – Kent and Stopkewich, Scarfe and Greenwood, Scholte and Haddock – are not as well known as some of the personalities involved in British Columbia's "bigger" productions in 2003, names such as Jennifer Lopez, Vin Diesel, and Scooby Doo.

But writing about the movies for the Vancouver daily, *The Province*, in the early years of the twenty-first century, I've come to know the work of the city's independents. They make their movies with the passion of the moviemakers of early Hollywood or mid-century Europe, and as they scrape together their projects, I find it impossible not to be increasingly drawn by their enthusiasm and belief that the movies can still matter, in stark contrast to many of the producers behind the city's U.S.-based service industry.

§

The best-known of those involved with the two *Hasting Street* films, Greenwood, like a number of expats in Los Angeles these days, often returns to the Canadian independent scene. "It's not just patriotic, it's not done out of pure sense of being Canadian," he says, in his trailer between scenes. "For me, it just makes sense to do projects that I think are good. You don't always do good projects – a lot of times you do stuff that, you know, can make you a lot of money very quickly. Sometimes you take that stuff. But this is not that. I'm not doing this for money. I'm doing this because the script is really strong. I read the first script for [CBC TV's] *Da Vinci's Inquest* and I went 'Oh, man, who is this guy? This is great writing.'"

A couple of evenings earlier, at Kent's retrospective at the Pacific Cinémathèque – "Exile on Main Street (& Hastings)" – the warmth among his Vancouver ensemble of the 1960s, including actors Lynn Stewart, Alan Scarfe, Scott Hylands, Patricia Dahlquist, Diane Griffith, and Angela Gann, had lit up the room when they joined him at the front of the theatre for a Q&A. As the evening drew to a close, I overheard Kent, saying softly to himself: "This evening was magical."

Now, back on the rooftop, Greenwood's movie's publicist Bill Vigars says that on the night of the retrospective, his old friend Hylands stayed over at his suburban Burnaby home.

"Scott was really high before he went," he says. "When he came home he was like a giddy little kid."

§

Vancouver's film and television production industry has become so diverse that entire books could be written about animation, documentary, short and experimental films, or television. The focus of *Dreaming in the Rain* is narrative feature films, though it does touch on a couple of particularly influential tv series (*Da Vinci's Inquest* and *The X-Files*).

The quotes in *Dreaming in the Rain*, with a few exceptions attributed to other sources, are from interviews I conducted for this book or, in some cases, publications I've written for (particularly *The Province*).

Among those I interviewed: Beverly Aadland, Lindsay Allen, Robert Altman, John Arnett, Jennifer Beals, Sonja Bennett, Frida Betrani, Beret Borsos, Jay Brazeau, Kim Campbell, Nicholas Campbell, Stephen J. Cannell, Chris Carter, Christine Chatelain, Gina Chiarelli, Babz Chula, Rachael Lee Cook, Gavin Craig, Martin Cummins, Patricia Dahlquist, Jack Darcus, Benicio Del Toro, Alex Diakun, Robert Dauphne, Jack DeGovia, Marya Delver, Kathleen Duborg, Madeleine Duff, Dean English, Jessica Fraser, Patricia Gage, Vincent Gale, Al Gowan, John Gray, Siobhan Gray, Bruce Greenwood, Chris Haddock, Piers Handling, Joshua Jackson, Katie Keating, Larry Kent, Greg Krizman, Michael Lambert, Nicholas Lea, Nick Mancuso, Sue Mathew, Sarah McLachlan, Beverlee Miller, Michael Moriarty, Carrie-Anne Moss, Jane Mundy, Christopher Nolan, Lee Novak, Sandra Oh, Ken Olin, Al Pacino, Gwyneth Paltrow, Molly Parker, Barbara Parkins, Frank Partiak, Carol Pastinsky, Hugh Pickett, Carly Pope, Parker Posey, John Pozer, Peter Prior, Ben Ratner, Sarah-Jane Redmond, Donnelly Rhodes, Dal Richards, Morrie Ruvinsky, Alan Scarfe, Leonard Schein, Tom Scholte, Michael Seel, Pia Shandel, Helen Shaver, Mina Shum, Nancy Sivak, Scott Smith, Sylvia Spring, Sylvester Stallone, Lynne Stopkewich, Hilary Swank, Bruce Sweeney, Lee Tamahori, Ian Tracey, John Travolta, Mel Tuck, Geoff Turner, Bill Vigars, Ross Weber, Anne Wheeler, Mike White, Barbara Williams, Sandy Wilson. I thank them all.

For providing photographs, special gratitude to Luke Carroll, Larrry Kent, Beverlee Miller, John Pozer, Morrie Ruvinsky, Mina Shum, Lynne Stopkewich, Bruce Sweeney, and all at the Pacific Press library.

BABY PICTURES

1

The last time I had seen director Lynne Stopkewich she was glammed up, standing in an overdressed lineup waiting to get into a Vancouver International Film Festival gala party. This time, Stopkewich's face peeks through her jacket's hood as she stands in pouring rain, waist-deep in a freezing-cold river in Maple Ridge, the town near Vancouver where she's directing her second feature, *Suspicious River*.

"Just so everyone's knows – our legs are frozen," someone in the river shouts to the crew huddled on the muddy shore. Stopkewich finally emerges from the water, gives her wet gloves a shake and exchanges knowing expressions with actor Molly Parker, who sits under a plastic canopy on a small dock, trying to light a match.

"Molly's mom lives a block away," says soaked hair-stylist Lee Novak. "She brought over baked potatoes and a jar of roasted assorted nuts and some special tea. Typical mom."

"Are you cold?" Stopkewich asks child actor Katie Keating, who plays a young version of Parker in the movie.

"Really cold," Keating says with a nod.

"It's a nightmare," Stopkewich says. "Thank god it's a dark story."

§

Lynne Stopkewich is one of those people so utterly suited to her calling that she actually looks far more content making a movie in ice water than schmoozing at a warm, well-fed movie gala. And Stopkewich is not alone. She's one of a talented group of filmmakers who met while attending the film studies program at the University of British Columbia in the late 1980s and would go on to form the nuclei of a West Coast Wave that's among the most innovative and provocative film scenes anywhere.

The UBC group is just one part of the Vancouver film story. Another part features the parade of American film and TV personalities, from John Travolta to Stephen J. Cannell, who have made Vancouver the third largest film industry in North America, and the target of Hollywood protests. But the Vancouver film story goes way back to the beginning of movie-making itself.

§

Stopkewich, in one way, is the perfect Vancouver director. She made a movie, after all, about a seemingly all-Canadian young woman who, underneath her commonplace surface, was having sex with dead guys.

Truth be told, Vancouver is not a particularly lively city. It doesn't have the noisy nightlife of Montreal or the diverse ethnic neighbourhoods of Toronto. What Vancouver does have, like Stopkewich's art, is an alluring dichotomy. On Vancouver's surface, there is a stillness, a ravishing natural beauty that seems to leave some dumbstruck, content to sit and marvel at the vista with nothing to say. In the city's underground, though, there have always been restive social and cultural movements, chafing to shout about plenty.

Polarization is intrinsic to Vancouver's history. For practically the entire second half of the twentieth century provincial politics was dominated by the Social Credit Party, one of the last remnants of the far-right movements of the 1930s, and the New Democratic Party, a vestige of the democratic socialist populism from the same period. Vancouver's hippie and punk scenes would become known throughout the international underground, while most people in the city barely knew they existed. Even Vancouver's physical setting contributes to the dichotomy – it's a place where the natural world is minutes from downtown, where the skyline is a mixed marriage of skyscrapers and mountains.

So, it's not surprising that polarization would define the relationship between the two film groupings in Vancouver. The better-known U.S. service industry, which produces mainstream "product," is a reflection of the Vancouver that's staid and risk-free. The city's independent filmmakers, from Larry Kent's group in the 1960s to Stopkewich and her friends today, are a particularly feisty bunch that reflects the Vancouver that's nervy and defiant.

The movie-making that has emerged in the city, almost entirely since the 1960s, is a microcosm of the larger film world. Nowhere else, though, is its two paths – the choice facing filmmakers everywhere – more clear, more polarized than in Vancouver.

The movies and the city of Vancouver have virtually identical birthdates. They have grown parallel to each other, so it's fitting that the film world's two divergent roads would meet in Vancouver at the beginning of the twenty-first century.

§

The actual moment of birth of the movies is uncertain, with inventors in several countries pursuing the notion of moving pictures in the 1870s and 1880s. France's Etienne Jules Marey unveiled in 1882 a photographic gun that could take twelve pictures a second. His images of birds are the oldest pictures in motion. In 1885, George Eastman and William Walker replaced Marey's glass plates with a gelatin-coated roll of paper called film. Four years later, it would be replaced by a plastic roll called celluloid.

While all this moving-picture conceiving was going on, the city of Vancouver was being born. On the west coast of Canada, immigrant workers were bringing the Canadian Pacific Railway to Burrard Inlet and, finally, in April 1886, the town of Granville was renamed Vancouver. In the decade after Vancouver's incorporation, electric lighting arrived, Stanley Park was opened, streetcar lines appeared, and the first Granville Street Bridge was constructed.

Meanwhile, in the reel world, inventors in the U.S. and Europe were racing to perfect cameras and projectors. "Peep show" viewing machines with ninety-second images made their debut at the 1893 Chicago World's Fair. Following the fair, they were installed in "kinetoscope parlours" across North America. The marketing of new movie technology wasn't nearly the instant, efficient machine it would become in the twentieth century. By the time the kinetoscope finally arrived in Vancouver for an exhibition in August 1897, the first large movie projector had been exhibiting big-screen motion pictures in New York vaudeville theatres for two years.

The following year, on October 7, John Schuberg set up a projector in an empty warehouse on Vancouver's Cordova Street and showed what was billed as newsreels from the Spanish-American War, but was shot in New Jersey. In 1902, John Schuberg opened the city's first movie theatre, The Edison Electric, on Cordova. A couple of years later, images of Vancouver were screened in theatres for the first time – shots of horses boarding a steamship for the Klondike.

The earliest films shot in B.C. were documents of mining, logging, and fishing. These "educational" films showed off the province's spectacular scenery, with The Edison Electric showing early movie audiences across North America and Europe images of the gold rush or the Rockies, as seen from moving trains. The Canadian Pacific Railway produced its own promotional films too, dispatching British cinematographer Joseph Rosenthal to create *Living Canada* in 1901, a series with such stirring titles as *During a Blizzard* and *Through the Beavermouth Canyon*. The railroad company was also behind the first narrative films, shorts shot in 1910 to glamourize west coast opportunities for love and employment, including the indelible *A Wedding Trip from Montreal Through Canada to Hong Kong*.

The best of the early documentaries made in B.C. was Edward Curtis's extraordinary 1914 feature *In the Land of the Head Hunters*, about native culture on the west coast. There were a handful of silent features made in B.C., including *The Alaskan* (1924) and *Wilderness Patrol* (1928). A.D. (Arthur David) Kean was the most prolific of the silent filmmakers who shot in B.C. "Cowboy" Kean, born in Manitoba and raised in the U.S., followed his newsreels, documentaries, and an early feature, *Told in the Hills* (1917), with his grandiose *Policing the Plains*, a $100,000-plus history of the North West Mounted Police shot in the Kamloops area in 1927.

Victoria's Nell Shipman became the first born-in-B.C. filmmaker of note. At fifteen, she was starring in a touring company's production of *The Barrier*. By twenty, she was in Hollywood, writing scripts. After writing and starring in a string of films, including *God's Country and the Woman* (1915), Shipman returned to Canada to star in *Back to God's Country* (1919), which she also scripted. Shot in Alberta, it was the most popular Canadian film of the era. Returning to the U.S., Shipman would go on to form her own production company and direct films.

Unlike Shipman, B.C. during the silent era was pretty reserved overall, and complaints of lewd, suggestive cinema resulted in the formation of the B.C. Motion Picture Act of 1913, establishing a provincial censor. It was particularly hard-nosed, banning everything from Sergei Eisenstein's *Battleship Potemkin* to the politically charged protests featured in newsreels of the 1930s. Scenes would sometimes be edited to replace the U.S. flag with the Union Jack.

Movies weren't the only target. In 1912, city council passed a measure banning public gatherings. But while one segment of Vancouver was devising ways to censor, another was waging a free-speech fight against the ban, drawing thousands of protesters to the Powell Street grounds. One of the organizations behind the campaign was the Industrial Workers of the World, a rabble-rousing syndicalist union which was given its famous nickname, the Wobblies, in Vancouver in 1911 when, according to lore, an immigrant Chinese restaurateur's pronunciation of iww was "I wobble wobble."

This city of immigrants, mostly from the British Isles, was drawn to the new entertainment from the beginning. There were eight movie theatres in the city by 1913. Vancouver would remain overwhelmingly British much longer than Toronto or Winnipeg, but in its downtown Strathcona district, Chinese, Italians, Jews, Japanese, Croatians, and other immigrant cultures each had its own street or more. The movies were a dream world for waves of new Canadians who packed local cinemas, learning to speak the language while the movies were learning to talk.

Following the success of the first movie with sound, *The Jazz Singer*, in 1927, Hollywood studios scrambled to assemble the talent to make talking pictures. Like most anyone who saw them, Vancouverites were entranced by the talkies and a few who would go on to make their lives in the movies.

In the first half of the twentieth century, one had to leave Vancouver if determined to be in pictures. One of the early starstruck locals to make her way south was Peggy Yvonne Middleton, who grew up on Comox Street in Vancouver's West End, working as an usher at the Orpheum when she wasn't watching the movies herself. One of her first jobs was in the chorus line at the old Palomar supper club.

"She was in the line and she kept agitating with the owner, Hymie Singer, and me to do a solo spot," said veteran Vancouver band leader Dal Richards. "Hymie was kind of reluctant, she was such a kid." But they gave Middleton a chance and she performed "Top Hat" complete with top hat and cane. "It was good," Richards recalled. "With her persistence, it was clear that she had ambitions, no wish to stay in a chorus line."

"She was a terrific Spanish dancer," said Robert Dauphne, who attended the June Roper School of Dancing with Middleton, "and then the next thing I knew she was in a movie doing the dance of the seventh veil or something."

Middleton made the move to Hollywood, taking her Italian mother's maiden name, De Carlo, along the way. Publicists billed Yvonne De Carlo "the most beautiful girl in the world," and she would become the first celebrated movie star from Vancouver. After arriving in Hollywood in 1942, she landed bit parts (*Road to Morocco, Shanghai Gesture*) before starring in 1945's *Salome – Where She Danced*. She became a fan magazine "cover girl," the exotic seductress in a succession of 1940s' films (*Slave Girl, Black Bart*). Most of her pictures were B-grade but she also appeared in bigger-budgeted productions such as *Captain's Paradise* and *The Ten Commandments*.

When De Carlo became involved with Howard Hughes, she returned to the city with the billionaire playboy and they stopped by the Panorama Roof nightclub at the Hotel Vancouver, where Richards was playing. "I sat down," Richards recalls, "and he said, 'How do you do?'

And that's the last I heard of from Howard Hughes." The billionaire recluse sat quietly while De Carlo asked her old friend for a Vancouver update. "She was extremely friendly, a very nice person. Strictly down to earth. Whatever she was doing down in Hollywood didn't influence her personality."

De Carlo may have been the best-known but she was hardly the only British Columbian to go Hollywood in the 1930s and '40s. There was art director Richard Day, of Victoria, who won seven Oscars for films such

Yvonne De Carlo.

20

as *How Green Was My Valley, The Little Foxes, A Streetcar Named Desire,* and *On the Waterfront.* There were actors such as John Ireland, Raymond Burr, and Alexis Smith. And there was Mary Livingstone.

When vaudeville comic Benny Kubelsky was in Vancouver playing the Orpheum with the Marx Brothers in 1922, he met Sadie Marks at her family's Passover seder at 1649 Nelson Street. In his autobiography, *Sunday Nights at Seven,* Kubelsky would write that during dinner the four traditional Passover questions were asked, "the first of which I should have heeded: 'Why is this night different from all other nights?' It was the most important night of my life, but I didn't know it." Sadie Marks, who would change her name to Mary Livingstone, would marry Kubelsky, who would change his name to Jack Benny. They became a legendary comedy team in movies, radio, and television.

There were others with more passing connections to Vancouver, including Vancouver-born Katherine DeMille (adopted by producer Cecil DeMille, she had supporting roles in films such as *Charlie Chan at the Olympics*), June Havoc (born in Vancouver when her parents were passing through on the vaudeville circuit, she had supporting roles in *Gentleman's Agreement, My Sister Eileen*), Anne Rutherford (shortly after she was born in Vancouver, her family moved to California, where she become an actor best known as Polly Benedict in the Andy Hardy movie series), and Victor Jory (Yukon-born but attended school in Vancouver before heading south to appear in many films, including *Gone With the Wind* and *Dodge City*).

Others with Hollywood connections would show up on B.C.'s doorstep. As June Havoc or Mary Livingstone could attest, Vancouver was a popular stop on the old vaudeville circuit. One Saturday night in October 1933, Texas Guinan – movie actor, singer, risque entertainer, New York nightclub owner renowned for flouting prohibition liquor laws – played the Beacon Theatre. After performing, she looked forward to a day off in the prohibition-free town. "I like these Canadian Sundays," she said. By Monday, however, Guinan was too ill to perform, and was booked into Vancouver General Hospital, where on November 5 she died from an abdominal infection.

The first Oscar winner to make his mark in Vancouver actually did so as a boxer. Jack Johnson, scorned by much of white America, had taken his title on the road. But the first black heavyweight champ received a chilly reception in B.C. He travelled first to Victoria, where he was refused lodging at the St Francis Hotel, whose manager claimed it was observing the "colour line." In Vancouver, he agreed to fight a boxer from Tacoma, a last-minute replacement for Denver Ed Martin. The boxer turned out to be Victor McLaglen, who would go on to win a best-actor Academy Award in 1935 for his role in *The Informer*. But to a Vancouver fight crowd on March 10, 1909, the future Oscar winner was just a little-known, awkward brawler who was knocked down in the first round and didn't fare much better for the rest of the bout.

The next year, an itinerant young Englishman, William Henry Pratt, arrived in the city he called "the metropolis of the west." Applying for a job with the Ray Brandon Players of Kamloops in the B.C. Interior, Pratt changed his name to Boris Karloff. He would remain with the touring company for more than a year but in those pre-Hollywood North days, there was little employment for an acting hopeful, so he eventually wound up working construction on what would be the Pacific National Exhibition. The ten-hour days and blistered hands were horrifying to the future movie monster, so Karloff tried his hand at selling real estate. "Probably one of the greatest things that happened to me was in Vancouver when I was twenty-two years old," Karloff would recall (in Peter Underwood's *Horror Man: The Life of Boris Karloff*). "Someone offered me a half interest in a gold mine for 100 pounds. I had the money, too. I asked the advice of a banker friend and he said, 'No.' That mine was subsequently sold for three-million pounds. But imagine what would happened to me. It would have ruined me." Instead, he moved on to Hollywood and *Frankenstein*.

SOME BRITISH COLUMBIANS WHO ENTERED THE FILM WORLD OF THE 1930s AND 1940s

Raymond Burr (New Westminster). Descended from a pioneering New Westminster family, he moved to Hollywood in the mid-1940s. Played the heavy in Hitchcock's superb *Rear Window* and other films but is best known as television's Perry Mason and Ironside.

Edward Dmytryk (Grand Forks). Directed some great performances by Bogart and others in some good movies (*Crossfire*, *The Caine Mutiny*) but is best known as a member of the blacklisted Hollywood 10 who turned on the others, naming names during the McCarthy era.

Victoria Hopper (Vancouver). A lead in British films of the 1930s (*Lorna Doone*, *The Mill on the Floss*).

§

Although Vancouver was enthralled with the new talking pictures, some even daring to head south to participate, the movies were not actually made in Vancouver. There were several failed attempts to start a film industry in the province, most notably Lion's Gate Cinemas of Canada in 1927. Lion's Gate (no relation to the current film studio with the same name) was to be a Hollywood-style studio built on fifty acres on Vancouver's North Shore, surrounded by a Beverly Hills-like neighbourhood. But the inclement weather and small population made the real Hollywood a more attractive location.

When talking-picture production did arrive in B.C. it would first come to Victoria, not Vancouver, and it had more to do with England than Canada. In 1927, the British parliament passed the Cinematograph Films Act, guaranteeing that a percentage of screen time in the United Kingdom's theatres would be devoted to films produced in the British Empire. To take advantage of the Act, Kenneth Bishop came to Victoria from California in 1932, with plans to transform the small city into the first Hollywood North. He enlisted Kathleen Dunsmuir, of the wealthy Dunsmuir family, to join in developing Commonwealth Productions.

Bishop and Dunsmuir, who had visions of her own movie stardom, leased a show building from the B.C. Agricultural Association in the Willows Park area and converted it into an unadorned studio. They started with *Crimson Paradise*, the first talkie shot in B.C., funded by $40,000 of the Dunsmuir family's money. Directed by Bob Hill, it's the story of young man who leaves the

John Ireland (Vernon). First went to England, where he acted in repertory groups, then Hollywood, where he received an Oscar nomination for *All the King's Men* and appeared in the western classic *Red River*.

John Qualen (Vancouver). A favourite of John Ford, he was a supporting player in *Arrowsmith*, *The Searchers*, *The Man Who Shot Liberty Vallance*, and *The Grapes of Wrath*.

Alexis Smith (Penticton). Starred in Hollywood films of the 1940s, including *Of Human Bondage* and *Conflict*. Decades later, appeared with fellow British Columbian Yvonne De Carlo in *Broadway's Follies*, for which she won a Tony.

Alan Young (Victoria). Debuted in the 1946 hit *Margie* but is better known for his role much later in TV's *Mr Ed*.

Baby Pictures

23

urban pressures of Victoria circa 1933 for the Cariboo.

Ivan Ackery, the manager of Victoria's Capitol Theatre, felt compelled to go all out with a gala premiere on December 14, 1933. "I had a hell of a time to sell my home office [Famous Players] on it," Ackery told *The Province* newspaper. "They said they'd give me the week before Christmas – that's the worst week in the year in show business. I had 20,000 leaflets dropped from a plane. They said: 'Come to the premiere of the first all-Canadian talking picture made in Victoria.' People thought I was mad. But I wanted action."

Victoria residents apparently embraced the opportunity to see on screen such local landmarks as Beacon Hill Park and Craigdarroch Castle (where the Dunsmuirs had once lived). According to a newspaper account: "Every notable Victorian was present and the picture itself, as well as its premiere, was regarded as the season's social event . . . shown in the middle of the night to the city's highest circle of society."

Filling the Capitol's 1,312 seats was the highlight of Crimson Paradise's short life. Afterward, it moved on the Vancouver's Pantages Theatre for a week, then went nowhere. "It was a real turkey," said Ackery. "So lousy it was good. Everyone wanted to see the local people and local scenes."

Bishop's next production, *The Secrets of Chinatown*, drew groans from audiences and complaints from the Chinese consul in Vancouver that it stereotyped Asians as criminals. Having bombed twice, Bishop left town, leaving Dunsmuir $50,000 the poorer. Still, Bishop was unswayed. Back in Hollywood, he pitched his Victoria concept to Columbia Pictures and, eager to break into the British market with B-grade pictures, the studio bought it. Bishop returned to B.C. to operate Central Films and produce a series of third-rate Hollywood films (none cost more than $65,000) in Victoria during the next few years, including one of Rita Hayworth's early movies, *Convicted*. Most (*Lucky Corrigan, Across the Border*) were instantly forgettable.

In 1938 Britain's parliament revamped the Cinematograph Films Act to close the loophole, thus eliminating the need for films produced in the "colonies." Central Film Studios was scrapped in April 1939 and Bishop died in Vancouver two years later.

Central did not produce quality films but it left a mark nonetheless: the first sustained feature-film production in B.C. The Bishop films were also the first "runaway" productions – the beginning of the low-budget film schlock an American service industry would bring to B.C. because of some perceived commercial advantage.

But B.C. movie audiences in the 1930s barely noticed the Victoria productions. They wanted to see the made-in-Hollywood screwball comedies, gangster pictures, musicals, and westerns in which, like a dream, you might catch a glimpse of yourself in the dark. Could be Peggy Yvonne Middleton transported by Ginger Rogers, Steve Brodie looking up at Tom Joad.

§

Another Vancouver day, sixty years before Lynne Stopkewich stood in the rain shooting *Suspicious River*, Steve Brodie was nearly beaten to death on a downtown street. It would be known as Vancouver's Bloody Sunday – June 19, 1938. Hundreds of unemployed workers had been occupying the art gallery and post office for a month to protest the desperate poverty and unemployment of the Depression. That Sunday, the RCMP tear-gassed the art gallery and stormed the post office, swinging clubs and whips, sending organizer Brodie and thirty-six others to hospital, some of the "sitdowners" breaking downtown windows as they retreated. That same day, more than 10,000 people showed up at the Powell Street grounds to protest the attack. Alderwoman Helena Gutteridge drew huge cheers upon addressing the matter of broken windows. "If the beaten and gassed men fleeing Hastings Street happened to damage a little property in retaliation, who are we to say that they were wrong?"

Such was the mood in 1930s Vancouver. Many who occupied the downtown buildings would be in downtown theatres not long after to see *The Grapes of Wrath*, with its depiction of Depression-era defiance. "I'm right here to tell you, mister, there ain't nobody gonna push me off my land," Dust Bowl refugee Ulee Graves vows. "My grandpa took up this land seventy years ago. My pa was born here. We was all born on it and some of us was killed on it. And some of us died on it. And that's what makes it ours, being born on it and working on it and dying on it. And not no piece of paper with writing on it. . . ."

Having endured the Depression, many in that audience watching Ulee Graves had the sense they were seeing themselves, a connection between a Vancouver audience and a Hollywood movie that had happened before and would occur again and again. And the actor playing Ulee Graves was more like them, at least in one way, than most might imagine – John Qualen was from Vancouver.

LAST DAYS

2

The Cadillac ambulance was flashing red as it raced Errol Flynn's body through the neon night, wailing down city streets, over the rickety Cambie Street Bridge, to the Vancouver General emergency room.

"They came out and they said, 'We've done everything we could, I'm sorry,' and I guess I went hysterical," recalls Flynn's companion Beverly Aadland. "I was banging my head and my hands on the ground and they took me off to a room. I think I was in a straitjacket because I was trying to get into the room with him."

The fifty-year-old Flynn, one of Hollywood's most famous movie stars, had come with seventeen-year-old Aadland to sell his yacht. His sudden death put Vancouver on front pages around the world and a spotlight on Aadland, who for years would be vilified in the press as a "bad girl." Reached in a southern California town she doesn't want mentioned, with a married name she doesn't want printed ("My life is very private now"), Aadland spoke forty years after the movie star's death that made her a household name in Vancouver.

Aadland and Flynn liked the view of the bay from the tony British Properties. "The lights of the city, just beautiful," Aadland says. "When we were there it happened to be the time of the year where it's just crystal clear."

The Vancouver night they watched was bathed in neon. The city had come through the Depression and the war and, in the 1950s, was trying on a pretence of picture-perfect normalcy. It was a sensibility reflected on the city's movie screens. The Hollywood glamourization of everyday life was at its peak, with the stylized imaginings of director Douglas Sirk's work (*Written on the Wind*) and other popular films (*A Summer Place*).

But when Aadland and Flynn showed up in October 1959, a new decade was looming that would bring huge cultural shifts. So, their days in Vancouver weren't just the last of a movie star, they were the last days of an era.

And even in the 1950s, past the manicured hedges of the Kerrisdale and British Properties neighbourhoods, the little port city had a nightlife with the swagger of a Jersey saloon singer and steakhouses and lounges out of *L.A. Confidential*. CABARET PERMIT SUSPENDED AS CITY PURGES NIGHT CLUBS, shouted the *Vancouver Province*'s banner headline on October 14, 1959 – the day Flynn died.

"I liked the way everybody dressed," Aadland says. "They dressed up to go to the store, to do things. I don't understand today. People get on an airplane like they're ready to clean the car. And I still dress."

To some, Flynn was a charming cad, a devilish Tasmanian who had swashbuckled his way to stardom in such movies as *Captain Blood* and *The Adventures of Robin Hood*. To others, he was simply a cad. His autobiography was titled *My Wicked, Wicked Ways*. He had been up on statutory rape charges; there were also stories that he had wanted to fight alongside the fascists in 1930s Spain and had even been a Nazi agent. Flynn's defenders claimed he was a double agent for the allies. There is little doubt, however, Flynn made his a "double" whenever possible. When he arrived to sell his yacht, *The Zaca*, to West Vancouver stockbroker George Caldough, he was a notorious drinker whose star was falling.

John Arnett was a young reporter with the *Vancouver Province* covering Flynn's October 8 airport arrival. "Suddenly this elderly looking guy walked off the plane with this young girl on his arm," Arnett says. "He had been drinking on the plane and he threw up and there was a

Errol Flynn with Beverly Aadland.

little bit of vomit on his shirt. Even as we stood around interviewing him he was knocking back the vodka."

Aadland remembers the rain that first day in Vancouver. "That's why he had a bowler hat on and my hair was all wet in that one picture that was taken at the airport."

Michael Lambert was an assistant manager at the Hotel Georgia when Flynn registered. "I remember him well. He came downstairs with some other people and I escorted them to a car that was waiting on Howe Street. I recall him being such a physical wreck that we helped him into the seat next to the driver and I had to lift his leg into the car."

Frank Partiak, a Hotel Georgia bartender at the time, recalled Flynn's cool companion, forever in sunglasses, who easily passed for twenty-one, the then-legal drinking age. "He was with this young lady who was underage we all know now," Partiak said.

"Because I was with Errol Flynn," Aadland says, "nobody ever questioned."

§

There were a couple of events in 1950s Vancouver that were portents of a more unruly future, indicators that politics and culture weren't so homogeneous as some liked to pretend. The man at the centre of each occasion was a film star, although that profession didn't top either's resume: Paul Robeson and Elvis Presley.

The first incident involved Robeson – opera singer, Shakespearean actor, writer, movie star, social critic, folk singer, all-America football player, lawyer. All this and a socialist too, which was enough to get him blacklisted during McCarthy's decade. The U.S. State Department, learning Robeson planned to give a concert presented by the miners' union in Vancouver in January 1952, used legislation enabling it, "during the existence of the national emergency," to prevent the departure of certain citizens. When Robeson arrived by car at the Canadian border in Blaine, Washington, he was stopped by Immigration and Naturalization Service officials who told the press they were acting on authority of the State Department. Robeson returned to Seattle, and the following day used a long-distance telephone hookup to sing and speak to 2,000 trade unionists at the miners' convention in Vancouver. The fired-up union decided to organize a concert at the Peace Arch border park. In May, Robeson stood at the border singing to 5,000 Americans, watching from the U.S. side of the line, and more than 25,000 Canadians who had gathered on the Vancouver side.

The second event took place at Empire Stadium in the summer of 1957. Presley's Northwest U.S. tour had passed relatively quietly, but when he started up his pelvis in Vancouver the crowd gave a thundering roar and vaulted the barricades. During the thirty-five-minute show, young Vancouverites repeatedly charged a police line protecting the stage. And when Elvis's performance ended, rock 'n' rollers tossed bottles and went toe-to-toe with police. The next day, Presley's manager, Colonel Tom Parker, merrily read aloud a local newspaper account of the chaos.

§

Beverly Aadland was named after the legendary Beverly Hills Hotel, where her father had been a bartender. She was a bright child actor who had bits in several movies (*Gigi*, *The Eddie Cantor Story*) and grew up quickly. "I went from eleven to twelve and five-foot tall to five-foot-six and I couldn't work as a child actor."

Aadland skipped a couple of grades, so her classmates were older and the people she worked with were even older. At thirteen, she was a dancer at the Las Vegas Sahara. "I had kind of that smart-aleck attitude. It wasn't so much that I knew what I was talking about. It was just that I was around so many dancers and stage people that I picked up their conversation."

She met Flynn while shooting *Marjorie Morningstar* a month after turning fifteen. "He wanted me to read for a play, believe it or not. That's what he said. I bought it."

Aaland's father disowned her over the relationship. "My mother thought he was just a benefactor who wanted to further my career."

By the time she came to Vancouver they had been together for two years. "I didn't really understand what love was but I felt a very strange sensation and I never wanted to be apart from him and we very rarely were."

One thing Flynn couldn't do was drive a car "worth a hoot," she says. Did they have drivers? "I drove occasionally." Did she have a licence? "No, but I drove."

During their six days in B.C., they moved out of the Georgia and into the Caldough home on Eyremont in the British Properties. They also went on the town, dining at the Hotel Vancouver's Panorama Roof, visiting nightclubs. Promoter Hugh Pickett was at the Cave nightclub to see the Kirby Stone Four when Flynn and Aadland walked in. "He just looked terrible. He just looked drunk, to start. I wouldn't have known it was Errol Flynn from the movies." *Last Days*

§

With no film industry to attract Hollywood notables, they were a rare sight in the Vancouver of 1959. National Film Board documentaries and television production existed through the 1950s but features were scarce once Columbia's Victoria studio departed in 1937. The last spurt of cinematic activity occurred during the Second World War. The 1942 Columbia picture *Commandos Strike at Dawn* brought actors' actor Paul Muni to B.C. as Vancouver Island subbed for German-occupied Norway. In 1945, Norway was portrayed by the Rocky Mountains in *Son of Lassie* with Peter Lawford.

The Canadian Co-operative Project was a somewhat cynical plan by studios to maintain cordial relations with Canada's authorities by making the odd film with a Canadian theme. *Canadian Pacific*, about the building of the railway, was shot in B.C. in 1948, as was *Cariboo Trail* a year later. They were hardly authentic, though, and no one noticed when the project faded.

There was a lot of talk, but virtually no production, during the next decade. Something called Dominion Productions had big, but ill-fated, plans for a Vancouver studio in the late 1940s. In 1952, local actor-gone Hollywood Yvonne De Carlo arrived to announce the formation of the Vancouver Film Company. Again, nothing.

The 1950s were a time when the arrival of Hollywood personalities, even apparently wholesome ones, was unusual enough to pique the collective curiosity of much of the city. The visit of Aadland and the rarely wholesome Flynn was enough to shake one's belief in Hollywood glamour.

§

The day Aadland and Flynn were to return to L.A., a newspaper column mentioned that he had taken a bow at the Cave. The same column noted that pianist Glenn Gould was coming to town and his uncle, Dr Grant Gould, would entertain him.

Caldough started to drive his guests to the old Vancouver airport on suburban Lulu Island. But during the trip, Flynn had so much back pain that near West 10th Avenue, Caldough turned the car around and made for the West End apartment of a doctor he knew: Grant Gould. In Gould's penthouse at 1310 Burnaby Street, Flynn regaled everyone with Hollywood stories, then excused himself to lay down in the doctor's bedroom. At the door, he turned and said: "I shall return."

Aadland used Gould's telephone to rescheduled their flight for the next day. "I came in to tell him what I had done and give him a kiss and he said, 'Wake me up in about an hour.' So about an hour later I went in and he was very cold. And I tried to wake him up and I. . . ." Her voice breaks and she pauses a moment. "Oh, this is hard . . . and I screamed for help and started mouth to mouth and . . . then the paramedics got there and as I said, the rest is fuzzy. They shooed me out of the room and I went out on the veranda. . . . It was clear and the moon was full. I remember looking up at the moon and praying."

Fire department paramedics were trying to revive Flynn when ambulance driver Al Gowan arrived. "He was over the hill but he was well-known. We carried a lot of people from time to time that were wheels. We treated everyone well but we knew we had to treat him with kid gloves – just to protect your own butt."

Gowan says Aadland was "totally distraught. She was in love with the guy and she's losing her guy, so she should be upset. She wanted to go with him and no one was going to stop her from going to the hospital."

Aadland sat next to Gowan as he rushed Flynn to hospital.

"She was standing beside me at the hospital. When she was told that he was DOA, she caved. She fainted and fell into my arms and I took her to a chair. Nurses came to help. That was the last I saw of her."

The Province's police reporter Terry Ross was at the station when word came to get the "blue sheet" report on Flynn's death. "Poor Errol," he recalls, "died of everything." The death certificate listed myocardial infarction, coronary thrombosis, coronary atherosclerosis, liver degeneration, liver sclerosis, and diverticulosis of the colon.

Aadland returned to the British Properties "a walking zombie" and was besieged by the media. She was taken to a funeral home to select Flynn's casket. "I pointed to a grey one and turned around and walked out . . . it wasn't handled well, let's put it that way. I wouldn't put anybody else through it."

Flynn's body was sent by train to L.A. Aadland's plane home stopped in Seattle. "The reporters were jumping over the partition to take pictures of me." The pandemonium was repeated in L.A. "I was in a fog for six months."

But she would remain in the news for years. There were suits over the will, battles with her mother, lie-detector tests, barroom confrontations, a boyfriend-turned-assailant who wound up dead. In her twenties, she crooned standards in nightclubs across the U.S. An *L.A. Examiner* story about her was headlined: CASE HISTORY OF A BAD GIRL.

"I had no preparation for death or the bombardment of the press," she says. "I was in places I wasn't at, I was doing things I wasn't doing, I was with people I wasn't with . . . I was called a hooker. I was called all kinds of things."

For instance, a *National Enquirer* reporter wrote she had caused a drunken scene at an L.A. club. Later, he was pointed out to her in a restaurant and she "picked up his eggs and put them in his lap. And then I turned around and walked back to my table and continued to eat my breakfast.

"I probably don't have the most tact in the world."

It's the stuff that would have won a young man the James Dean Memorial Rebel Hero Award but there's a double standard that makes one man's "cool guy," one woman's "bad girl." What is more appalling than anything Aadland might have done was the media of the day's refusal to cut any slack to a spirited young woman who had been through several degrees of hell.

Two brief marriages ended when her husbands strayed. "I didn't have the patience to work it out or try to. I just grabbed my gowns, my music, my jewelry and split," she says. "They wanted the notoriety of being my husband. . . . And I wanted to have a home and children."

Today, Aadland has been married for more than thirty years and has a daughter. "We swim and dance around the house and talk a lot." She also watches movies, enjoying *My Favorite Year*, a 1982 comedy about a flamboyant actor loosely based on Flynn. "I thought it was the funniest thing I'd ever seen."

There are a thousand good reasons why in retrospect Aadland should hate Flynn. But she doesn't. And in an age of convenient, easy disavowals of the past, there's something refreshing about someone so unrepentant after all these years.

When did she settle down?

"I still haven't," she says with a laugh. "I haven't lost my spirit. I still wear sunglasses all the time."

THE PEOPLE VERSUS LARRY KENT

3

The spirit of the 1950s lived well into the sixties in Vancouver. In July 1962, comic Lenny Bruce, who had an abrasive, honest approach that would revolutionize stand-up, opened to a packed house at Isy's Supper Club in Vancouver. The following day, his caustic performance was attacked in the *Vancouver Sun* by columnist Jack Wasserman. That evening, the Morality Squad showed up at Isy's and told owner Isy Walters his licence would be suspended unless Bruce's run was cancelled. When the operator of the Inquisition Coffee House found out, he stepped forward with an offer to present the remainder of the performances. Bruce agreed, but the city's licensing boss announced that the Inquisition's licence would be lifted if he performed. Bruce finally threw up his hands, vowing never again to perform in Vancouver.

Not everyone in the city agreed with the way Bruce had been treated. Some were part of a small artsy bohemian community that hung out at the Bunk House, which featured folk music and poetry readings, and the Cellar, a jazzy club that was literally underground at Main and Broadway. There was also a group of students itching to break out of the confines of the theatre department at the University of British Columbia.

On the university campus, a group around Larry Kent was about to embark on its own, made-in-Vancouver project that would bring down the same wrath Bruce had attracted. Kent would become Vancouver's first independent filmmaker, but in 1962, he was a UBC student who had the audacious conviction that he could make feature films in Vancouver. This despite the fact that virtually no English-language films were being made in Canada, and in Vancouver there were no crews, equipment, film actors, or film directors.

"I had written a play called *The Afrikaner*, which was an anti-apartheid play, in '62," Kent recalls. "I was in the theatre department at UBC and it was a little constricting. I was not happy with the way things were going."

Kent, who had moved as a youth to Vancouver from South Africa, says Vancouver was "devastatingly conservative" at the time. "There were sort of two elements of Vancouver. There was a very small bohemian arts community and then a very large conservative community that came out of the ethos of the '50s. And the theatre department was very autocratic."

The idea of making a film started percolating the moment Kent met amateur cinematographer Dick Bellamy. Kent was in love with the new cinema he would watch at the Varsity Theatre, near the gates of UBC – from Federico Fellini's *La Dolce Vita* to British "kitchen-sink" films such as *Room at the Top*. "You wanted to see something that dealt more with reality. Films that dealt with what it was like to really be young, alive.

"I think that in theatre there was already becoming a stronger reality. There was a movement to the absurd or to kitchen sink but there was much more a feeling of trying to explore what was actually happening. Pinter was becoming popular, and Ionesco. There were all sorts of different things happening in the theatre that were slowly translating into film in Europe, especially into the nouvelle vogue, the Italian neorealism."

Scott Douglas and Alan Scarfe in *The Street.* *courtesy Larry Kent*

36

Kent teamed with Bellamy, by day a glass-blower at UBC, and three actors from the university's theatre department – Alan Scarfe, Scott Douglas, and Patricia Dahlquist – and started work on a short called *The Street*, filming as they wandered the pavement and bars of East Hastings Street's Skid Row. "And I decided at that stage that we were going to make a feature. I just said, 'Let's make a feature film.' Over the summer of '63 we shot *Bitter Ash*."

In 1963, there was a small feature-film industry in Quebec but nothing in English-speaking Canada. This was before Torontonian Don Owen's groundbreaking film *Nobody Waved Goodbye*; before Vancouver knew about John Cassavetes. Kent literally willed into completion the first three independent films made in Vancouver – making movies on nothing budgets, casting extraordinary improvisational actors, and pushing the envelope over the Lions Gate Bridge.

Since Kent and his UBC friends were virtually inventing Vancouver independent film, there was no one to turn to for assistance. "Nobody," Kent says. "The big advantage I had was that I was studying theatre at UBC and we had a lot of people in the theatre department who were very talented. The only sort of crew we had was Dick and myself. Dick had a camera and we bought some film and we went ahead. It was a four-week shoot. We shot for two weeks and then Dick Bellamy decided he was going on holidays to England for six weeks. When he came back we shot the final two weeks."

The *Bitter Ash* storyline involved a pretentious poet/playwright and his pregnant wife meeting head-on with an angry, alienated working-class youth. The budget was $5,000, much of it scraped together by Kent, who also worked as a printer at the *Sun* and *Province* newspapers.

Tickets were dispatched to bookstores and *Bitter Ash* opened at UBC's Brock Hall on a Monday afternoon in the fall of 1963. "Right after the screening there was this big, big brouhaha both at the university and downtown. . . . We could only show it at Brock Hall. The censor board banned it downtown. They banned it without seeing it. They hadn't seen bare breasts on the screen before and of course the words "shit" and "piss" were said and they were very upset at that. It was banned for everybody but UBC students. It was banned in B.C., not only Vancouver. On the one hand suddenly we had all this notoriety and people wanted to see it and on the other hand once we ran through the students nobody else could see it."

The banning of *Bitter Ash* did nothing to dissuade Kent and his friends.

"The virginal, puritanical attitude that was held by the establishment had nothing to do with reality," Kent says. "Sexuality in *Bitter Ash* is used in a way which is very, very painful and upsetting to everybody because it was very angry, you know, all of those things that are there. And that's what I wanted to talk about. You couldn't go sort of pretending that everything was sort of hunky dory and sexually everybody's living quietly in their lives. They just didn't want to show it or didn't even want to think it existed."

In those days filmmakers, because there weren't any, didn't fret over distribution. In fact, this was a small student film that Kent didn't anticipate would have much shelf life. But the controversy wasn't restricted to Vancouver. "We were banned at the University of Toronto. We were banned in Calgary and Saskatchewan and everywhere else."

∫

The film's star, Alan Scarfe, says the atmosphere in the UBC auditorium was electric the day *Bitter Ash* was shown. "It was as if you had done a banned play behind the Iron Curtain."

Scarfe, whose father was the dean of education at UBC, grew up a

On the Squamish Highway shooting *Bitter Ash*: (back row l–r) Dick Bellemy, Larry Kent, Alan Scarfe; (front row l–r) Sharon Bunce, Lynn Stewart. *courtesy Larry Kent*

couple of blocks from Spanish Banks beach, acting in Lord Byng high school productions. Kent instantly recognized Scarfe's talent when the young actor enrolled at UBC, and the fledgling director cast him in his play *The Afrikaner* and then in his first two films.

"I kind of looked up to him like an older brother," says Scarfe. "I felt safe with him. I think I believed in a core of integrity in the guy."

UBC theatre students of the day were intrigued at having a filmmaker among them. "Well, he got them all pretty excited about it," says Scarfe. *Bitter Ash* was set all over the Vancouver area, from the Squamish Highway to the old Beatty Street Pacific Press building, but the big buzz around the campus theatre scene was about the party sequence, shot in an old clapboard house in what is now Coal Harbour. Everyone in the theatre department was invited to the on-screen party which is classic pre-hippie hip, down to the bongo drums. The scene took a long time to shoot and the hot summer day turned into a muggy evening, and the staged party became a real party inside the packed house.

"Everybody got pissed and stoned and everything else. Good fun," says Scarfe. It was also where they shot the scene with Scarfe and Lynn Stewart that got the film banned. "It's a love-making scene. There I was on top of this girl, everybody's sweating and Larry's getting off on it probably. Who knows? I don't know how many people were in the room. It was incredibly hot in this room and there's Dick Bellamy probably sweating bullets with his camera hand-held. And there's a shot in which she's scratching my back with passion, you know, but there's no makeup girl or anything to deal with that, so she really has to do it. So she's gouging her nails into my back and Larry's saying, 'Deeper, deeper! Harder, harder!' And I finally say, 'Well, fuck off, Larry! That hurts.'"

∫

In the summer of 1964, Kent shot his second feature, *Sweet Substitute*. Again he assembled a strong cast, including Carol Pastinsky, who had just returned to Vancouver from California after two years studying at the Pasadena Playhouse. "When I came back, a friend of mine, Bobby Silverman called me and said, 'This guy's making a film and he wanted to know if I knew any actors.'

The 1960s rebellion wasn't all about the hippie counter-culture (which didn't take hold until 1967). Before that, as the western world slowly woke from its postwar somnambulism in the early 1960s, a prescient cool was taking shape, drawn to European films and method actors, avant-garde theatre, folk music, left-leaning politics (with an interest in the U.S. civil rights movement) – guys who looked like Leonard Cohen, women like, well, Carol Pastinsky. She was the grand-daughter of the city's first Orthodox rabbi, passionate about Dylan and Brando, Pinter and Fellini, social justice and bohemian culture.

For Pastinsky, the controversy around *Bitter Ash* made meeting with Kent all the more attractive. "It made it very appealing when you heard that part of the story because this would have been a fairly interesting guy, you would have thought. Bobby Silverman took me over to Larry's apartment one afternoon near the corner of Broadway and Macdonald, in that area, where he was with his wife Mary and their daughter. We met and he said, okay, there was no script, there was nothing, there was just this idea in his head."

Sweet Substitute, about another alienated young man (Bob Howay), probing his sexuality and the rest of his life as he grapples with the choice between conformity (represented by his relationship with a Sandra Dee wannabe, played by Angela Gann) or rebellion (represented by his studymate, played by Pastinsky).

On the set of *Sweet Substitute*. *courtesy Larry Kent*

The shoot was largely impromptu, Pastinsky recalls, with Kent supplying dialogue, "now and then." There was, for instance, the moment Kent suggested "something about Andorra" when she and Howay's characters were about to study. The result was a sweet, memorable scene in which two young Vancouverites, about to step out into the 1960s, dream aloud of how they'll pursue adventure in their lives, how they'd love to travel to an out of the way spot . . . such as Andorra, the tiny principality nestled in the Pyrenees.

"You fed off that [Kent's suggestions] because here we were, none of us knew what we were doing. I mean, not in a huge way," says Pastinsky. "And so, if Larry wanted to do it, we did it. And he had no script. He just had these ideas. He'd give them to us and every now and then there'd be scripted things and you'd go from that. There was an infectiousness about him that kept you going with it. And he did have a definite point of view. It was to get to the end his way, basically. He would look at me and say to Bob Howay, 'Why would you choose this person over that person?' I mean, one is so much less interesting or one is so much more interesting. And he would talk about it for hours. You would get into it.

"Larry was fascinated about all of it. He really was. We shot the entire thing in his one-bedroom apartment. There was no money whatsoever and we would go there and we'd have to clean the place up before we could shoot. And he liked it. He loved having everybody around, he loved it being in his apartment. You know, we all used to feel bad for Mary, 'cause we were always there."

Again, Kent released his film at UBC in the fall. *Sweet Substitute* was distributed in the U.S., played the London Film Festival, and was awarded a citation at the 1965 Canadian Film Awards (later renamed the Genies). It read: "For the very great promise and already substantial accomplishment clearly shown by director and actors alike, and for the sensitive and imaginative handling of the story."

§

The following year, Kent was back with his third film *When Tomorrow Dies*, which he wrote with UBC professor Bob Harlow. It is a precursor to feminist-influenced movies such as *Diary of a Mad Housewife* and *Woman Under the Influence*, about a mother of two who escapes a lonely marriage with a career-driven husband and returns to UBC where she develops a close relationship with her English professor. "There was such an anti-feminist feeling at the time, it was a very hard sell," says Kent. "So, we sort of hit a real brick wall when we did it."

When Tomorrow Dies was shot exquisitely in black and white by cinematographer Doug McKay, and its star, Patricia Gage, delivered one of the standout performances in Canadian film.

Born in Scotland, Gage moved to Vancouver with her mother in 1958 and trained with Anthony Holland, an acting teacher who would later head the Langara theatre program. "These were the days when you didn't have agents, people just called you. And I had been doing so much work in theatre in Vancouver. Larry was holding auditions and they called me in to do a screen test for the lead in the show. And I got it," she says.

Although Gage was one of Vancouver's most consistently working stage actors of the era, a pervasive presence in the first years of the Playhouse Theatre, *When Tomorrow Dies* was her first film work.

"We were all in uncharted waters, just diving in there and saying, 'Oh, I hope this works.' And oddly enough, it did," she recalls. "To do an independent film with no money, you were basically putting together your own makeup, your costumes, everything. . . . It was very, very exciting, because we were going into territory that absolutely no one knew. We didn't have the technology that we have today. We were relying so much on the elements as opposed to artificially putting it all together. If the scene was set in a sunny day in the park and it happened to be pouring rain that day, you had to switch the scene right away and make it in the rain.

"*When Tomorrow Dies* wasn't his [Larry's] first. But it was his most ambitious, I would say, because he actually put together a script rather than just working day by day and let's see what happens."

For a young man of the time, Kent seemed uniquely observant of the tribulations of a young married woman.

"I don't know if he knew, at the time, what he was doing," says Gage. "He just knew something had to be said about it. But he was never into saying, 'This is an important film because we've got a message.'

"This is the time that we were tapping in to the fact that it's simply not enough for women to have babies and look after a house any more, at least for the majority of women. And households were starting to need two incomes instead of one. I mean, two or three years later, yes,

42

we were very conscious of the feminist movement. But I wasn't conscious of it when we were shooting *When Tomorrow Dies*. I just knew we were tapping in to something that was very important and had to be spoken about."

Gage would appear in one of David Cronenberg's first films, *Rabid*, and his attitude reminded her of Kent. "In the sense of, 'I'm going to do this. It doesn't matter what anybody thinks of it.' A perfect example of that is *Crash*. I mean, talk about pushing the envelope. I personally can't watch it.

"I think the difference between David and Larry is the fact that David is able to combine his creativity with the commercialism, with the budgeting, with the casting, with the whole star concept. Larry hasn't really been able to do that. It's an area he is not happy or comfortable in, with the suits." Had Kent been willing to accommodate producers? "I think he would be in a place like where David Cronenberg is."

§

After the three features, Kent moved to Montreal. "I was broke and I got a job at the film board. That only lasted six months." His first Montreal film, *High*, about the dark side of the counter-culture, was banned at Montreal's Expo 67 by the Quebec Board of Censors.

Kent kept making films in Montreal (*Façade, Fleur-Bleue, Mothers and Daughters*) and he continues to develop scripts. There has been a recent groundswell of interest in Kent, with tributes at festivals and cinémathèques and a documentary in the works. He also plans, finally, to complete his first film, *The Street*, now titled *Hastings Street*.

Kent tried his hand at a couple of mainstream productions (*Keep it in the Family, High Stakes*) but he wasn't satisfied. "I want to make my own films. The wonderful thing is that I can look back forty years and there's a film that I screen for an audience and they really like it and understand it, you know, whereas some of the stuff that I've done commercially, you put your heart and soul into it then the producer comes in and fucks it up. In the end you sort of want to shoot yourself."

All these decades later, Kent keeps one eye on his old city. "Vancouver's doing some very interesting sfuff – people like Bruce Sweeney and so forth and the girl who did, what's her name, you know the one about the dead."

$$\int$$

Kent and his creative circle set a standard and ethos for Vancouver independent filmmaking that continues, a willingness to show the raw truth. And in Kent's films, Vancouver is Vancouver – it doesn't stand in for another (i.e., American) city. "Well, it was a Vancouver film, you know. It was about living in Vancouver." As for those who would call it America in search of U.S. distributors? "Well, it seems to me that you're starting on a false premise right from the beginning. I think that you're always trying to deal with the environment you live in and if you say Vancouver is Seattle you start off with a lie because Vancouver's not like Seattle. It's a completely different emotional feeling."

Larry Kent was the founding father of Vancouver independent film, and a founding parent of indie cinema, anywhere, period.

Another former UBC student, Jack Darcus, who has been making films in Vancouver since 1969's *Great Coups of History*, has had a first-hand look at the impact Kent had on Vancouver. "Those first two films had a very great impact," Darcus says. "They showed it could be done. Larry either had that blind naïvete or tremendous courage. Usually, one film finishes most people off. The fact that he went on to another and then a third one just was, for everyone working in theatre or acting or the arts, an amazing achievement."

And those who comprised the extended Kent Group have kept in touch, to varying degrees, through the decades. "Larry did have an eye for casting," says Pastinsky. "I think that probably he knew way more than any of us ever thought he knew."

Working in Kent's ensemble has had an enduring impact on everyone involved. "It became a major thing in all our lives," says Pastinsky. "Not so much even the film, but where it led us. And brought us all together. We've all stayed in touch and our lives have taken strange routes."

Sweet Substitute's Bob Howay would die in a mountain climbing accident. ("Tragic. He was a really lovely, wonderful guy," says Scarfe.) His costar, Bobby Silverman, would be involved in a severe car accident. But Gage, Scarfe, Douglas, and others have had long professional careers after starting on Kent's no-budget shoots.

Scarfe became a director, writer, acclaimed Shakespearean actor, performed on Broadway, lived in Toronto and L.A., was a regular in Vancouver director Jack Darcus's films, and has appeared in TV series

44

(*Seven Days, Tour of Duty*) and studio films (*The Wrong Guy, Lethal Weapon 3*). He returned to B.C. in 2002.

Douglas left for the U.S., where he changed his name to Scott Hylands (Scott Douglas was already taken by another member of the Screen Actors Guild) and continued performing in theatre, films (*The Boys in Company C*), and tv (the lead role on ctv's *Night Heat*).

Gage went on to live and act at Niagara on the Lake, then in New York for twelve years, continued acting in tv (*As the World Turns*), films (*American Psycho, Waking the Dead*), and theatre. She lives near Toronto. "I have recurring roles on three series at the moment – *Queer as Folk, Doc*, and *Tracker*," she said in 2002. " I have no intention whatsoever, ever to retire. I have, all of my life, considered myself a working actor. That's how I make my living. It's what I pay income tax on, it's what I do in life."

As for Pastinsky, Kent says: "She was a terrific actress. I don't know why she didn't continue."

After escorting *Bitter Ash* to the London Film Festival, Pastinsky and Howay stayed on in England for two years, doing repertory Shakespeare. When Pastinsky returned to Vancouver, alone, the city was not a viable place for making a living as an actor and there were other things that seemed to need doing. "I got very involved politically in what was going on, particularly against the war. We helped people

Carol Pastinsky. *courtesy Larry Kent*

come across the border, we found places for them to live."

Pastinsky, who now lives in the coastal B.C. town of Gibsons, also worked at CBC before contracting a debilitating circulatory illness. "I'm a lot better now than I was twenty years ago. I got married, we both stayed active, and eventually, Harvey, my husband, worked for CBC. We came up here with *The Beachcombers*."

There is one thing Pastinsky never did get around to doing, something that's been in the back of her mind since Larry Kent said the word "Andorra" before she and Howay studied geography in *Sweet Substitute*.

"I never visited the place," says Pastinsky. But she thought about it: "Always. 'I want to go to Andorra.' And that was absolutely Larry. That was the one line I honestly remember being written and that whole sort of thing went from there.

"I would love to have gone there. No, I haven't thought about it in a long time."

§

"I'm just going to describe to you an event that happened on my high school graduation," Scarfe says.

"This is at Lord Byng high school – very staid, fairly affluent, little old Point Grey. And on the day of my graduation a bunch of ringleaders, of which I was one, had organized a demonstration on the basketball court. We hated these teachers, we hated the guy who was the principal of the school. There were a thousand kids on that basketball court, all screaming at the top of their lungs, 'We hate Lyman, we hate Lyman,' which was the first name of the principal.

"And Carol Pastinsky's husband – I don't know whether she's still married to this guy or not – Harvey McCracken was his name and he was one of our bunch. He just lived down the block, and we concocted an effigy of the principal, and he brought it [to school during] lunch hour after having a couple of snorts. It was hung up from the basketball hoops and burned as the kids stormed around chanting.

"I remember standing up a block away like, you know, Field Marshal Rommel, watching this happen. Several police cars turned up. They were pelted with eggs. It was like the beginning of the '60s. Hello, here we are."

46

THE SIXTIES

Clyde Barrow and an *Easy Rider* arrived in Vancouver at the same time. Two separate groups of renegade Hollywood filmmakers came to the city in 1970 to shoot *Carnal Knowledge* and *McCabe and Mrs Miller*. Just before shooting began, the groups convened for a party at the Austin Taylor manor at 54th and Granville.

The *McCabe* (Robert Altman, Warren Beatty, Julie Christie) and *Carnal* (Mike Nichols, Jack Nicholson, Candice Bergen, Art Garfunkel) ensembles bore some responsibility for a large chunk of the seminal films of the late 1960s/early 1970s – *Bonnie and Clyde, Easy Rider, The Graduate, M*A*S*H, The Last Detail, The Long Goodbye, Don't Look Now, Chinatown, Five Easy Pieces.*

"I remember talking to Jack Nicholson and my wife sitting on Warren Beatty's lap the whole evening," says Alex Diakun, a stage actor fresh out of Alberta, who had landed a role in *McCabe and Mrs Miller.*

Over the next months, Beatty and Christie would host a continuing party at their rented, Arthur Erickson-designed West Vancouver home above the ocean. It was in Vancouver that Beatty and Nicholson would become fast friends, Altman would construct an entire hippie village on the side of a mountain, and Bergen would do her best film work in Nichols' second-best film (after *The Graduate*).

But this story actually begins a couple of years earlier when Robert Altman arrived in town to shoot another movie.

§

The little park in Vancouver's Kitsilano neighbourhood is quiet on a fall afternoon – a stroller being pushed on to a small wooden bridge, a young man in a suit hurrying along the dirt pathway, a young woman reading on a bench.

Kitsilano is one of those old working-class neighbourhoods that

47

seems to get more gentrified the more the baby-boom generation ages. In 1968, though, when Robert Altman came to shoot *That Cold Day in the Park* in Tatlow Park, the neighbourhood was one of the capitals of the counter-culture's borderless "New Nation." ("A nation of alienated young people," Abbie Hoffman said. "We carry it around with us as a state of mind.")

The rebellion expressed by the Larry Kent group and others who were very much outsiders in the early 1960s had, in just a few years, crashed through Vancouver's staid surface and, by the time Altman arrived, was changing the face of the entire city.

In the counter-culture centres, from Berkeley to Amsterdam to Madison, Wisconsin, to New York's Lower East Side, it seemed as though a generation raised in bland, assimilated suburbia was creating something akin to the tight-knit, urban neighbourhoods their parents had abandoned – virtually inventing their own ethnic group. And in Vancouver, Kitsilano's main street, Fourth Avenue, as much as an immigrant enclave in New York, had its own music, language, dress, food, and politics. Suddenly, everything was on the agenda in this revolution – street protests, feminism, marijuana, gay rights, Vietnam, ecology, student radicalism, culture.

In 1969, one of the founding conferences of the women's movement was held at UBC and more than 100 students were arrested for occupying an administration building at SFU. In 1970, Greenpeace was founded in Vancouver and the city's Yippies invaded the border town of Blaine, Washington, after Nixon invaded Cambodia.

"It was an exciting time for the theatre, for film, for women, for all kinds of things," says Patricia Gage. "It was a very exciting time to be in Canada and be in Vancouver.

"A lot of the American draft dodgers came to Vancouver because of the weather and things like that. And we were doing a lot of innovative things. I did a very, very controversial play called *The Ecstasy of Rita Joe* with Chief Dan George, at the Playhouse. So we were dealing with that situation. And we were dealing with the whole drug culture. George Riga, who wrote *The Ecstasy of Rita Joe*, then came out with *Grass and Wild Strawberries*. It was a time of . . . well, it was explosive. It was taking the lid off all this stuff that we knew was going on but no one was talking about."

People from every era of Vancouver filmmaking would be touched by this cultural combustion. There would be those from the Kent group (Carol Pastinsky, for one) who would become part of the counter-culture of the late 1960s, others who were active in the culture (Babz Chula, for another) who would later play roles in the indie film scene, and some who were children (Molly Parker, yet another) of hippies.

Like earlier times, this era in Vancouver would be reflected on screen. Through the first half of the twentieth century most everyone in Vancouver, regardless of politics, culture or predisposition, had watched the same films. But there were increasing cultural divisions, beginning in the 1950s with music, as young people embraced rock 'n' roll while their parents kept listening to derivatives of the music they had grown up with. And alongside a wholesome family mythology like *Please Don't Eat the Daisies*, the studios were churning out films aimed at the alienated-youth market. Some were bad (*High School Confidential*), some were great (*Rebel Without a Cause*), some were quickie Elvis musicals.

The counter-culture's arrival in the late '60s was accompanied by a parade of made-in-America films specifically about it (*Easy Rider, Wild in the Streets, Medium Cool*) or with its sensibility (*Bonnie and Clyde, Cool Hand Luke, M*A*S*H*).

The old-style studios were going through their death throes and their last gasp was a long, good one, lasting from 1967 until the mid-1970s, including everything from *The Graduate* to *The Godfather*. It is not surprising that the last great era of studio films was also the best of times for American movies shot in B.C. – Altman (*That Cold Day in the Park, McCabe and Mrs Miller*), Mike Nichols (*Carnal Knowledge*) and Bob Rafelson (*Five Easy Pieces*).

§

The year 1962 quietly marked the beginning of the two film industries that would come of age more than thirty years later. While Larry Kent and friends at UBC were taking the domestic independent scene through its formative days, the service film industry took its first step into Vancouver when, in June 1962, *The Sweet and the Bitter* was shot in West Vancouver.

After decades of fruitless talk about building a film industry in Vancouver, on November 11, 1960, something finally happened. Czech

49

immigrant Oldrich Vaclavek, the spokesman for British investors behind Panorama Estates Ltd, announced that construction was about to start on a movie studio on Hollyburn Ridge, just off the Upper Levels Highway in West Vancouver. Unlike earlier announcements, this one was real. The plan was to operate Vaclavek's Commonwealth Film Productions out of the studio and to lease its facilities to American and British producers making features and television.

Commonwealth Film Productions planned to make a couple of features a year. The first production, *The Sweet and the Bitter*, about a Japanese woman seeking revenge for the Second World War internment of her father, was directed and written by British novelist James Clavell, who would be better known to moviegoers for *To Sir With Love* and far better known to readers of novels such as *Shogun* and *King Rat*. After *The Sweet and the Bitter* was shot in twenty-three days, Commonwealth announced Clavell would shoot his second feature, *No Hands on the Clock*, in Vancouver, too. (Apparently the company didn't feel the title was lengthy enough because it was quickly changed to *At the Break of a Wave There is Madness Beyond*.)

But that movie, regardless of its name, was never made. *The Sweet and the Bitter* was set for a London premiere in 1963, but its producer Commonwealth Productions was evicted from Panorama and post-production was shelved in England. Apparently, *The Sweet and the Bitter*'s budget had risen from $175,000 to $450,000 during the shoot. Commonwealth Films and Panorama Estates fought it out in the courts and the film wouldn't premiere until 1967 at Vancouver's Orpheum Theatre.

Peter Prior worked construction on *The Sweet and the Bitter*. "We don't talk about that one. It had an awful lot wrong with it. I don't know how much directing [Clavell] had done before but we probably had enough in the can to make about six movies," says Prior. "Clavell was known for the fact that everything had to stop in the afternoon. He used to have to have a silver tea service on a silver tray every afternoon. We used to think it was quite amusing."

Despite the trouble, Panorama's facilities became a minor draw. Another company, Hollyburn Films, took over the studio and in 1964, British producers, including J. Arthur Rank, decided to shoot the feature, *The Trap*, on Bowen Island and at Panorama. Set at the beginning of the twentieth century, Oliver Reed, as a kind of Quebecois Grizzly

Adams gone wrong, buys a mute wife played by Rita Tushingham. This intense film does, along with providing epic treatment of the B.C. terrain, confirm that marriage can be slavery.

"We had a huge set built on the main stage up at Panorama which was a forest set," Prior recalls. "We didn't actually finish it here. The British crew that had come over was promised they'd be back home for Christmas. So the final scenes were shot somewhere in Britain. It didn't look like B.C. forest. It was typical European, you know, where the trees have all kinds of space in between them. It's not like here, where it's all undergrowth and brush."

§

The 1960s would end with the arrival of some of Hollywood's best young directors. In Hollywood, film pioneers go back a century but Vancouver's pioneers arrived in the 1960s and 1970s, and the handful of movies made then are among the best American movies filmed in B.C.

The first of these films shot in Vancouver was also one of Robert Altman's first.

"It was wet but I loved it," says Altman, who stayed in West Vancouver's British Properties for about three months while working on *That Cold Day in the Park*, an independently financed film. "We had a great time in Vancouver. We cast most everybody from there, other than Sandy Dennis and Michael Burns and I think John Garfield Jr and another girl. But everybody else we cast up there. We shot locations in Vancouver, in the city and around and then we had that set we built on the stage."

What was the attraction, with virtually no crews or infrastructure or profitable exchange rate? "We found that studio up there, I didn't have union problems to deal with that I had down here at that time, and it was cheaper for us to do it because we built a rather large set. In fact, we filled that stage, that old Panorama studio. We brought in a certain amount of people. We brought in our camera. I forget what the break was but, you know, we fettered out as many people as we could up there and many of them were not particularly experienced at that time."

But the decision wasn't entirely a matter of economics. At the time, Vancouver was far removed from L.A.'s film world and the irascibly independent Altman says his good time making *That Cold Day in the Park* was largely the result of having no bosses around. He was also drawn by the city's look. "It gave me a little bit of a strange, I would say, foreign look to the film," Altman recalls. "It wasn't familiar territory. I was originally going to shoot that film in England. To transpose it to San Francisco or Portland or someplace like that seemed to hurt it. And by going to Vancouver I was able to keep the attitude. It was written by an English woman and it just fit better."

The film opens with the words "Vancouver, B.C.," then Dennis tells dinner guests, "It's starting to rain," and city landmark after landmark follows, from the Burrard Building to Granville Street. Dennis's character informs her dinner party that's she's noticed a young man (Burns) sitting in the rain in the park next to her apartment. "Nobody's forcing him to sit out in the rain. Perhaps he likes it," she's warned by a guest, but in this more innocent time she takes him in from the rain and decides to keep him. The movie touches on the anti-war sentiments of the era, with John Garfield Jr, the son of the great blacklisted actor John Garfield, playing an American drifter.

This is not great cinema from Altman, who would go on to become one of America's better directors, albeit a wildly hit-and-miss one. But *That Cold Day in the Park* would result in Altman returning two years later to shoot *The Presbyterian Church Wager*, a gritty Warner Bros western starring Warren Beatty and Julie Christie that would be renamed *McCabe and Mrs Miller*. "Well, I had had the experience from *That Cold Day in the Park* and we just decided it was a good place to go and build, because we had to build that whole town and we built it as we shot it," says Altman. "I just was familiar with the territory and it just seemed like a good place to go.

"I just thought it was the best place to do it. I got the weather that I wanted, I knew I had that virgin territory. I don't

Robert Altman.

know where I would have gone in California or anywhere to build that set. And I knew people up there."

McCabe and Mrs Miller was shot at the tail-end of the western genre, when gritty, real-life depictions of the West were in vogue. The Vancouver area, for the first time, plays Washington State in this dark, muddy western. Cast and crew formed a real community, living in a mining town constructed in West Vancouver's Cyprus Park.

"We put together for that film kind of a family, kind of a hippie family," Altman recalls. "Most of those guys that built the town of Presbyterian Church actually were living there on the property. In other words, in those buildings and tents and that bar that we built which was the first thing we put up.

"Every night when these guys would finish work they would all go down there. That's where they'd meet. In fact, they built a still up there which I had to have destroyed because I was afraid somebody would go blind. Where we shot *McCabe* was right in the British Properties. I mean, it was really not far away [from the city]. In those days, you drove up through a bunch of $100,000 houses and then went over a little knoll and you looked down on this big kind of gully that led down to the sea and that's where we built the town. And then we went to Squamish to do the town of Bear Paw."

Diakun recalls that the original screenplay was quickly discarded. "We had this whole script but not a word of it was used. The movie was made up every day between Altman and all the people there."

Beatty and Altman's strong wills would, on occasion, collide. There was an instance in which they had shot twenty takes, with Beatty wanting more, when Altman simply announced he was satisfied and done for the day. Beatty continued shooting the scene with first assistant director Tommy Thompson at the helm.

In the late 1990s, Altman, back in Vancouver as a producer, took a drive with Thompson along West Vancouver's Upper Levels Highway searching for traces of *McCabe and Mrs Miller*. "We drove up around there. It's kind of built over. We couldn't find it. We just couldn't. The roads have changed and our memories have grown fainter."

Still, they kept driving, looking for this piece of filmmaking history they couldn't resist revisiting. "Oh, just nostalgia," says Altman. "We were just driving around and said, 'Let's go see if we can find that place and see what it looks like now.'"

Not long after Altman was done with *That Cold Day in the Park*, BBS Productions arrived on Vancouver Island, fresh off the summer success of its *Easy Rider*. BBS (Bert Schneider, Bob Rafelson, Steve Blauner) was at the heart of the counter-culture inside Hollywood and would go on to make the great Peter Bogdanovich movie *The Last Picture Show* and the Oscar-winning Vietnam documentary *Hearts and Minds*. They had come to B.C. to film segments of a low-budget picture called *Five Easy Pieces*. (They also shot in the U.S.) The filmmakers included director Rafelson, who had just made a movie starring the Monkees called *Head*; cinematographer Leslie Kovacs, who was the director of photography on *Easy Rider* and *That Cold Day in the Park*, and a skinny young actor, Jack Nicholson.

Nicholson's scene with an irritable, officious waitress has become a classic anti-heroic film bit. He tries to order a chicken sandwich without the chicken. "Hold the chicken?" she sneers. "I want you to hold it between your knees," he explains.

Five Easy Pieces would be chosen best picture of 1970 by the New York Film Critics Circle and would influence generations of indie filmmakers with its stark, deliberate look at an alienated young pianist in conflict with his proper, dysfunctional family (brother with a wrecked neck, father with a stroke, sister he can't relate to, brother's fiance he wants to relate to). "Tell you one thing," he tells Karen Black upon heading north from California, "where we're going it's going to get colder than hell."

This did not prevent Nicholson from coming back a few months later, with Mike Nichols, whose first films were *Who's Afraid of Virginia Woolf?*, *The Graduate*, and *Catch-22*. Nichols' fourth film, *Carnal Knowledge*, was shot at Panorama and the old Taylor family manor, which became New England's Amherst College. The film, which was also shot in New York, follows the sexual travails of two exasperated, alienated young men (Nicholson, Art Garfunkel), giving hints of the lecherous, leering Nicholson to come. It also starred Candice Bergen and Ann-Margret, whose performance drew an Oscar nomination.

§

Although Hollywood movies, for the first time, were being made in Vancouver in the late 1960s, there wasn't enough film work to sustain an acting career so some aspiring Vancouverites experienced the tumultuous decade in California, New York or London.

In 1969, Vancouver's Barbara Parkins, a star of the 1960s' TV hit *Peyton Place*, was at London party for Roman Polanski when he learned that his wife, her friend Sharon Tate, had been murdered in L.A. by the Manson family. "A friend of Roman's was having a dinner party for him. I rushed over 'cause I heard that some people had been killed and she was hurt. And then when the news came to him at his friend's house everyone was just freaking out. They immediately got on a private jet and flew to L.A. That was a sad time. I mean, it was the end of our innocence at the time because it was so horrific."

Born in Vancouver, Parkins grew up in the East End and Richmond, bussing to her aunt's Marge Berry Dance School, near Slocan and Kingsway, where her mother played piano. Parkins performed in the Theatre Under the Stars ballet production of *Rhapsody in Blue* and dreamed of dancing in New York. Vancouver, at the time, "was very simple, very non-happening. We would always go to the White Spot [restaurant] because that was the big thing when I was a kid in Vancouver. We would sit in the car and have our hamburgers. When you drove down to Stanley Park, there were no high-rises, a very pretty place to live."

Barbara Parkins.

Parkins hadn't studied acting at Gladstone high school and, unlike De Carlo and others who left Vancouver starstruck, she just kind of fell into it. "My uncle who lived in L.A. said to my mother, 'I can get you double, triple the money to play piano for a dance school down here.' So we sold our little house on Slocan Street and she got this job at Falcon Dance School on Hollywood Boulevard."

At seventeen, Parkins was attending Hollywood High, living in a one-room apartment with her mother, studying tap, ballet, fencing and acting at the Falcon school.

Students staged scenes at the school one weekend and agents showed up. "They signed me and six months later I got *Peyton Place.*

"The pilot sold and the series came on the air, with little fanfare strangely enough. And then it just exploded. And then it became the biggest series of all time.... We were filming two episodes a week and it go so popular we were filming three episodes a week."

The show ran for six years and Mia Farrow, Ryan O'Neal, and Parkins, who was nominated for a best-actress Emmy, became stars as a result. "When she came to town you couldn't go anywhere with her," says Madeleine Duff, a longtime Vancouver friend. "People would come up to her all the time."

She had a style all her own, a voice that at once sounded Canadian, American, and British. "I think it's transatlantic. As a kid in Vancouver in school, my mother was brought in for a big discussion with the music teacher and I was told that I could not be in the choir anymore because my voice was too different, which totally devastated me."

Parkins was signed to a two-picture deal with 20th Century Fox. "I was very excited, very scared and very in awe of this whole idea of a contract with a studio. If I had been less naïve I would have been aware of the power of the situation possibly that I was going into – dealmaking, getting involved in the whole aspect of filmmaking and television. It would have been interesting how my career would have evolved."

She starred in *Valley of the Dolls* but quickly tired of the L.A. industry and started to reject offers, including

SOME WHO EXCHANGED B.C. FOR HOLLYWOOD IN THE 1950s AND 1960s

Beverly Adams (Vancouver). Appeared in several pictures the 1960s (*How to Stuff a Wild Bikini*, *The Silencers*) but retired after marrying hair-product mogul Vidal Sassoon.

James Doohan (Vancouver). Had minor film roles (*The Wheeler Deelers*, *Bus Riley's Back in Town*) before arriving as *Star Trek*'s Scotty.

Don Francks (Vancouver). Made his studio film debut in 1968's *Finian's Rainbow* with Fred Astaire and Petula Clark. Also appeared in many films shot in Canada, including *The Drylanders* and *McCabe and Mrs Miller*. He's worked continuously in North American film and TV since the 1950s.

Arthur Hill (Vancouver). Raised in Saskatchewan but started acting while attending UBC. Did community theatre in Vancouver before moving on to England, then Hollywood, where he appeared in features (*Harper*, *Petulia*) and starred in TV's *Own Marshall, Counselor at Law*.

the lead in *Love Story*. "I got bored, I got disenchanted with Hollywood. I guess I wanted to do different, more interesting roles, they weren't coming my way."

Parkins did accept an offer from Tate, her *Valley of the Dolls* co-star, and Polanski, and moved into their empty London flat, working out of England for a time, shooting John Huston's *The Kremlin Letters* in Ireland.

She was the first Hollywood star from Vancouver to return to her hometown to shoot, starring in the 1974 film *Christina*, a psycho drama about a woman who pays someone to marry her so she can get a U.S. passport. "I wanted to do this film and it was being done in Vancouver and I thought, 'How great. I'm home, that's nice, I'm home, I'm around my family.' And I liked the script. I thought it was interesting but he wasn't a very good director, so. . . ."

Christina was directed by Paul Krasny and produced by Trevor Wallace, who was trying to established himself as a Vancouver-based producer following his 1971 sci-fi feature *The Groundstar Conspiracy*.

During the shoot, Parkins stayed at her mother's place. "It wasn't the big industry that it is now and a lot of the press would come by, a lot of people would want to take me to lunch. It was a very big thing for a home-town girl coming back and doing a film in Vancouver." She was invited to the Vancouver opening at the Capitol Theatre. "I couldn't go there so my mother represented me and they had her up on the stage. It

Robert Ito (Vancouver). Survived Second World War internment camps to go on to an acting career in theatre, TV (*Quincy*), and film (*The Terminal Man*, *Some Kind of Nut*).

Margot Kidder (Vancouver). Born in the Northwest Territories, she moved down to Vancouver, working as an usher at the Varsity Theatre while attending UBC. She made her film debut in Norman Jewison's 1969 comedy *Gaily, Gaily*. Best known for her portrayal of Lois Lane in the *Superman* movie series, but she's had a varied career, including some fine work on Canadian films (won a best-actress Genie for 1981's *Heartaches*).

Patricia Owens (Golden). A familiar face in 1950s features, Owens starred in the original *The Fly* and appeared with Marlon Brando in *Sayonara*.

Lee Patterson (Vancouver). He starred in British and Hollywood B-grades (*Passing Stranger*, *The Ceremony*).

actually became a cult film, it was so bad."

It was in Vancouver again, in the 1990s, that the performing career that started in the city would pretty much end. At first, she was pleased to back in Vancouver, working in Stephen J. Cannell's CBS series *CrimeTime After Primetime*. But things started to turn.

"I had just had my daughter. Certain things that were promised in regards to the helping with her never came to fruition. One day they broke for lunch and I came off the set and I came outside, sat, and the sun was shining, it was a beautiful afternoon. And I was just crying my eyes out. And my dresser came up to me and said, 'What's the matter?' And I said, 'I don't want to do this anymore. I don't want to act anymore.' Much to the dismay of my agents I picked up my child and I moved back to London.

"I'm asked all the time to do daytime soap operas or do a Joan Collins-type character and it makes me want to go to the bathroom and vomit. It's so commercial, it's so one-dimensional, I've done those things and I don't need to do them again. I'd like to try one more time to do something really on the other side of my coin, so to speak, a really interesting role."

These days Parkins' focus is photography, travelling to locales such as Alaska, Japan, and Italy, shooting for British publications. She lives in Beverly Hills with her daughter but, in a way, she never fully returned to Hollywood after the "innocence" died.

Parkins was part of the '60s scene that partied at the Polanski place in L.A.'s Benedict Canyon ("Sharon was wonderful. Kind, sweet, she was like a doe, very gentle, very soft. Roman was Roman Polanski, very bizarre, very black sense of humour. He could be very manipulative in a harsh way and very manipulative in a charming way.") and at the Mamas and the Papas' manor in Bel Air. At the time, she was dating Christopher Jones, who had a brief taste of stardom when he led a youth rebellion in the hit 1968 movie *Wild in the Streets*. ("I don't know where he is but he was the 'new James Dean.' He disliked the industry, he disliked the way people tried to control his life, he was his own spirit, so he moved up to Big Sur Carmel and became an artist.")

Although Parkins lived outside of the Hollywood mainstream, she didn't identify with the counter-culture either. "I was a loner, basically. Still am."

∫

Morrie Ruvinsky, having arrived from Montreal to study creative writing at UBC, had no trouble identifying with the Kitsilano counter-culture.

"It was Canada's equivalent of Haight-Ashbury," he says. "I was very much in the heart of it, absolutely. It was a great time to come to Vancouver. It was just alive. New things were being tried out in the arts. There was something fresh and wild about it."

Ruvinsky took time from his graduate studies to become Vancouver's second independent filmmaker, combining personal savings with Canada Council writing grants to fund *The Plastic Mile* ("It was about me making a movie about a filmmaker making a movie") in 1968.

The female leads, Beverlee Miller and Pia Shandel, were Ruvinsky's friends, but the male star, Jace Van Der Veen, was discovered in an unconventional casting session. "He was hitchhiking one day as I was driving home from UBC and I picked him up. I said, 'What are you doing?' He said, 'I'm a graduate student in drama at UBC,' and I said, 'Oh, terrific, you want to be in the movie?'"

The night before *The Plastic Mile* was scheduled to premiere at the

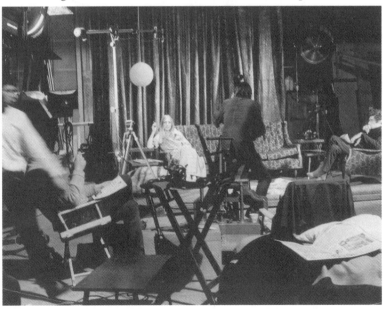

Morrie Ruvinsky directs Pia Shandel on the set of *The Plastic Mile*. *courtesy Beverlee Miller*

1969 Vancouver Film Festival awards-night gala at the Queen Elizabeth Theatre, B.C. censor Ray McDonald banned it because of a scene involving Shandel's character and an orgasm.

"I was stunned because there was no reason to censor it," Ruvinsky says. "Vancouver at the time was a very, very provincial place. It was isolated from the rest of the world and it was very backward in a lot of its thinking. That was one of the exciting things about Vancouver: There was this invasion of the hippie revolution in a town that was really super conservative in its cultural attitudes. And it was a big clash."

Dreaming
in the Rain

Shandel says cancellation of the screening was a huge letdown for the assembled relatives, cast, and crew. "This wasn't Larry Kent. Larry Kent came out of UBC and was considered a little bit sordid, and he was kind of a bit wicked. But this was going to be a legitimate movie, you know. And the director Morrie was from Montreal so it had a bit of pan-Canadianism to it," Shandel says.

"Morrie's managed to pull this off in Vancouver. Who cares what it was about? Who cares how good it was? He made a movie, a feature film, the reel is there, the audience is there, and some little pinhead won't let it go because there's a little scene where Pia fakes an orgasm. So, Morrie gets steamed."

There was a protest in front of the theatre

(l–r) Morrie Ruvinsky on stage at the Queen Elizabeth Theatre with Jace Van Der Veen and Ben Metcalfe.
courtesy Morrie Ruvinsky

60

as festival-goers wandered in to watch a replacement film. "At some point, somebody said, 'You better come in and say something,' so I said 'Okay,'" recalls Ruvinsky, "and I remember coming into the theatre and then behind me I heard all of this singing ["We Shall Overcome"]. I turned around and there were the troops marching in behind me. I marched up on the stage and they all marched up behind me and sat up on the stage."

Ruvinsky addressed the audience about how unfair the decision was and again asked festival organizers if the film would be shown. Again, no. Festival president Ben Metcalfe expressed support for Ruvinsky, but projectionists refused to defy the censor.

"So I went up to the projection booth and I got the film. I put the five reels up on the stage and I said, 'Well, now, here you can see *The Plastic Mile*.' And everybody laughed. Then I thought, 'Well fuck, I can do better than that.'

"I picked up a reel, I got a pair of scissors, and we went up and down the aisles cutting off little pieces of the film so everybody could have their own piece of *The Plastic Mile* and get to see a little bit of it."

The Plastic Mile episode was one of those vivid 1960s events which, like the decade itself, would stick with its participants in oddly cinematic ways. Although Beverlee Miller was one of the leads, she has never seen the film. Nor did she make it to the Queen Elizabeth Theatre, having moved to New Jersey to attend Rutgers University. "But someone sent me a piece of *The Plastic Mile*," she says. "I kept it for many years."

THE DECLINE OF WEST COAST
CIVILIZATION

5

Dennis Hopper stood at a microphone on stage at East Vancouver's Viking Hall desperately trying to control the uncontrollable. He was shooting a punk rock concert scene for his movie *Out of the Blue* and the real-life 1979 Vancouver punks brought on as extras wouldn't do as they were told. Finally, someone let out a loud "Fuck Hollywood" at the actor/director. The self-styled "renegade" filmmaker saw his opportunity to bond and said, "Yeah, that's right, fuck Hollywood." But the audience wasn't buying and before Hopper could explain that he knew James Dean and Captain America too, the shouting got louder.

"Fuck Hollywood," they screamed, many not knowing, or caring, who Dennis Hopper was.

§

There was a moment in the mid-1970s when it looked as though Vancouver might revert to the somnambulism of the 1950s. Then punk rock showed its sneering face. At the time, it seemed like the new anti-hippie culture, but take a slightly longer view now and you notice there were only a couple years between the death of the hip counter-culture in the early mid-'70s and the birth of the punk counter-culture in the late mid-'70s. They were, by and large, at different ends of the same generation and while hip culture was far tougher and more intelligent than the saccharine portrayal it's received in the mass media, punk at its best was softer and more intelligent than it's often been portrayed.

At least punk was during its first years in the late 1970s when its heart was in London, represented by working-class bands like The Clash and The Sex Pistols. Later, when its heart moved to L.A.'s beaches, it became less melodic and far less socially conscious. It was a move from punks whose parents voted Labour to punks whose parents voted Republican. The punk that emerged in Vancouver in the late 1970s predated the large scene in Southern California suburbia, so it was influenced by London, not L.A. And true to Vancouver form, it had that nagging west coast Canadian social conscience. D.O.A., The Subhumans, and other Vancouver bands were quick to "rock against" any bad cause and defiantly shouted lyrics delighting in a general strike or decrying greedy "sickoid" culture.

Chris Haddock, the producer-creator of CBC's hit series *Da Vinci's Inquest*, first got involved in film as a stand-in for Ray Winston (*Sexy Beast*), who was starring in the punk movie *Ladies and Gentlemen – The Fabulous Stains*. "[The film also featured] the bass player from The Clash, Paul Simonon; two players from The Sex Pistols, Steve [Jones] and Cookie [Paul Cook], and the Tubes. Lou Adler was the director. Joe Roth, who's now the head of Revolution Studios, ex-head of Disney, was the producer," says Haddock.

"There was a fantastic assortment of talent. Lou Adler's previous big hit had been *The Rocky Horror Picture Show* and he was trying to create another cult movie. So I was working as a stand-in and got to know all the guys in the band. I came out of that and went directly into music. I actually formed a band shortly after all those guys left town."

Haddock's musical endeavours were helped by the guitar that Sex Pistol Jones had stolen from the props truck. "I was up in Steve's hotel room and there was a bunch of guitars that were used for the props in the band they were playing. We were just hanging around after set and he asked me if I wanted to buy this '56 Telecaster that had been used as a prop in the band. So I said yeah and laid down seventy-five bucks to buy it. About two years later I was short on rent and gave it to my roomie, who was the landlord, and he took it and played with it for a long time. And then he sold it to another guy who eventually got it stolen from him, so there's a hot '56 Telecaster out there somewhere."

Vancouver film did not reflect punk as overtly as it did the sixties counter-culture. Punk was not as large, demographically speaking, as the hip counter-culture, and there were not a lot of movies directly involving punk, though there were some such as *Ladies and Gentlemen – the Fabulous Stains* (also known as *All Washed Up*), *Out of the Blue*, and *Terminal City Ricochet*. It affected Vancouver film more through the personalities who would later emerge (including former punks and current film directors Mina Shum and Lynne Stopkewich), the unique connection between film and music in Vancouver, and the determined do-it-yourself ethos, which would change the culture of filmmaking in the city.

§

Much of the punk impact on movie-making would emerge years later with the arrival of a film scene as fiercely independent as the punk scene had been. But there were other influences at work in the decade following the Vancouver appearance of Altman and other Hollywood mavericks. If the independent film scene was punk, the emerging U.S. service industry was disco.

Despite high-profile films such as *Carnal Knowledge* and *McCabe and Mrs Miller* – which premiered a week apart in June 1971 – Vancouver's studio space and movie-making infrastructure were too embryonic in the early 1970s to attract Hollywood in big numbers. There was the occasional feature, notably *The Groundstar Conspiracy* (1971) and *Russian Roulette* (1975).

The Groundstar Conspiracy was a science fiction thriller shot at Panorama and Simon Fraser University, which played a futuristic space complex. Originally called *The Alien*, then *Plastic Man*, it starred George Peppard and Michael Sarrazin. Vancouver plays Vancouver in *Russian Roulette*, a bit of Cold War intrigue also known as *Kosygin is Coming*. It features mountie George Segal in hand-to-hand combat on the Hotel Vancouver rooftop.

The federal government's Capital Cost Allowance tax shelter, which allowed film investors to write off 100 percent of their costs, prompted a late-decade filmmaking boon, moving starstruck dentists and accountants to invest in a spate of bad movies aimed at the international market.

The Canadian Film Development Corporation, founded in 1967 to develop the country's feature-film industry, also played a substantial role in the sudden increase in production. The federal funding precursor of Telefilm, the CFDC provided financing for thirty-four Canadian features in 1979. Gratien Gelinas, the organization's first head, had argued for film quotas and a box-office tax on American films but, fearing the U.S. industry's response would be a boycott, the government instead opted in 1974 for the Capital Cost Allowance writeoff that would, so the theory went, develop international coproductions, thereby establishing Canadian producers who would then finance smaller Canadian films. But the boon in production wasn't joined by one in distribution, and the Capital Cost Allowance films that did find distribution were mostly critical disasters.

The 1979 film *The Changeling* (Canadian-financed by Garth Drabinsky's Chessman Productions) was the best known of the made-in-Vancouver films produced as a result of the tax-shelter initiative (although the program's big "success" story was *Meatballs*, a comedy which was shot in Ontario for CDN$1.6 million and grossed more than US$40 million). In *The Changeling*, George C. Scott is a composer/visiting professor who, for reasons even more mysterious than the ghostly goings-on, decides to live alone in an enormous mansion during his spooky stay in "Seattle." Hollywood cameras depicting Vancouver landmarks (the Lions Gate Bridge, the Europe Hotel, and Gastown's Maple Tree Square in *The Changeling*) as places elsewhere would become annoyingly commonplace as the service industry grew.

At the time, Montreal was still Canada's film centre, home to thirty-nine features in 1979. That year Toronto had seventeen and twelve were spread across the rest of the country. Although the writeoff had more impact in eastern Canada, it was felt in Vancouver, too, with nine features in 1979: *The Changeling, Bear Island, Out of the Blue, Element of Risk, Klondike Fever, Patman, Prophecy, Strange Companions,* and *A Man, A Woman and A Bank*.

Bear Island, a thriller set on a mysterious Arctic isle, has one of the more eclectic casts assembled for a B.C. movie, including Donald Sutherland, Richard Widmark, Vanessa Redgrave, Christopher Lee, Barbara Parkins, Lloyd Bridges, and a very young Bruce Greenwood.

§

From the early 1970s until the mid-1980s, there were a handful of local feature filmmakers, but still no film scene.

The locals included Daryl Duke, a veteran of early Vancouver television, who returned home in the 1970s after a long stay in Hollywood primarily working as a TV director-producer. Back in Canada, he directed the Toronto feature *The Silent Runner*, with Elliott Gould, which won several prizes – best film, director – at the 1978 Canadian Film Awards, precursor of the Genies. Although Duke directed television in B.C., including the 1973 TV movie *I Heard the Owl Call My Name*, he didn't really work as a Vancouver-based feature director, instead focussing on CKVU, a new TV station he owned in the city, and directing TV miniseries (*The Thorn Birds*) in the U.S.

There was the odd Canadian feature made in Vancouver the first years after Larry Kent departed. Sylvia Spring, newly arrived from Ontario, had a bit part in Morrie Ruvinsky's *The Plastic Mile* (1969) and not long after she would direct her own, *Madeleine is...* (1971), starring Nicki Lipman as a young woman from Montreal residing in Vancouver's hippie milieu. Madeleine is dressing a shop window when she sees a man, identical to her fantasy clown, looking in from the street. The film provides a glimpse of bits of Vancouver that are long gone, such as the Stanley Park zoo and the pre-touristy Gastown.

"I came to Vancouver in '67, which was a very high time, and I fell in love with the place and so I decided to move here," says Spring, who had worked as a documentary writer-director at CBC and CTV. "So, I freelanced and I did little odd jobs here and there. I did a film with [Vancouver filmmaker] David Rimmer for CBC. And then there was a little bit of money that the film board was giving out to do pilot films so I did a pilot for *Madeleine Is...*"

The *Madeleine Is...* short was well-received so Spring developed it into a feature screenplay and, with money from the CFDC and private investors, she became the first woman to direct a Canadian feature film. (Nell Shipman had directed silent pictures in the U.S.)

"I had chutzpah. Well, you know, I was ambitious. I thought I could do anything," she recalls. "I had no feature experience, I had no training but what I did was I hired very good people. I hired Doug McKay, who was the best cameraman, everybody told me. He shot one of Kent's films. He was wonderfully supportive."

Toronto distributors put the film into theatres across Canada but, says Spring: "They didn't do any pushing in the States. They were supposed to take it to Cannes and they didn't promote it all. So it just disappeared."

The thin ranks of early local filmmakers also included Peter Bryant (*The Supreme Kid*), Byron Black (*Master of Images*), Tom Shandel (*Another Smith for Paradise*), and Zale Dalen (*Skip Tracer*).

Then there was Jack Darcus.

§

Not long after the original Vancouver indie filmmaker, Larry Kent, left for Montreal, another appeared on the scene just as determined to make his own movies. Jack Darcus was the second Vancouver director to leave his stamp on the city with a series of features. He also was the city's most prolific filmmaker in the 1970s.

Darcus grew up in Vancouver's Marpole district, skipped a grade ("That was their way of handling people who were looking bored, I guess"), and in 1957, when he was sixteen, enrolled at UBC (philosophy and art history). He also studied painting at the old Vancouver School of Art at Hamilton and Dunsmuir.

"After I left university, I showed paintings, taught night school. I sort of segued into designing sets for a company called the Gallimaufry, which was an independent theatre company. That company ended up becoming Tamanhous later on. So, I was painting and designing sets and seeing a lot of great films."

Darcus's infatuation with the movies started at the Saturday matinees in the neighbourhood Marpole Theatre, but there were other films and motivations that would move him to make movies.

"The thing that happened that I think that got me into film in the late '60s was the Vietnam War. I was involved in a lot of protest things. Painting was not a vehicle to address that though. At the same time, because Hollywood lost its grip on what was happening for a while there, we had some of the best European films coming in – Bergman, Truffaut, Goddard, Antonioni, Fellini. All these films came in that now would never play in North America. They had long runs. The Varsity Theatre had Don Barnes who was the manager at the time. And it was known as an art house."

In 1968, he took his idea for a movie, *Great Coups of History*, to the film society at UBC. "They had some money and wanted to make a film. They had no subject. I had a subject."

The genesis of *Great Coups in History* was in "an amazingly raunchy raconteur" whose portrait he was commissioned to paint. "While I was painting her, she told these incredible stories about men she had picked up. She was living off men but she was manipulating and designing the relationships so they were looking after her interests – long-term relationships, six months, a year or so, usually with immigrants who wanted an English-speaking woman who had some class. And she did. So she could take them to good restaurants, she could show them Canada, and they could look after her.

"So, I was painting her and listening to her and I thought, 'Wow, what an incredible subject you are.' And also, the fact is the painting, being as mute as it was, just wasn't reflecting her at all."

He began visiting once a week to tape her stories, at first thinking it might become a stage play. "One was called 'The Little Lunch,' where she'd pick up a strange man in a restaurant. As soon as she saw a man alone she knew all the moves to get to his table and to get him to pay her lunch and set up something for the future.

"We finally honed these things down so I had some very nice versions of her principal story. Then I, at that point, connected with the film society." The society backed the project and with Darcus digging into his own pockets too, he soon found himself directing his first feature.

"I had the wit to hire Terry Hudson, who had just shot Morrie Ruvinsky's first feature. And Terry was a wonderful, young, talented cameraman. I knew nothing about directing other than what I'd watched in rehearsals of theatre and I knew nothing about film language. And so we started shooting. I was very quickly in over my eyebrows in debt and also learning very fast. I was writing nights and shooting days and it was the wildest ride I'd had up to that point. We shot for a month. I guess in today's terms it would be a couple of hundred thousand. In those days it was purely the lab costs so it was something like about, I think, I spent $7,000."

He ended up shooting 20,000 feet of 16-millimetre film. "And I started cutting. I had never cut before. Eight months later I came out with a film. I fell in love with film during editing because then I started to understand how to use it, and how to pace scenes, how to collapse time, how to extend time if you wanted to. It's a wonderful art, editing. I was doing portraits every afternoon and editing at night.

"I got the film finished and then Odeon theatres picked it up and opened it at the Varsity. They gave me one week, in between Bogdanovich's *Targets* and *Z*."

Great Coups of History, released in 1970, only played Vancouver and the Edinburgh festival. But in 1973, Darcus's second film, *Proxy-hawks*, about birds of prey, Vietnam, and a west coast couple reuniting, was accepted to Cannes.

His first CFDC funding (CDN$60,000 towards the CDN$100,000 budget) came with his third film, 1975's *The Wolfen Principle*, about a Holocaust survivor's plan to free the wolves in Stanley Park. "At that point, I had to learn how to write. I'd managed to do the first two films with just an event structure and some dialogue but I hadn't formally had to write a screenplay or impressed anybody with my writing skills because I had started the movie and then written it as we went along. When it came to the third film, I had to send in screenplays to the government bureaucrats. And they had to read and approve what I wrote, which was for me another whole art to learn."

Early on, Darcus was inspired by fellow UBC student Larry Kent, and he's formed a lasting bond with *Bitter Ash* star Alan Scarfe, another old friend from the university.

"I remember sitting down with him in that grungy old cafeteria below the old auditorium and having lots of philosophical discussions," says Scarfe. They went on to work together at Gallimaufry and other theatre projects before Darcus asked Scarfe and his wife, actor Barbara March, to star in *Deserters*, a 1983 feature about a confrontation in Canada between a Vietnam War-era U.S. army officer and a deserter. Darcus drew directing and screenwriting Genie nominations for the film, which addressed the matter that had led him to filmmaking: the implications of war, in particular Vietnam.

"A lot of people's comment about *Deserters* was it was so good that it was worth remaking with a budget sufficient to really make it work," says Scarfe, noting that the acclaim didn't translate into distribution. "Even the fact that it got nominated for a number of Genie Awards – both Barbara and I got nominated – that didn't help. It didn't seem to matter a darn. So I think they wind up getting on Citytv. They keep playing. They're all playing constantly on the Bravo! Channel. Jack and I have done five movies, actually talking about a sixth one now.

"We're just very comfortable together. We work very easily together on the scripts and I've worked with him on the scripts in each case. I just like him. We've always liked each other. And I recognize him as an unique and adventurous spirit."

Some of Darcus's witty, nuanced tales are easily as entertaining as movies that get distribution, but his films came along at a time when Vancouver indies received little attention. Their failure to get more recognition was due to their low-budget look and an almost impossible distribution system.

"Jack's scripts are always wonderful," says Scarfe, who also costarred in *Overnight* (1986), a comic look at the absurdity of the film industry, and *Kingsgate* (1990), a look at intellectuals coming apart at a country retreat.

"*Overnight*, which is now called *Not Just a Dirty Little Movie*, is one of the funniest scripts I've ever read. I mean, we sat down at the first reading before we shot that movie and we were in absolute hysterics with it. But of course translating an enormously comical script on to film is very difficult. So, it only partly works.

"*Kingsgate* comes from a real event that Jack and I and my wife were all involved in, with a girlfriend of his. We used to have a place in southern Ontario called Kingsgate Farm. I actually threw the girlfriend out of the house. That film is the least successful of all of them, I think. That film should have worked."

And there are the Darcus films that never got made. "There was a wonderful film script called *The Falcon and the Ballerina*, which we were going to make with Karen Kain way back when in the early '80s. Never got made. It is just very difficult for him to get people to fund him," says Scarfe. "He's made a remarkable number of films but of course people like Alliance, where you're going to get the money from, say, 'Well, none of them made any money.' So that's the toughie."

Darcus isn't complaining, though he has few illusions. "As a person who's managed to make eight features – managed to get my writing on the screen so that I could see whether it worked or not – I've had a very charmed existence in filmmaking terms, just because I've had the opportunity to do that." There is an upside, too, to not attracting attention from the mainstream film industry. While he has received little distribution, Darcus's noncommercial style is actually key to his longevity.

"I'm essentially very much on the periphery of everything. The only way I've managed to do what I've done and am continuing to do is to stay way, way out there, just because my approach doesn't fit. But there's a little enclave of continued cultural interest going on in Canada, where the CRTC [Canadian Radio-television and Telecommunications Commission] compels broadcasters to license Canadian product simply as a token gesture and therefore someone like me can have an existence making movies. If the CRTC went away, there's no reason that the Movie Network would ever want to pay a licence to me. They could buy twelve American movies for the same price."

THE STUDIO SYSTEM

6

Vancouver's current studio system started with a Hollywood conversation between a Toronto actor and a Los Angeles producer. Nick Mancuso, of Toronto, was talking with Stephen J. Cannell, of L.A., on the set of the TV series *Stingray*, which was being produced for NBC. "He [Cannell] is losing his shirt because these shows are costing about $400,000 more than what the networks are licensing them for," recalls Mancuso. "It was killing me. I said, 'Steve, let's go to Canada.' He said, 'No.' This is in '86 when nobody was coming up. After about three, four meetings he changes his mind. The next thing you know we're shooting in Calgary and Vancouver. And then he brought up *Wiseguy* and he brought everybody else up. And that's how it started."

After Mancuso's suggestion, Cannell checked out Toronto, but didn't like the time zone; checked out Vancouver, but couldn't get a crew; checked out the favourable exchange rate and decided that practically anywhere in Canada would be fine. He started in Calgary but quickly moved his operations to Vancouver, shooting in warehouses and other locations around town.

Cannell would build North Shore Studios (now Lions Gate Studios) on a fourteen-acre site in North Vancouver. "It started because Nick Mancuso was the star of *Stingray*," Cannell says. "He was a Canadian. I didn't know why we would shoot in such a distant location."

Cannell was hardly the first to consider building a studio in B.C. But Columbia's studio in Victoria was an old story and the Panorama site, in starts and stops since the early 1970s, was shrinking as pricey West Vancouver real estate developers encroached and the last of it wound up as a condominium development after the "for sale" sign went up in 1985. The old Dominion Bridge site in Burnaby, where sections of the Lions Gate and Golden Gate bridges were built, was being utilized as a sound stage, and nearby Vancouver Film Studios was being built in slow gradations. As well, sound stages were being concocted in warehouses and other buildings around town. And there had been talk in the newspapers of a new studio in Delta or Surrey or Squamish or even Blaine, Washington.

Cannell's North Shore Studios, though, was more than a headline that went nowhere. It was built quickly and would fundamentally change the U.S. service industry in Vancouver. (Although Cannell was the driving force behind it, funding also came from the B.C. government and Paul Bronfman's Comweb Corp. "I wanted to bring in a Canadian partner so we wouldn't look like a bunch of carpetbaggers," Cannell says.)

It was the country's largest filmmaking centre, the city's first multi-sound, all-purpose stage facility built for the express purpose of making movies. It would accelerate the growth of Vancouver's film-making infrastructure and local crew members used the U.S. shows shot there as training schools.

It's where producer Chris Carter's TV shows, including *The X-Files*, would later be shot. Before that, upon its grand opening in 1989, Cannell's own programs, *21 Jump Street* and *Wiseguy*, put the studio on the map. "I shot fifteen primetime series up there. It was thriving long before *The X-Files* ever arrived. [*21 Jump Street*'s] Johnny Depp was white hot," he says.

As well as boosting the infrastructure, the popularity of *21 Jump Street* and *The X-Files*, and of Depp and *The X-Files* stars David Duchovny and Gillian Anderson, changed the perception of Vancouver as a tax-shelter dumping ground. Not that the overall quality of productions increased appreciably, but now the service industry was entrenching.

The Bridge Studio's expansion quickly followed North Shore's opening. Proponents of a permanent studio on the old Dominion Bridge site had won out over a mega-shopping centre proposal from the developers of the West Edmonton Mall. The renovated facility featured the largest special-effects stage in North America.

The increased studio space was a turning point for the U.S. service industry but it didn't singlehandedly create the film industry in Vancouver. As much as Cannell's arrival was a catalyst, there's no doubt that someone eventually would have filled the demand for highly profitable studio space. The city's locale and look were just too much for U.S. producers to ignore. Expansion and entrenchment, in some form, was the inevitable consequence of an industry that had been growing during the 1980s due to a sliding Canadian dollar, inviting government policies, Hollywood's shift from shooting in studios to shooting on location, and the growing professionalism of Vancouver crews.

The crews had a local face by the 1980s. In one five-year period during the decade, the Canadian content of Vancouver crews rose from forty to ninety-seven percent. "The crews here are exceptional," noted Martin Sheen, while in town shooting *Cold Front*. "They're professional and friendly, and willing to go that extra step to get things right."

The crew members that came together in Vancouver had disparate backgrounds. Gavin Craig, local head of the film union IATSE (International Alliance of Theatrical Stage Employees), which formed in B.C. in 1962, notes: "Don't forget about the evolution of motion pictures. Our union per se as a whole started on stage, the migration from stage to motion pictures was a natural. So there were qualified people. There's a big difference between a carpenter and a scenic carpenter. A carpenter, as you know, makes things to last. A scenic carpenter makes things so he can pick them up with his little finger and after it's finished, he can throw it away. So you want to make it as cheaply as possible and only last for the period of paying for the motion picture. That's what you have to educate a carpenter to do. Instead of making it out of two-by-fours and four-by-fours and one inch plywood you've got to make it out of banana board and one-by-threes and Styrofoam and everything like that. We have sculptors and such within our organization as well.

"So that has evolved. Also, the lighting people migrated from CBC and *The Beachcombers*. And a lot of our members came from the rental houses of the equipment as well. There was also a migration from Toronto and the Prairies to Vancouver because it was becoming the nucleus of the industry in Western Canada."

By the mid-'80s, Vancouver had pulled away from the rest of Western Canada. In Alberta, for instance, filmmakers spent about $8 million in 1984, down from $25 million in 1983, a decline attributed to Vancouver's proximity to Hollywood. "They [Vancouver] did really well last year because nobody wanted to shoot in Los Angeles during the Olympics and Vancouver was relatively close," Michael Hamm, president of the Alberta Motion Picture Industry Association, said in a 1985 Canadian Press story.

The budgets of film and television production in B.C. increased from $12.5 million in 1978 to $65.8 million in 1980 to more than $200 million in 1989. Thousands of film industry employees felt secure enough to stop plotting backup careers.

In 1978, the B.C. Film Commission was established to scout locations and generally make life easy for producers considering a B.C. shoot. "We're cheap and we're close," commissioner Dianne Neufeld said in a Canadian Press story in 1984. "Mexico is cheap and close, too, but the difference is they don't have a skilled pool of technicians and facilities."

By 1985, the annual *Reel West Digest* was listing virtually every component of the industry that you would find in Los Angeles, from gaffers and stunt performers to talent agents and computer graphics designers. Locals such as Paul Sharpe would become fixtures in the industry, with his Sharpe Sound Studios enabling filmmakers to complete post-production in Vancouver, mixing sound for hundreds of productions from *Dick Tracy* to *Double Happiness*.

Jane Mundy, for one, had dreamed of being in the movies back at her suburban Toronto high school, and the first time she prepared food on a set, she found herself living out the fantasy. "They hauled me off and gave me a part in an episode of [the TV series] *Bordertown*. I was the mail-order bride. I sent my mother the tape. She loved it."

In 1987, Mundy started working at Reel Appetites, a Vancouver film catering company, and purchased

TEN MEMORABLE U.S. SHOOTS IN B.C. DURING THE 1980s

First Blood (1982). Sylvester Stallone's first Rambo film; he returned three years later for *Rambo: First Blood II*, directed by Victoria's George Pan Cosmatos.

Star 80 (1983). The last movie shot at Panorama Studios; Mariel Hemingway plays Dorothy Stratten, the murdered actor/playmate from the Vancouver suburb of Coquitlam.

Rocky IV (1985). Like film follow-ups such as *Jurassic Park 2* and *Men in Black 2*, the Rocky sequels were so bad that they actually diminished the public perception of the original movie, even though the first *Rocky* wasn't half bad.

Knights of the City (1987). A band of New Yorkers can't decide if they want to be a street gang or a music group.

Roxanne (1987). Steve Martin's update of the Cyrano de Bergerac story, shot in beatific Nelson.

The Accused (1988). The only shot-in-Vancouver movie to win a major Oscar: Jodie Foster was named

76

the firm five years later. Her first big catering gig was for the film *We're No Angels*, which was shot in Mission, B.C. "It was horrible for us, cooking for 200 people a day, sixteen or seventeen hours, freezing, had to go through six feet of snow. We were so cold, after breakfast we put pancakes in our bras to keep warm." But she was hooked on the work. "It was exciting. I like the fact that I had freedom." She also learned a lot about eating patterns. For instance, *We're No Angels'* Sean Penn: "If he was a good boy the night before he'd have scrambled eggs, bacon, hash browns – a regular breakfast. If he was a bad boy he would have a fresh vegetable and fruit plate."

Actors, too, were setting up shop. John Travolta actually moved to Vancouver in 1989, purchasing a condo near the north end of the Burrard Street Bridge. He had a couple of projects in Vancouver and other actors were moving to the city, too. "I thought, 'I'm going to be there anyway, why don't I just live there?'" Travolta says. "George Segal moved upstairs because it looked like it was Hollywood North and people were going to be there. I liked roller blading around the park. I used to do that every day. I literally would go the four or five or six miles or whatever it is around the park. And I went up the mountains to ski once or twice. I felt very much a part of it."

Travolta shot four movies in Vancouver (the three *Look Who's Talking* films and *The Experts*) but when a year went by without work in the city, he sold the condo and headed back to L.A.

best actress for playing a woman defiantly demanding justice after being gang-raped.

Friday the 13th, Part VIII (1988). More mindless mayhem from the producers of this movie series of the '80s.

Cousins (1989). Ted Danson and Isabella Rosselini, distant relatives by marriage, cavort at Hycroft Manor and other Vancouver landmarks.

The Fly II (1989). Simon Fraser University – apparently Arthur Erickson's architectural contribution to bad science fiction – is again the futuristic setting in this poorly conceived sequel.

Look Who's Talking (1989). During one of the frequent lulls in Travolta's career, the Vancouver-shot *Look Who's Talking* series was all that stood between him and *Return to Welcome Back, Kotter*.

Also: *Eureka* (1983), *Runaway* (1984), *Iceman* (1984), *Year of the Dragon* (1985), *The Journey of Natty Gann* (1985), *Clan of the Cave Bear* (1986), *Stakeout* (1987), *The Experts* (1989), *Cold Front* (1989), *Who's Harry Crumb?* (1989).

Some left their mark a little more loudly than Travolta. In 1989, Mike Tyson arrived to spend time with his estranged wife Robin Givens, who was shooting a TV movie called *The Penthouse*. Greeted by newspaper and television reporters at the Hotel Vancouver, he grabbed a camera from a *Vancouver Sun* photographer and threw it against the wall, then lunged at a BCTV camera, ripping away its viewfinder and smashing it to the floor. Tyson then tried to grab the television camera, but the cameraman escaped through a revolving door, with minor injuries to his hand.

That same year, Johnny Depp was starring in *21 Jump Street* when he got into a brawl and let his opinion be known about Canada's national winter sport. "He said we were a bunch of Moosehead-drinking hockey players. He was pretty insulting to Canadians," Coast Plaza Hotel security guard David Sulina told the *Vancouver Sun*, after Depp was charged with assault. Depp pleaded guilty to spitting in Sulina's face and kneeing him in the groin.

Throughout the 1980s and into the '90s, the Canadian dollar would fluctuate (worth 76 cents to every US$1 in 1987, 85 cents in 1989) and the occasional government proposal to tax visiting American filmmakers would cause a stir, but Vancouver's studios were open for business, the infrastructure was falling into place, the dollar would stay relatively cheap, and the industry would continue to grow.

§

There was a moment – just before the American service industry started to regard Vancouver as Hollywood North –when it seemed that 100 years of B.C. polarities had come to a head. By the early 1980s, Vancouver's cultural underground had moved on from Fourth Avenue to Commercial Drive and far-flung Gulf Islands. Some conventional "wisdom" maintained that the in-your-face manner of Larry Kent or Morrie Ruvinsky was passé, that artistic and social upheaval was something more in tune with the late 1960s or early 1970s. But Vancouver's great social street fight (and that of the entire province) happened much later than that, during the rainy season of late 1983, when suddenly it seemed as though the entire city was racing through a cranked-up newsreel from the French general strike of May-June 1968.

It started when the Social Credit provincial government proposed large-scale cuts to social services and restrictions on labour organizing. The cultural and political communities that had been for decades fomenting separately joined forces in a "Solidarity" movement, which organized picket lines, occupations and huge rallies, and called for a general strike. B.C. Federation of Labour president Art Kube was among those advocating a syndicalist-style action in which striking workers stay on the job and take over the management of their workplaces. All this was brought to a screeching halt by a last-minute backroom deal between a squeamish union leader (the International Woodworkers of America's Jack Munro) and a jittery premier (the Social Credit's Bill Bennett), but for a time Vancouver's streets looked like something out of Costa-Gavras's *Z* or Warren Beatty's *Reds*.

§

While the U.S. service industry grew in Vancouver through the 1980s, there wasn't a sustained independent film scene. A movie made by Vancouverites in the city was still a rarity. There was, however, the occasional significant independent film.

Phillip Borsos' 1983 film *The Grey Fox* was a benchmark for Vancouver filmmakers. Borsos, who grew up in the Okanagan and Maple Ridge, had made several acclaimed shorts, including the Oscar-nominated *Nails*, before directing this story about train robber Bill Miner, beautifully shot throughout the B.C. Interior. American actor Richard Farnsworth portrayed Miner, a "gentleman" outlaw who began a second life of crime in B.C. after serving thirty-three years in San Quentin.

The Grey Fox was the first Vancouver film to win the Genie Award for best picture, and it attracted raves during its North American-wide distribution. When Hollywood came calling, Borsos answered, following up *The Grey Fox* with the studio films *The Mean Season*, a thriller with Kurt Russell and Mariel Hemingway, and the seasonal *One Magic Christmas*. His last film was the epic story of Canadian doctor/radical/ adventurer Norman Bethune. The production was wracked by creative differences between Borsos, screenwriter Ted Allan, and lead actor Donald Sutherland, but the resulting film, *Bethune: The Making of a Hero*, is not entirely without merit. Where the great promise shown in *The Grey Fox* may, or may not, have taken Borsos ended when he was taken by cancer at age forty-two.

79

Borsos had known Sandy Wilson, whose *My American Cousin* was the other breakout B.C. film of the era, since their youths in the Penticton area.

"Phil Borsos' dad was my high school art teacher," says Wilson. "I knew him when we were kids. I helped him to get some money to do his first short film, *Nails,* and he was the one who read my script, *My American Cousin,* and convinced Peter O'Brien to produce it. And Phil made a point to visit us on the first day of our film shoot."

My American Cousin is an autobiographical, coming-of-age story set in 1950s' Penticton, a summer holiday destination in B.C.'s Okanagan. Wilson, who had lived in Vancouver since the mid-'60s, came up with the idea for the movie while vacationing at her Okanagan cabin in August 1982. "I heard the Johnny Horton song 'The Battle of New Orleans' come on the radio and I said, 'Oh, this reminds me of my American cousin.' And I thought, 'What a great title for a film.' So I got out my lipstick and I wrote it on the plate-glass window and it looked really good. I started thinking about it. It's that golden summer of 1959 – the innocence, the beauty of the Okanagan, the boy, the girl, the Americans, the Canadians, that sense of where are you from and what is family and what is home. I thought, 'Oh, this is a movie I would like to see when I'm an old lady in the old folks' home.' That's basically the reason that I make any of the films. I thought, it's not a short film and it's not a documentary. I guess it's a feature. So I started writing."

Although Wilson was writing her first feature, she had been involved in film since 1967, when she was a student at Simon Fraser University. "We were all involved in the student politics up there and I was a cartoonist for the student newspaper, *The Peak.* Then some women came up from Berkeley and talked about this idea that women needed to be liberated and that was like a real big surprise, a radical notion. And it was right around that time I heard there were some cute guys in the Simon Fraser Film Workshop. So, I put the two together and signed up for film."

This was before there were film studies programs on Vancouver campuses, but the student group, including future filmmakers such as Peter Bryant (*The Supreme Kid*) and Terre Nash (*If You Love This Planet*), had made super-8 movies. Soon, Wilson had graduated to directing documentaries and shorts and working on such early Vancouver indies as Sylvia Spring's *Madeleine Is . . .* (as assistant director) and Jack Darcus's *Proxyhawks* (assistant editor).

As Wilson wrote *My American Cousin*, she began lining up her crew and cast, including her Vancouver neighbour, Margret Langrick, as her precocious adolescent self. "That little Margaret Langrick definitely fit the bill. She had what I always look for for working with anybody, which is what I consider to be a kind of a generosity of spirit."

Vancouver actor Babz Chula, who would appear in many Canadian films, had only done American service-industry work before *My American Cousin*. "I was called in to audition for Sandy and I really appreciated that before we did anything they talked to me, which is so unusual. Right away, I knew that I was hooked on Canadian independent film – local community projects. There wasn't any celebrity stuff. It was me and them. I could say, 'Oh, I just had oral surgery, I'm a little groggy,' and I didn't feel like I blew the audition. There was no way to blow the audition. It was just people in the room, you know, it was really cool.

"Then it carried its way through all the way to the shoot. It was relaxed, it was fun, we laughed our asses off. We were in Penticton – you couldn't have been in a more beautiful place. It was an exquisite summer, just one of our dry, high beautiful blue sky summers. We're sitting out overlooking Lake Okanagan and shooting a movie. I mean, it was just heaven."

Wilson shot much of the movie in the place where she grew up, Paradise Ranch, at the end of a dirt road seventeen miles north of Penticton. "That was a big kick," says Wilson, "to write a film and reinvent your family and have control over making your younger brother, who used to tease you, look like an idiot. That was very satisfying."

My American Cousin would win every major Genie Award and be distributed throughout North America.

"It was a little bit before the days we knew to be excited about stuff like that," says Chula. "There wasn't a screening for the cast. There was none of that kind of preparation for the festival circuit, where you know you're going to participate in the whole process that films go through now. There was no process."

When the film opened in Vancouver in 1985, Chula was shooting *The Accused*, the movie that would win Jodie Foster an Oscar.

"Well, let me tell you, they went to see it. I remember [*The Accused* director] Jonathan Kaplan and all these people went to see *My American*

Cousin because it was like this award-winning big blockbuster Canadian movie. And they didn't get it at all. They thought it was hokey. They ranted about how unprofessional it was and, you know, 'What's the big deal?' and 'It was like a coming-of-age movie.' They couldn't believe it had been best film in Canada, winning the Genie or 'whatever that award is you people have.' They said it was slow, they thought it was amateur."

There are things about *My American Cousin* that don't work (some of the supporting players' acting is uneven). Still, Wilson captured the era and place and the sense of being Canadian in a most unusual movie for 1986 – a teen movie with a brain. (Remember, Canada was about to give the world *Meatballs III*.) This was not just an American coming-of-age story, it was a North American story, set in the most Americanized of Canadian towns, Penticton, when the Okanagan town was doing its best impression of a Southern California beach community.

"In the States we got rock 'n' roll all day long," the older American cousin Butch (John Wildman) explains to Wilson's alter ego, Sandy Wilcox (Langrick). "Anything you want, you get in the U.S.A."

The film's magic was missing in Wilson's 1989 sequel, *American Boyfriends*. Chula, however, does recall one telling incident, shot at a cemetery on a day so cold that the frozen rain was blowing sideways.

"We were ankle deep in ice water and dressed in light frocks, so that in between every shot we were running over to heaters and drying our hair. We were shivering and trying not to have our breath show on screen. And it's a funeral. There's a lot of people there. . . . We think we're wrapped and then she [Wilson] called us all back out of the vans. She said, 'I made the worst mistake. We have to shoot that again.' People just went, 'Okay, let's go.' I don't even remember the mistake. I'm not sure it was even hers, but she took it.

"I will say that one of the remarkable things that happened for me in that experience was to work with a woman director who, when she made a mistake, would own up to it to cast and crew. That's the first time it ever happened to me as an actor in any experience ever. I mean, you know how everybody's always, always blaming the little guy."

My American Cousin and *The Grey Fox*, independent rarities in the Vancouver of the 1980s, were portents of what was to come in the next decade, when the acting, directing, and infrastructure that were emerging separately would come together.

For people working in film, there are places to go to and there are places to leave. Vancouver has become a place to go to, but in the 1970s and '80s, it was still a place for actors to leave. As the soundstages and studios went up during Vancouver film's formative years, the old studio system still enticed Canadians down to Hollywood. Vancouver actors were virtually never given lead roles in the new service industry and independent film was almost nonexistent, so actors wanting to be in the movies had little choice but to leave. Among those who left B.C. in the 1970s and '80s: Michael J. Fox, Kim Cattrall, Bruce Greenwood, and Jennifer and Meg Tilly.

§

The day Barbara Williams moved away from Vancouver, it was pouring rain and tears. These days, Williams is an actor in Los Angeles with a long list of television and movie credits. In 1979, though, she was a gifted stage actor in Vancouver planning to move to Toronto, but before heading east she planned to give her possessions to her brother Randy in Victoria. It had been a difficult time for her brother, a year older, who had been in a mental institution.

"He had reemerged and I had been trying to help him. He lived with me for awhile. I was always trying to get him jobs," Williams says. "I had a deep psychic connection to him and had been having a recurring dream through all his turbulence – we were circling each other, he had a knife, I had to talk him out of the knife, I took the knife and I killed him."

The night before going to Victoria, Williams was unable to sleep at her place at Second and Trafalgar in Kitsilano. "I got up, it was pouring rain, my car had been stolen." In the morning, the police discovered the car, which had been taken for a joy ride.

"I went and got the car, drove to Victoria in the pouring rain. My windshield wipers had been torn off. I was crying uncontrollably. I was crying in the rain, driving in the rain, weeping like I was leaving my life behind. Finally, I got on the ferry. The sun came out at Discovery Passage and I felt this weight lift out of my heart. I knew my brother had killed himself. I knew when the sun came out at Discovery Passage that was the moment he died."

In Victoria, Williams drove to her mother's home where Randy had been staying and his neighbours came out said, 'Would you like us to call your sister?'

"I knew. It was never even spoken."

∫

Williams was born in Hecate Channel on a tugboat coming into Esperanza, a small village on the Northwest Coast of Vancouver Island. Her mom Simone was a waitress, her dad Jack a sometimes sailor and welterweight boxer but mostly a logger.

The young Williams grew used to being the new kid in class, living in logging camps, usually on Vancouver Island or the B.C. coastline. Her family had moved twenty-seven times by the time she was eleven, when they finally stopped for awhile, in the town formerly known as Gibson's Landing.

"I didn't grow up in a city, so what really shaped my imagination was nature. I was always deep into fantasy. When I was little, all my

dolls were like people. Movies had a big impact on me and TV. I remember my dad was Paladin from *Have Gun Will Travel* and my mom was Lucy from *I Love Lucy*."

Well, sort of. There was a lot of love in her family and her dad was quick to speak out about social injustice but there was a sadness in that home too. "I wasn't raised in a high-achieving family. My dad was a big drinker. It was a hard, harsh, rainy, alcoholic culture. I wanted the light. I just found a way to channel all this pain I was in."

Barbara Williams. *photo by Jason Payne, courtesy* The Province

At first, her way was music, playing guitar at twelve. "I was a flower child. I used to walk around everywhere with my guitar," she says. It was the heady days of the Kitsilano counter-culture and young Barbara found her way into a music festival in the nearby town of Aldergrove. "I somehow snuck in. It was amazing," she says. "I was sitting in the barn on this bale of hay. Someone said, 'Why don't you sing a song, Joni?' And the woman next to me picked up a guitar and started singing 'Both Sides Now.' It just blew me away. It had a very, very big impact on me. Joni Mitchell and Hank Williams, those were my two biggest influences."

Williams started acting, too, and at eighteen won the best-actress award at the provincial drama festival for her performance in *Suddenly Last Summer*. "I was working at Brian's Drive-in right across from high school. I didn't know if I was going to be a waitress all my life or what," she says, "but I got put in *Suddenly Last Summer* and suddenly it catapulted me into theatre."

She moved to Vancouver, studying at Studio 58, at the Langara campus of Vancouver Community College, then on to the Tamanhous House theatre group, starring in thirty plays from 1974 to 1979 – everything from *Dracula* to *St Joan of the Stockyards* to *The Tempest*. "It was one of the most creative periods of my life. I didn't develop my auditioning skills or preparing myself for the business. It wasn't great preparation for Hollywood but it did give me the freedom to access my creativity in a way that I just am not permitted to anymore. You don't get to do that when you're doing movies and television. I had more fun back then than I've ever had since. I wasn't thinking about career. It was being part of this collective of creative people. I mean, it was serious fun. We were serious about what we were doing."

Tamanhous founder John Gray was teaching a class at Langara when Williams enrolled. "She has enormous talent. It was obvious when she first showed up at Langara. Everyone thought, 'Yeah, there's the one,'" says Gray, who has continued to work with Williams over the years. "She was smart and very honest and of course she was gorgeous – still is. She was like something out of a Joni Mitchell song."

§

Every move by an actor is not a career move. After her brother's funeral in Victoria, Williams left for Toronto but "it was just too painful to even consider acting," so she disappeared, spending her days doing cabinet work on her uncle's boat.

Eventually, she acted in Toronto, and moved to Hollywood in 1984 after meeting actor Nick Mancuso, whom she would eventually marry. "I met Nick on a film shoot in Israel, a Canadian-Israeli co-production, and followed him down to L.A. and was seen at a birthday party. This person asked if I was an actress and wanted to see me on film. She liked my look and I went in and auditioned. I read for the casting director, then she asked me to read for the producers and then they made a decision to screen test me. It just happened so quickly. I wasn't even living in L.A. I remember I tested with Steven Bauer, and Nicolas Cage was screen testing. Anyway, so then I went back to Toronto because Nick was sort of half in Toronto, half in L.A. And they called me saying I got the role."

Williams was cast in the starring role in *Thief of Hearts*, a highly hyped Paramount feature about sexual fantasy and manipulation. "I was just swept up into this whole process and I immediately had tensions with one of the producers, Don Simpson, God rest his soul. At the time I guess he was doing a lot of cocaine and stuff. He was very, very abrasive and I was kind of shocked at how rude he was. So, very early on the experience was soured for me. It was a unanimous decision to cast me when they saw my screen test, you know, the studio and producers and everything, and then they just decided that they had

AMONG THOSE WHO LEFT B.C. TO TRY HOLLYWOOD IN THE 1970s AND 1980s

Fairuza Balk (Vancouver). At age nine, she was selected to play Dorothy in a hyped sequel to *The Wizard of Oz*, 1986's *Return to Oz*. Balk has continued acting in the U.S., including roles in *Almost Famous* and *Personal Velocity*.

Kim Cattrall (Vancouver Island). Cattrall left the island town of Comox early and was offered a Universal contract after being sighted in the Toronto stage production of *The Rocky Horror Show*. In L.A., she appeared in television and movies, including *Porky's*, *Police Academy*, and *The Bonfire of the Vanities*. These days is best known for her role in television's *Sex and the City*.

Tommy Chong (Vancouver). Born in Edmonton, Chong spent his formative counter-cultural years in Vancouver, where he teamed with American Cheech Marin to form Cheech and Chong, the most popular movie comedy team since Abbot and Costello (*Cheech & Chong's Next Movie*, *Still Smokin'*).

to change what I looked like. They cut my hair, dyed it, permed it, then dyed it again. When I look at that film, I think it's like SCTV."

The production may look like a bad parody of an SCTV parody but there was some serious behind-the-scenes conflict. Williams had gone to L.A. to work, with no aversion to the prospect of movie stardom, but she was not about to allow anyone to exploit her, regardless of the payoff.

"I had made a big stink. They wanted to shoot more explicit stuff than I was willing to let them. I wasn't going to do it myself and I certainly didn't want them using an image of me. But they went ahead and cast a body double and shot this scene and I didn't even know about. And then they pressured me to get a release. It was a very unpleasant, unhappy experience."

Meanwhile, her manager was suing Paramount for overtime pay she was owed. "It was a precedent-setting case. The SAG [Screen Actors Guild] took it up. And so it ended up costing Paramount a lot of money because we won the case." Williams, though, didn't get a penny. "They hadn't established the precedent until my case."

Williams was excluded from *Thief of Hearts* promotion, the spotlight instead put on costar Steven Bauer. She was sitting in her West Hollywood apartment when she learned how excluded.

"Somebody called me and said, 'Oh, they're going to be reviewing *Thief of Hearts*, turn it on.' So I turned on the TV. [Movie critic] Gary Franklin comes on and he just gives

His daughter, actor Rae Dawn Chong (*Quest for Fire*), has also lived in Vancouver.

Michael J. Fox (Burnaby). Son of a career soldier, Fox spent his childhood on Canadian military bases before the family settled in Burnaby. Started at CBC Vancouver, then at eighteen moved to the U.S. and never looked back. Says director Sandy Wilson: "I was going to audition him for the part of my American cousin except they said, 'Oh, he's just got a TV series, something called *Family Ties*.'" Became famous as Michael Keaton and more famous for the 1985 hit film *Back to the Future*.

Chief Dan George (North Vancouver). He was a former chief of the Burrard Indian Reserve when he was Oscar-nominated for his performance as a Native elder in 1970's *Little Big Man*. Appeared in other 1970s' films (*Harry and Tonto*, *The Outlaw Josey Wales*).

Michael Ontkean (Vancouver). Highlights of his long Hollywood career include the hockey movie *Slap Shot* and TV's *The Rookies* and *Twin Peaks*.

me a rave review, said he didn't really care for this, didn't care for that, but on the basis of my performance he'll give this movie, you know, a 10-plus because I was such a stunning actress and blah, blah, blah, blah. And he says, 'I called the studio and said I wanted to interview her, that young girl, and they said, 'Well, unfortunately, she's gone back to her native Canada.'"

Williams' three-picture deal at Paramount was never exercised. "If the movie had been a huge success you can be sure that all would have been forgiven," she says. "That was my big Hollywood movie. I think I was hot for a while but the movie didn't do anything. Right after you do a movie, everybody's waiting to see what's going to happen. Like I could get meetings for anything.

"There was a moment where I was poised to be a star but I wasn't really so interest in being famous. I didn't have that driving ambition. I was still in creative mode."

Not a bad thing, right?

"In the big picture, sure," she says. In the smaller picture, however, she didn't get the big pictures. Still, steady work came her way – recording her music, acting on stage and TV (series lead in ABC's *Spenser for Hire* and NBC's *Country Estates*), in features. Among the highlights: John Sayles' *City of Hope*, Richard Pryor's *Jo Jo Dancer Your Life Is Calling*, and *Teamster: The Diana Kilmury Story*, for which she won a Gemini Award as Canada's best actress in a TV movie.

"I'm a working-class person and my sense of myself in the business is that I'm a working actress. I don't think all the work I've done is representative of who I am but I'm not ashamed of anything I've ever done. But I would definitely love to do more work that reflects my values."

Jason Priestley (North Vancouver). Made the move to L.A. in the late '80s and soon landed a role in *Beverly Hills, 90210*. Also appeared in films (*Tombstone, Heartbreak Hotel, Love and Death on Long Island*).

Dorothy Stratten (Coquitlam). Her short life story is the subject of the film *Star 80*. "Discovered" on the job at a Coquitlam Dairy Queen by an ambitious sleaze, she went on to *Playboy* magazine, then roles in *Americathon, Skatetown USA*, and *They All Laughed*. Murdered by her estranged husband. She also had a relationship with director Peter

∫

Bogdanovich, who married her sister after the murder.

Jennifer Tilly (Vancouver Island). Comic actress debuted in 1984's *No Small Affair*, then went on to *The Fabulous Baker Boys* and an Oscar nomination for *Bullets Over Broadway*. Grew up in Victoria and the Gulf Islands.

Meg Tilly (Vancouver Island). Jennifer's younger sister started as a dancer but after a back injury switched to acting. Followed her 1982 debut in *Tex* with *The Big Chill*, *Psycho II*, and an Oscar-nominated performance in *Agnes of God*.

In 1994, Williams married longtime activist-politician Tom Hayden, one of the Chicago Eight in the conspiracy trial that followed the riots at the 1968 Democratic Convention, and she's politically active in her own right. In her own way, she maintains a connection to B.C. in L.A. through an involvement in the campaign against the use of pulp from old-growth forests. "It's the continuing effort to save the last frontier on the west coast."

It's not surprising that Williams would be trying, long-distance from L.A., to protect the land she grew up on. She has never lost her bond with B.C. "There is always this gravitational pull. Any reason to go back up to Canada I do, to Vancouver in particular. There just a sympatico that doesn't exist down here. People sort of get me more. They don't get who I am here. I think being from the west coast of Canada, maybe it's the isolation, it's a unique place to come from. It's not like another place.

"Sometimes people in L.A. will say, 'You're not from here.' I'll say 'Canada' and they'll say, 'No, it seems like you're from some place,' like they think that I'm more cultivated or something. It cracks me up because, you know, I'm a logger's daughter."

Having had a long, closeup look at the L.A. industry, Williams knows there are more important things, especially after adopting a son, Liam, at birth in 2000. "The two biggest things that happened to me the last few years is holding my father's hand as he died and holding my [baby's] birth mother's hand when she gave birth."

Williams is part of the last generation of actors who worked Vancouver's stages before there was a film industry in the city. Now that an independent scene is developing in Canada, she's worked in Ontario (2000's *Love Come Down*, 2002's *Perfect Pie*) and has a keen interest in Vancouver film.

"I'd love to find a way back there," Williams says, adding that she's never been one to map out a career. "I didn't really have a strategy. I have to laugh – my niece wants to be an actress and asks me, 'Do you have any advice?' I have no advice, nothing except be strong."

§

While Williams hummed Joni Mitchell songs and dispensed fish and chips at the Gibson's Drive-In, Bruce Greenwood was on the west side of Vancouver daydreaming about ski slopes.

Greenwood, who grew up in the Kerrisdale area, had no interest in acting ("I wanted to be a skier or a writer") in 1976 when he enrolled in a theatre course at UBC, where his mother was a nurse and his father was head of the geology department. "I needed three easy credits at university. I was taking a heavy course load, so I needed something that was totally subjective, that you couldn't be failed at. You can't fail acting. You can be a bad actor but you can't fail. And then, of course, it caught my interest and that's all I cared about."

He was on stage at the campus Frederic Wood Theatre, then the Arts Club. "It was so clear that that's what I suddenly felt like doing that I left school and started working professionally." Greenwood would spend years in Canada working the stage, the odd TV show or film (did a *Beachcombers* episode, a bit in *Bear Island*) and drill rigs before moving to L.A. "on a whim" in 1984.

Greenwood would become one of the most successful Canadian expatriates ever to settle in Hollywood, with critical acclaim for his starring role in *Thirteen Days* and box-office acclaim for *Double Jeopardy*.

Back in 1984, though, like any aspiring actor just arrived in L.A., Greenwood was apprehensive about a future in Hollywood. And any actor from Canada wanting to work in film and television in the early '80s had little more than bit parts waiting for them back home. That would soon start to change, and as much as any Vancouver actor, Greenwood's rising fortunes would be the result of the growth of filmmaking in Canada. But that first uncertain night in L.A., he fell asleep, on a friend's floor.

THE WEST COAST WAVE

The Vancouver of 1963, when Larry Kent gathered together his friends and his cameras, in some ways barely resembled the city of 1989, when a second UBC filmmaking group emerged.

In between, there had been a quarter-century of cultural upheaval, and British Columbia's political polarization had culminated in a near general strike in 1983. But while fedoras and bouffants had been discarded, some things hadn't changed. Vancouver feature filmmaking, apart from the American-constructed infrastructure that was now in place, was practically as underdeveloped in 1989 as it had been twenty-five years earlier.

"There was a lot of film-industry service, television. You know, *MacGyver*, *21 Jump Street* – American-style shows," says John Pozer, who would play a pivotal role in the second UBC group. "There wasn't really anything Canadian to touch on other than *My American Cousin* and *The Grey Fox* – two great movies. So, there wasn't a lot of identity or a track record to build on."

And those two movies didn't come from a community of filmmakers with a distinctive Vancouver sensibility. Although there was an ongoing French-language Quebec film industry, Canadian English-language cinema was virtually nonexistent until the 1980s. There were the Larry Kents and Jack Darcuses in Vancouver, the Don Shebibs and Allan Kings in Toronto, but little consistency, no sustained scene. Almost the entire generation of Canadian actors and directors to come of age before the 1980s – from Norman Jewison and Arthur Hiller to William Shatner and Barbara Parkins – did not for a moment believe they could make a living in film in Canada. It wasn't until the early '80s that the first English-language scene developed in Canada. And it wasn't in Vancouver.

In the late 1970s, Toronto's David Cronenberg was the first to turn down Hollywood offers, determined to stay home, where he'd made early features such as *Shivers* and *Rabid*. He was followed by a group of filmmakers at least as determined to stay in Toronto and build a Canadian cinema. The Toronto group that emerged in the mid-1980s, largely out of the LIFT (Liaison of Independent Filmmakers of Toronto) cooperative, included Atom Egoyan (1984's *Next of Kin* was his first feature), Patricia Rozema (*I've Heard the Mermaids Singing*), Ron Mann (*Comic Book Confidential*), Bruce McDonald (*Highway 61*), Peter Mettler (*Scissere*), Don McKellar (*Last Night*), and John Greyson (*Zero Patience*).

The arrival of these Toronto filmmakers in the 1980s was a sea change for English-language Canadian cinema. By choosing to stay in Canada, they were creating a scene that would enable other talented Canadians to stay, too, for the first time. For several years, it would remain the only such scene in the country.

Then, in 1989, something remarkable happened at the University of British Columbia. That year, a particularly talented group that would become the heart of the Vancouver independent film scene of the 1990s were enrolled in the UBC film studies program. The gathering at UBC and the subsequent production of the student film, *The Grocer's Wife*, were not only the nuclei for the first Vancouver indie scene, they were crucial to the development of a cross-country Canadian cinema, adding a West Coast Wave to the Canadian film scene centred in Toronto.

"You've got to actually go back all the way to 1989, because that's when John Pozer shot *The Grocer's Wife*," says Ross Weber, an alumni of Pozer's film. "I did location sound mixing. I had never met my boom man and we had to drive to Trail. It was the first time I met the guy. And it's Bruce Sweeney. He's my boom man. And so Bruce and I were the sound team on *The Grocer's Wife*."

The Grocer's Wife would play Cannes. Even more impressive was the lineup of UBC film studies students who worked on the movie. The production involved eight future feature directors: Pozer; Sweeney (*Last Wedding, Dirty*), boom operator; Lynne Stopkewich (*Kissed, Suspicious River*), production designer; Mina Shum (*Double Happiness, Long Life, Happiness & Prosperity*), assistant director and casting director; Weber (*No More Monkeys Jumpin' on the Bed*), sound; Reg Harkema (*A Girl is A Girl*), editor; Greg Wild (*Highway to Heartache*) and Kathy Garneau (*Tokyo Cowboy*), art department. And there were more than directors involved – future cinematographers Greg Middleton (*Kissed, Suspicious*

River), Brian Pearson (*Dark Angel*), and Glen Winter (*Smallville*) were camera operators, and future producer Steve Hegyes (*Double Happiness, Last Wedding*) was a producing consultant. And there were others at UBC who weren't involved in *The Grocer's Wife* but would play major roles in Vancouver film, including actor Tom Scholte (*Live Bait, Dirty*), production designer Tony Devenyi (*Last Wedding*), and director Erik Whittaker (*Airport In*).

"John's feature caused a chain reaction," says Sweeney. "His feature was made and everything fell like dominoes. Everyone just got their features out after that.

"I didn't realize you even could make a feature until after *The Grocer's Wife*. It didn't cross my mind. I go to UBC and just happen to meet John and then we made this film. I thought, 'Shit, I could make one.' But I didn't go to school thinking, 'I'm going to make a feature.' That wasn't my goal going in, but it was my goal after the first year."

The film students who met at UBC in the late 1980s would become a close community who partied together and made movies together and by the middle of the 1990s were making films as smart and tough as any indie scene anywhere.

The crew of *The Grocer's Wife*: (back row l–r) Lynne Stopkewich, Brian Pearson, John Pozer, Peter Wunstorf, Ross Weber, Rovin Basi, Bruce Sweeney, Mina Shum, Wes Robertson, Deb Slonowski, Bettina Kuklinski; (middle row l–r) Greg Lavier, Greg Middleton, Glen Winter; (front row l–r) Carmen Thibault, Karin Brooks. *courtesy John Pozer*

John Pozer was born in Kamloops, B.C., in 1956 and moved to Vancouver before starting elementary school. Although he graduated from the west side's Prince of Wales high school, he spent much of his youth with relatives in the small-towns of B.C.'s Interior. Pozer also spent time in Vancouver's East End, taking classes at the Dadye Rutherford School for the Dramatic Arts.

His podiatrist father and costume-designer mother encouraged his involvement in the arts and by age nine Pozer was a member of the Equity actors union. He performed in professional musical theatre productions at the Queen Elizabeth Theatre, the Vancouver Playhouse, and the National Arts Centre in Ottawa, and was on stage in Stanley Park the day the venerable Theatre Under the Stars' Malkin Bowl made its return after being gutted by fire. "I actually reopened the Theatre Under the Stars, the first year, in the title role of *Oliver*," he said.

Pozer's first memorable film experience occurred when he was fourteen. "My father took me to see *Easy Rider*. I had to have parental supervision. He took me twice. And I was very keen, having a natural interest in the arts. My parents were very liberal. With my own earnings, I bought my own first camera and I started to take the movies from the back seat of the car."

After high school, Pozer had an assortment of jobs (from selling real estate to delivering auto parts for Plimley-Chrysler Dodge on Fourth Avenue), travelled, and studied fine arts at Langara and broadcast journalism at BCIT. He moved on to UBC, studying photography, sculpture, painting, and, finally, film.

His first movie shoot was Scottish director Bill Forsythe's *Housekeeping*, filmed in the B.C. Interior town of Nelson in 1987. "I wrote him a letter saying I'd like to watch him work on set as a director apprentice. I'd seen a lot of his films at the film festival. I was a big fan of *Local Hero* and *That Sinking Feeling* and when I heard he was going to shoot in Vancouver I jumped at the chance to at least write him a letter and try, through a couple of channels and contacts I had, to get it to him. And then I got a response from him via the line producer saying, 'Okay, come on set.' Bill put me in the position of being a lamp operator. He called me a 'portable solid.' So when he'd ask everyone to leave the room and it's a very closed set – the first AD and everyone would all be leaving – he'd just look over and say, 'John, you hold the lamp.' And I'd sit there and hold the lamp and watch him work the scene out while everyone else was watching video monitors outside. It was a good introduction.

"I never lost my love of the theatre – going to the theatre, going to movies. Directing suddenly became an idea of using all the experience and the background I had, some of the great people I worked with. It seemed like it could be a viable business, a viable income but ultimately it was the expression. You see, in the theatre, every night it's always different. In the film, you can nail it and it can be there forever."

§

The first time Mina Shum applied to UBC, she sent her application ransom-note style, with cut-out letters like the album cover of The Sex Pistols' *Anarchy in the U.K.* "I thought they'd think it was artistic," she says with a laugh. Maybe the UBC film program wasn't looking for artsy kidnappers – Shum's application was rejected twice. But she would eventually be accepted and become one of the most renowned filmmakers to come out of any Vancouver film program.

Shortly after Shum was born in 1965, her family left Hong Kong for Vancouver. As she moved from school to school in East Vancouver and suburbia, there was one constant – she loved to watch television, particularly old movie musicals. One of her earliest memories is lying upside down on a couch, watching Fred Astaire and Ginger Rogers. "Something about the image of this woman saying goodbye to this man in black and white while I was upside down brought me to tears. I knew there was something powerful about this."

At eighteen, Shum was already immersed in the arts – singing in the punk band Playdoh Republic, taking concert photographs, and attending theatre school – when a screening of Peter Weir's *Gallipoli* turned her toward film. "I saw that and I realized you can make art and film. I decided I was going to pursue film."

Shum and many of her UBC classmates were mature students oriented toward narrative features rather than experimental filmmaking. "We weren't coming out of high school going, 'We want to make a movie about a giant rat.' You choose which school you go to. I decided to go to UBC. Why? Because it was a marriage of the narrative and production values. That's what I wanted. I wanted to make films that looked great. They had the equipment and the expertise to do that. And so we all arrived expecting that because everyone wanted to make narrative films in my program."

§

Lynne Stopkewich was born in 1963 into an Anglophone family in a Francophone enclave in east end Montreal. She was an artsy kid, painting, acting, writing, making super-8 movies. Attending Montreal's Vanier College was a "renaissance" for her. Stopkewich became a politically active, anarchist punk rocker. She also discovered a world of foreign and art films and planned to enroll in graduate film studies at New York University or Columbia.

"I was going to go to New York. I got a big scholarship from the Quebec government. But I found out how expensive it was to go to the U.S. I decided I would take the money and sock it away to start saving to do a movie here because my movie was going to be my thesis. So, I decided I was going to stay in Canada rather than go to New York and be poor and have no way to raise money, because I knew I wanted to make a feature. That was the whole reason I went to grad school – you know, following the whole Susan Seidelman, Jim Jarmusch, Spike Lee model of making their first features out of their thesis film."

In 1987, she enrolled in UBC's film studies program. "There were only two schools in Canada that were doing graduate degrees at that point. One was the University of Toronto and the other one was out here. In Toronto, the focus was script-writing and it was a really regimented program. The program out here was self-directed. You tell them in your application what you thought your strengths and weaknesses were and what you wanted to focus on. To my mind it seemed like something that was really focused and specific and one-on-one and all those kinds of things. I thought that was cool. I figured I'd go to Vancouver for two years, write a script, maybe go back to Montreal and shoot it. But once I got here, everything changed. That's when I met the gang."

Making a feature film was not how a student got with the program in those days at UBC. "No one had that on their agenda . . . except for John. And on the first day of class, actually, I sat there in my black leather jacket and purple hair and said, 'I want to make a feature as my thesis.'"

After that first class, the students went for lunch at the students' union building. "We were all sitting there and John was kind of looking at me and he said, 'So, what do you want to do?' I basically said, 'Yeah, I want to make a feature.' He said, 'Yeah, I want to make a feature.' And that's how we sort of connected. The rest of it came after that.

"No one had ever done it before. They had been told the program can't sustain doing a feature. We argued that it could. So John and I hooked up and I said, 'Look, I'll help you produce your movie and you can help me do my film.'"

§

Born in Sarnia, Ontario, in 1962, Bruce Sweeney had grown up in love with the movies. "From an early age I was a movie nut. I watched the movies on the French channel. I didn't know I was watching Truffaut and Louis Malle and Godard and all these people. I was just watching it in French and, at that point, I thought if I watched the French movies I had a greater chance of seeing some nudity. So that drew me to it initially, but then I realized how many of those images and scenes resonated later."

Sweeney grew up a couple of hours from Toronto in a middle-class home, his father an engineer, his mother heavily involved in the arts community. "A lot of her friends were artists, painters. And we'd go to the art gallery all the time for art lessons. She just exposed me to the arts at a very young age."

After high school, he was eager to leave Sarnia. "But I had a good relationship with my parents and my friends and everything, so it wasn't a hostile thing at all. I wanted to live in a bigger city." Sweeney joined friends hanging out in the resort area of Lake Louise, Alberta. He planned to go on to university, probably Toronto, when he found a summer job in a mine near Campbell River, B.C. and got his first look at Canada's west coast. "It was summer and it was beautiful. It just struck me as being sheer beauty. I came and stayed."

Sweeney, who'd been drawing and painting forever, enrolled in the Simon Fraser University art program. While at SFU, he was increasingly drawn to film, transfixed by the European movies he'd see at the Van East Cinema and the Pacific Cinémathèque. Upon graduating with a BA in Art and Communication, Sweeney switched to UBC. And he switched to film. "Being a visual artist is just too damn solitary. You just have this tendency just to go out of your mind. I thought film would be good because it's social, you do it with other people."

§

Ross Weber learned the magic of cinema growing up in in Terrace, a town in central B.C.

"We used to go to Kelowna for the summer. We had a summer shack on the lake. And my mother, I think it was every Saturday night, she'd take us to the drive-in. I must have been eight or nine, and two movies really affected me – one was *Planet of the Apes* and the other was *Lawrence of Arabia*. Halfway through Lawrence of Arabia I remember the northern lights came up above the screen. My mother had put us in our pajamas, right, we'd sit in the car and maybe fall asleep. The movie's running and everybody walked outside and started looking at the northern lights while *Lawrence of Arabia* was playing on the screen."

After high school, Weber moved to Vancouver and was taking sciences at UBC when he learned he could study film on campus. "I didn't even know there was a film program. I'd always been interested in movies and got into the film program. Then I basically hung out there for five years, did a Master's."

§

There has been the occasional notable filmmaker from other Vancouver schools, including Vancouver Film School (Kevin Smith was a dropout), Emily Carr Institute of Art and Design (Oscar-nominated animators Wendy Tilby and Amanda Forbis), the Simon Fraser Film Workshop of the 1960s, and a strong contingent of experimental filmmakers from SFU (particularly the group of 1970s' directors/instructors that included David Rimmer, Al Razutis, and Patricia Gruben).

UBC, though, has had the edge on narrative feature filmmakers, producing an array of outstanding directors. There were the original UBC filmmakers (including Larry Kent and Jack Darcus), the second UBC bunch (including Bruce Sweeney, Lynne Stopkewich, and Mina

Shum), and there are those, while not part of either UBC group, became directors after attending the university (including Daryl Duke, Sturla Gunnarsson, and Allan King).

Darcus suggests the strong theatre department has had a lot to do with the narrative approach of UBC filmmakers. "When you have a theatre department, and you're hanging around next door to it, you tend to develop a literary outlook as opposed to experimental or documentary or whatever else," says Darcus.

"I had already left UBC, but my then-wife was working at UBC and was working at the Frederick Wood Theatre, so I was still connected very much with the theatre people. And all the people I worked with in the [Gallimaufry] theatre company were all ex-UBC students. It was almost an outreach from the UBC theatre department and I was connected with it because I designed the sets."

Some alumni suggest the reason UBC has become a filmmakers' breeding ground has less to do with the university than it does with the students who happened to show up there. They went to UBC but they weren't the sort to wear the university's sweatshirts or join singalongs at school football games. There are those among them who don't even have much good to say about the place. Some of the better filmmakers, from Kent to Pozer, were the rebels of their departments and, you suspect, would have been at odds with most any institution.

§

Pozer, for one, had confrontations with some faculty who didn't want him to make a student feature or use the department's filmmaking equipment. "You know what? That's the business of art. You get steeled up to that pretty quick. If anything, I just looked beyond the petty relationships and said, 'You know, I've got a good film.' And I think for me to finish it I needed a bit of encouragement and I got that through my friends and my family."

What was going on in that program in 1989 that produced so many filmmakers?

"Well, to tell you the truth, to blow my own horn, and I'm hardpressed to do so, but you know what? I don't think it was the program. I think it was the summer a lot of these people spent shooting *The Grocer's Wife*," says Pozer.

Pozer was the most driven student filmmaker to show up at UBC since Larry Kent. He vowed to do something no student in the film program had done: make a feature film as his thesis project. And the impact it had on the student crew would change the nature of Vancouver filmmaking. "They did it for free, they were watching it happen, watching it go. I didn't have a mentor or anyone showing me the way. I went out there and did it. Yes, I had apprenticed on Bill Forsythe's *Housekeeping*. But you know, I had Bruce Sweeney on boom, I had Ross Weber mixing sound, Mina Shum assistant directing, I had Reg Harkema cutting, I had Kathy Garneau set decorating – doing a fantastic job – and Greg Wild, and Lynne designing, Greg Middleton was a camera operator. Let me just say, I think I offered them an experience that allowed them to believe they could do it."

As a student, Pozer devised a way to shoot his feature using UBC equipment. "That's the only way I'd be able to do it. I never made any of my plans publicly known because they [the film program] didn't encourage features. I set a plan into operation wherein I'd be able to get all of the equipment out of the rental area. I wrote the script in creative writing class and then I just negotiated to sign out all the equipment for the summer, when the regular student classes weren't there. It just seemed to be a no-brainer for me. I mean, why is all this equipment sitting in the room? I figured I'd sign it all out, then bring it back before school opened again."

Not everyone agreed. No film student had ever made a feature. "I was not encouraged. Rather, they seemed very protective of the equipment."

Pozer would not be deterred, and eventually raised money through friends and family and returned to the B.C. Interior of his childhood, to the smoky smelter town of Trail, to create his surreal, twisted look at the underbelly of the picturesque B.C. that appears in travelogues. "I tried to show something completely different than what B.C. was supposed to be. You know, it was always waterfalls and bears and old-growth forests. And I just said, 'Hey man, let's turn the camera over here. You've got industry and sloth and greed and duplicity.'"

Stopkewich explains the financing: "The company was called Medusa Films and it was me and him and an old buddy of his, Greg Lavier, who had no background in film at all, who invested some money. It wasn't a huge tax break but you could write it off. John put money in, his family put money in, friends – $500 investments, $1,000 investments, whatever – and just cobbled it together. And we all went out and shot it in Trail. Peter Wunstorf [the director of photography] and John were the only people who had ever worked on a feature before."

Through the "absolute mayhem," Pozer learned early how to handle producers. He recalls telling Lavier, "If you invest $15,000 I'll let you do a day of directing." Lavier agreed and arrived in Trail on the first day of shooting. "He comes on set, says, 'Okay, I'm here, what do I do?'" recalls Pozer. "I said, 'Well, here's the stop sign, here's this little yellow coat, you go down to the far end and make sure no traffic gets up here.' And he says, 'Traffic director?' And I said, 'It's all right, man, it's all directing and I need your help today.' And you know what? He took it on the chin and he said, 'I'm in.'"

"It was great, but you know what?" says Stopkewich. "It was so not like a movie. I mean, it was a movie and we tried to run it like a regular movie, but because we were all friends we sort of did it as we went."

∫

(l–r) Director John Pozer, actor Simon Webb, camera operator Greg Middleton, and director of photography Peter Wunstorf on the set of *The Grocer's Wife*. *courtesy John Pozer*

Stopkewich and Pozer were at the social centre of the UBC film scene. "John is just a crazy man, very loud and very funny and very driven, and he was kind of the ringleader of getting everything going," says Sweeney. "He was the first to get the film cooking and the first to get the party started. And John and Lynne were together and any time you were anywhere that you had John and Lynne, you essentially had the makings of a good party right there.

"They lived in Chinatown but John spent a great deal of time living in his mother's basement in the west side. Lynne had another suite in the west side as well. Everyone had places so they could go out to UBC. And John edited *The Grocer's Wife* right in his mom's basement."

"Yeah, it was fun," says Stopkewich. "At first I was living in residence and then I lived in a one-room apartment in Kits for $200 a month. Because John had gone back to school, he had moved into the basement of his parents' place in Dunbar.

"Right from the beginning I remember there were people in the undergraduate program – Steve Hegyes, Greg Middleton, Samuel Berry (who's now a screenwriter in L.A.), Mina Shum, Reg Harkema, Greg Wild, all these people were all so passionate about filmmaking. At parties we'd always talk about movies. And it seemed like the department itself at that time was pretty west coast – a real low-key kind of department – and a lot of these students wanted that kind of structure. These were the people who would always be breaking the rules. There were rules where only certain projects got picked to get made and a lot of these guys were, 'I don't care, I'm going to make a movie anyway even if my project doesn't get picked.' These individuals were super focused. I'm not surprised that all of them have done really, really well."

Stopkewich says a key moment in the making of *The Grocer's Wife* occurred at the 1988 Vancouver International Film Festival. "We got passes where you go see tons of movies and I saw, like, fifty films. It was insane, like I was going crazy. I saw Guy Maddin's film *Tales From the Gimli Hospital* for the first time. I'll never forget it. We were sitting there in the third row. We knew that the film had been made for $20,000 and we were talking about wanting to make a feature and how do you get the money to do this. This was around the time when people were making films on credit cards and trying to do it themselves. And we just sort of looked at each other – 'My god, $20,000.'

Reg Harkema was great: 'If he can do it, we can do it. Right?' And so immediately John was working on the script."

§

The Vancouver International Film Festival had a major influence on the West Coast Wave, from Sweeney's experience at a forum with director Mike Leigh which inspired his improv style, to Shum's absorption at a Luis Bunuel retrospective which "really influenced my sensibility of what cinema could be," she says.

The Festival was founded in 1982 by Leonard Schein, who would go on to open the art-house Fifth Avenue Cinemas and direct, briefly, Toronto's film festival. After coming to Canada as a draft resister in 1972, Schein taught psychology at community colleges before turning to his passion: the movies. There had been two earlier Vancouver film festivals that had introduced foreign-language and art films to many moviegoers, but Schein's festival was larger and included a trade forum which, in 1985, would lead directly to Pozer's first on-set experience. "I brought in Bill Forsythe," recalls Schein, "because I did a tribute to him. He liked it so much here in B.C. that he made his next film *Housekeeping* here. And that was just because he came to the film festival. At that time, we had a lot fewer guests at the festival than now so you could spend more time with the people. He and his wife were here and we went out with them. He just really liked it here."

§

"John's parents had a cabin in the States and they would go away so we'd have people over to his parents' house," says Stopkewich, "or we'd have parties at Reg Harkema's house. He lived in this crazy house with all these guys. We'd have parties at Sweeney's house. He was living in Dunbar as well. It was great."

Shum: "Oh yeah. We'd go over to their house and eat. I remember eating many, many tuna and cucumber sandwiches over there. John and Lynne were mom and dad. It was their film, for one thing. I mean, *The Grocer's Wife* was theirs and we'd go over to their house and watch different edits and what-not. They'd throw parties."

But the university years were more than one long party for the UBC film group. "I'm not a very social person. I didn't do a lot of hanging out with the group," says Weber. "I remember hanging out with Bruce quite a bit. We'd watch movies. He'd have a whole pile of tapes we'd watch – the Bergman movie we hadn't seen. I remember I went to Montreal to cut sound on *The Grocer's Wife* and lived with John in this grotty little apartment in the Plateau area and froze my ass off during the winter."

"Ross was marking my papers. When I was an undergrad, he was already in the grad program," says Pozer. "Friendships were forged. Lynne and I, we had some parties. I don't really recall the partying so much as I do searching for the cut, searching for the scene, searching for the money, searching for the final mix."

Stopkewich, too, recalls the working side of the UBC years. "I still remember vividly these nights where John would just be working away on his script for *The Grocer's Wife*. And that was his thesis. I had to go through two years of coursework and paperwork before I could write my script. That's why it was kind of like, 'You're going to do your movie first. I'll do my movie second.'

In 1990, Stopkewich, Shum, and Steve Hegyes organized the first UBC student films festival. "Nobody else cared to put a festival together but we did, and that was a big triumph for us. It was also very empowering," says Shum, "because then you saw that they were real work, it wasn't just student films. It was my film, my first film, and this is what it's about and I will continue in this vein. That was very important in terms of the growth of that scene."

To Pozer, the personal friendships and the work were inseparable. "It's one of those things. It doesn't start through any sort of organization of any kind. It all starts because a friend knows a friend who knows a friend and the next thing you know you have a party going. And then the next thing you know you've created something, which has a kind of spirit that you just kind of go along with."

§

Making a feature was an entirely new experience for the crew Pozer culled from the film program. Shum was named first assistant director, although she had never been a second assistant director, and casting director because she had a degree in theatre and an acting background.

"We just all went, 'Hell yeah, we'll do it.' It was a forty-five-day shoot. John and I got in a car. We were the first two to go. We drove in his old beat-up Dart at fifty miles per hour all the way to Trail. It took us thirteen hours to get there. And we scouted the place and the crew arrived a day later and we started filming. It was really exciting. The place where the crew was staying was someone's house in Rosedale – sort of a ski village-type place – a friend of theirs who was away tree planting, so we got to take over their house.

"In one room it was Bruce Sweeney, Ross Weber, and me. We slept in this room together. I remember Ross had a bum neck and I lent him my pillow. It was really all in the family. We would wake up in the morning smelling of last night's beer, we'd all make coffee, drink some coffee, go and shoot.

"The experience of doing it meant that we could do it – as film-makers. Sure, John was the director on that film and it was his vision, and we followed his vision, all of these people who didn't know what they were doing. I mean, had Ross ever recorded sound for a feature? No. Had Bruce ever been a boom operator? No. Had I ever been an AD? No. But we all did it. And Lynne was the art director and that was probably her first big production design. But seeing that you could actually rain a group and inspire them meant that I, too, and Bruce, too, and Ross, too, and Lynne, too, could make their own work. I think that was a very big turning point. Everything we were doing was stuff that no one believed was possible and that bonds you, you know."

Weber, who would go on to be a film director and Genie-nominated editor, says the UBC group was characterized by a willingness to do it, rather than talk about it.

"They were a bunch of people that had a lot of chutzpah, let's face it. You know, to go out and make a movie. I mean, there's a lot of talented people that just can't get past talking. Doing it is eighty percent of making a movie, just simply doing it. Let's just say I've worked for a lot of different people and met a lot of people in the business and I find there's a lot of egomaniacal people. Sometimes I wonder, do people really just want to be famous or are they actually trying to make good art?"

What was the difference between the UBC group and every other film school class across Canada?

"It's so hard to answer that," says Sweeney. "I'm not the one who starts the party, I join the party. And I luckily joined that party. Having been skeptical of so many things and cynical on so many levels, I just enjoyed that this group had sort of a fun, cynical attitude. John was quite an openly confrontational man and just to watch him bull his way through all these different scenarios I learned a lot. When I went into school I was very timid. And I was taught that you can want something and not be ashamed and just go get it. John led by example in the sense that if you want to make a film, everyone says 'no,' but you just tell everyone, 'fuck you.' Just get what you need, right? And I don't think people had seen that spirit at all, because every step of the way you'd always be just taught the odds of how you can't make a film and how it won't be a success and no one's going to see it. So why start? I mean, UBC didn't want you to make features either. But the spirit and energy were infectious. So much came out of that."

Shum says the UBC group, as a social scene and filmmaking scene, may not have existed without the making of *The Grocer's Wife*. "I don't think so," she says. "I mean, we would have maybe worked disparately more. Bruce and I didn't know each other until we slept in the same room together, you know, literally. We were in a class together for a year but we really didn't get to know each other until *The Grocer's Wife*."

Pozer is not one to wax on when asked to name directors who influenced him. He's more likely to thank those who taught him what not to do. "I'd have to say not really focusing on any other film director or anything like that. I mean, Scorsese, you look at that. But really it's nothing to really reference low-budget. Spike Lee, of course. I saw Spike Lee's *She's Gotta Have It* and I thought it was very poorly mixed and a very poor sound recording so, I mean, when I'm working on sound I'd see that and say, 'We've got to do a better job than that. There's no way I'm going to have that kind of sound. That's terrible.' I'd look at Guy Madden's *Gimli Hospital* and I thought, 'Yes, it was surreal and odd. Looking for a little bit more of a narrative, looking for a little more of a dramatic narrative for myself.' Saw Bruce McDonald's *Highway 61* and I thought, 'Gee, we've got way better, way stronger exposure and cinematography than that.' I saw a bunch of stuff. At that period of time there was a lot of MTV culture – it was fast cutting, a lot of loud music and, you know, that was never my approach. I wanted to make a very long, boring film and, gee, I accomplished that. No,

I wanted to do everything that was not happening in contemporary culture – no gunshots, no car chases, no drugs, no murders, no sex, no fast music, no rock 'n' roll, no road show. And so I gave myself a bit of a challenge."

Not only did the shoot bring Pozer back to the B.C. Interior of his childhood, the stark beauty of his black-and-white images brought him home to the spectacular imagery of the Hollywood musicals he grew up on during the years he was singing and dancing at Theatre Under the Stars.

"Everyone said, 'Shoot in black and white? What are you, fuckin' nuts?' Well, black and white, how better to specify a narrative, rather than through some eye candy with your colour. Forget it, I'm not into it. You read the first paragraph of the script – billowy, grainy clouds of smoke over which the titles play. Well, that says black and white.

"I'll tell you when we made *The Grocer's Wife*, I just thought to myself, we would have people working for free because it was the kind of an experience where people would come on set just to see what was going to explode that day. People were not only coming, they were bringing their own fucking lunch. And people would never be allowed to have these jobs: I wouldn't be allowed to be a director, Simon Webb would never be a lead actor, Bruce Sweeney would never be on boom, Ross would never be mixing. There would never be any of these jobs. So by having no precedent but having an idea about how to do it, I have to think for me – and you got to remember I'm producing, writing, and directing – the experience was on set. And you would see these guys, they would get there, they would see the schedule collapse, they'd see Wunstorf and I trying to figure out how we were going to shoot this. We'd throw one thing away, we'd scratch something on paper, we'd type it up, pass it around, everything would change in a moment, we'd shoot something.

"It was a vibrant experience. I really believe everyone was there to learn, everyone was there to watch something. It was the best school that we had. And it was on the edge, it was dangerous, and it was so exciting to be there. I say that from my biased perspective because, Christ, man, I had to try and make it work, with the help of a lot of others."

Pozer would transfer to Concordia University in Montreal, where, along with Weber, he would complete post-production on *The Grocer's*

Wife. In 1992, the film premiered, and was selected for the Cannes Film Festival.

"They phoned me," recalls Shum. "I freaked. I was just like, 'Yeah! We did it! Yay!' I have so many great memories from that show. Just absurd things. We had to roll a fake smokestack down the street while all the Trailites were watching, wondering, 'What the hell's going on?'"

The film would be heralded at other festivals and play theatres across Canada. More than that, it gave birth to a West Coast Wave whose impact on Canadian film has just begun to be felt. When Sweeney's *Last Wedding* was chosen to open the 2001 Toronto International Film Festival, the fest's director Piers Handling acknowledged the UBC group. "It's nice for us to recognize and affirm that," said Handling, "and to make that movement of filmmakers feel as much at home at the Toronto festival as the Vancouver festival."

The Vancouver indie scene has grown beyond its UBC nucleus but Sweeney, Stopkewich, Shum, and the rest remain its heart. Simon Fraser University film grad Scott Smith, whose *rollercoaster* was popular on the festival circuit, pays tribute to the UBC group. "I met all these guys working on *Kissed* and *Live Bait*, so I'm sort of this SFU parasite in this UBC crowd."

Actor-director Martin Cummins, whose *We All Fall Down* also played festivals, says newer Vancouver directors can't help but be conscious of the presence of the wave of indie filmmaking that started at UBC. "It's out there. And I guess on some level I'm a part of it," he says. "I feel like I know that I am. And it's a cool thing. You know, all these people that are making these movies because they want to make the movies, not because they're getting rich doing it."

And the UBC alumni have continued to be friends, working together on occasion, more often leaving phone messages or sending flowers when a classmate is about to begin a shoot. Pozer, who has directed another film (*The Michelle Apartments*) as well as television, is a fan of his friends' work. "Mina's made a good spin of her 'Mina stories.' Bruce Sweeney's approach – fantastic approach. I had to kick his ass a few times. But you know what better part for him to play than boom, in there watching everything."

Pozer pauses a moment and suddenly he's talking about the making of *Close Encounters of the Third Kind*. Director Steven Spielberg, he notes, hired one of his favourite directors, Francois Truffaut, to play a scientist in the film. Afterward, someone asked the great French New Wave filmmaker if he learned anything working with Spielberg. "And he said, 'I didn't learn anything from Steven Spielberg but I learned that every time the director says, "Action," there are twenty people behind him who think they can do a better job.'

"And it couldn't be more to the word than on *The Grocer's Wife*, because everyone behind me was watching scrutinizingly, just going, 'You know what, I could do that.' And I don't mind that. I love all these guys. I think it's great. And good for them. And ultimately how wonderful to go and see their films and go, 'My god, they're great.'"

THE ACTORS

Nicholas Lea stood stark-naked in front of a room full of strangers. "Turn around a couple of times," the acting teacher said, "we'll take a look at you." Lea was thoroughly humiliated but compliant. "Then I remember the improv finished and I went and sat down in my chair and burst into tears. So that was my first experience and it hasn't really fucking changed that much, to be honest with you. It still feels like I'm taking my clothes off."

He would go on from that first acting class to lead parts in movies (*John Woo's Once a Thief, Vertical Limit*) and a regular role on TV's *The X-Files*. Lea, from the city's west side, was part of the first generation of Vancouver actors to learn the craft in their home town and face the decision of whether to leave.

In 1975, a Vancouver acting school called The Desimone Studio printed a flyer proclaiming: "You do not have to go to Hollywood to become a star . . . the opportunity is here." The statement was closer to the truth in 1995. By the early '90s, the Canadianization of bad American television had given actors a shot at survival in Vancouver and aspiring Canadian performers, who once would have made a beeline for Hollywood or New York, were relocating to the city.

The actors, along with the new directors and filmmaking infrastructure, helped create the foundation for a Vancouver independent cinema. While UBC turned out the directors, the American filmmakers brought sound stages and shiny new cameras and other infrastructure technology into the city that would enable Vancouver crews to surpass the look of *The Beachcombers* or *King of Kensington*.

The city's acting base was more plentiful and didn't arrive as suddenly as the UBC directors. Still, one acting group of the early '90s overshadowed the rest. There are many fine acting schools in Vancouver but you can no more talk about current Vancouver film without mentioning the Gastown Actors Studio than you could have talked about American film from the 1950s to the 1970s without mentioning New York's Actors Studio (Marlon Brando, James Dean, Paul Newman, Al Pacino, and Dustin Hoffman, to name a few).

Among the Gastown actors who would play major roles in Vancouver film and television: Lea, Molly Parker, Martin Cummins, David Cubitt, Suzy Joachim, Jed Rees, Brent Stait, Ben Ratner, John Cassini, Christianne Hirt, David Hewlett, Barry Pepper, Ian Tracey, Kim Restell, John Pyper-Ferguson. Although these actors and the UBC directors were developing their crafts at the same time, they were virtually unaware of each other until the mid-'90s when the filmmakers stepped out with a series of movies, including *Double Happiness*, *Kissed*, and *Dirty*.

Gastown Actors Studio founder Mel Tuck studied theatre at the University of Alberta in the mid-1960s and was a working actor-director in Toronto in the 1970s when he took a job teaching acting at Ryerson. "The teaching thing just hooked me. I loved doing it," he says. He had his share of teaching successes in Toronto, including students Nia Vardalos and Eric McCormack, but Vancouver was ripe for his approach when he arrived.

"I do what I do and I think I do it well, and I've had a pretty good batting average, but the timing was really excellent," says Tuck. "It was '88, just when the film industry was starting to really blossom here, in terms of the American stuff anyway. And it opened up a world for these people and they went at it."

Gastown alumni say Tuck's success is due to much more than timing, crediting him as an acting coach who understands individual needs rather than breaking someone down into "neutral," then remaking them in his image.

"He's an exceptional teacher," says Molly Parker. "This man worked with people on an individual basis. Because of that, we all got this training that was honed specifically for us."

Martin Cummins, who would go on to star in TV series (*Poltergeist*, *Dark Angel*) and films (*Love Come Down*, *We All Fall Down*), spent more than four years at Gastown Actors Studio. "I've got my own set of fears and idiosyncrasies and odd shit. And the deal is that I bring that stuff to the table when I act, so there's some areas where I find it difficult to go because of who I am personally. And Mel could see that and was able to address it in a way that didn't make you defensive or, if you were, then he could find his way around that and speak to you. It was a safe environment and it was a supportive environment to be able to work out stuff. He supported trying things out in there and falling on your face in there and making the stretch in there, so that when you went outside, your tool box was bigger, you had more things to use and you could expand yourself."

Says Tuck: "When I went to school I was taught to go to the neutral. I don't even know what neutral means but the thing is, if you know about you, if you're self-aware – not self-conscious but self-aware – then at least you're coming from some place that's true, then you take that to the script. I do very much teach to the individual. And I choose the material to help take them in those ways. I had them doing the Greeks, the Shakespeare, the modern, you name it, because the thing is that individual scenes or whatever make specific demands on actors in specific ways."

The students in Gastown developed a close personal bond that has continued. Many now teach at the Lyric acting school, which is operated by Gastown alumni Kate Twa and Michelle Lonsdale Smith. "Everybody hung out together," Cummins says. "I haven't experienced that since. There was a bar right across the street, Characters Taverna, and everyone would be over there. It'd be like a dozen or fifteen people. Everybody spent a lot of time together, you know, which was kind of odd."

§

Nicholas Lea grew up in Vancouver's Dunbar neighbourhood, more inclined to play in rock bands than act on stage. "I didn't become an actor until I was twenty-five because it just didn't seem viable to me," he says. "I'd always wanted to do it. It was something I had always been in love with. I still remember my friend giving me shit for not wanting to come out and play and wanting to stay in and watch movies. I was in love with the idea of actors and acting and stories."

He tried other acting classes – including the one that dressed him down – before finally discovering the Gastown Actors Studio. "Mel Tuck gave us a place to do it, he gave us the support to do it, kind of treated everybody as sons and daughters. I think it was really appealing because everybody liked to get hugged.

"I don't know what was going on at the other schools but I remember Mel saying things to us like: 'You're all really good. There's no reason why you shouldn't be working. You're as good as some of the people we watch in films and on television, so why not?' When you get that kind of support, it's going to propel you on to the next level. And it coincided with what [Stephen] Cannell was doing, which started to give those people a start doing television, in getting their feet wet."

Like Cummins, Lea sees Gastown as an innovative school where lasting bonds were forged. "I just remember the day that Molly was thinking about leaving and going to study at one of the universities. She thought that maybe that was the better place to learn how to act. And was more established. We all talked her out of it, said, 'No, no, no, you can't do that, you can't, no, you've got to stay here.' And she was like seventeen, eighteen at the time. She stayed and thank goodness. I've always felt that an independent, reasonably ground-breaking place is a much better place for an actor to learn to stretch."

§

Molly Parker has never regretted the decision to remain at Gastown. For one thing, a working-actors' culture pervaded the place. "We would all sort of go out drinking and talking. They were all older than me and they were really inspiring to me because they were working, these were people who were actually making a living as actors," says Parker, who would go on to star in the Vancouver film *Kissed*, then independent productions in the U.S. and Europe.

"I mean, Nick was, John Pyper-Ferguson was, Martin was, John Cassini was, Brent Stait was. I was really the baby of the group. I was the youngest of all these people and I didn't really know what to do. I was thinking about going to theatre school. I thought that was probably important. And I thought about going to New York, and I thought about going back to university. Through lots of discussions it was like, 'No, stay here, 'cause we can do this here.' And then I actually started working."

Parker started at the Gastown Actors Studio shortly after graduating from high school in Maple Ridge, with plans to study biology at Simon Fraser University. "But I won these acting burseries, just a couple thousand dollars from school," she says. "I thought, 'Well, I'll use those up, then I'll go to university in January.'"

The talent agency Parker had signed with in high school merged with another, so she dropped by and spoke to agent Murray Gibson. "I had long, long blue hair. I was, you know, totally out of my mind. And I went in and I said, 'What should I do? I have this money, I want to study.' This agency had sort of come together. They had so many clients, they didn't know who was who, they were just letting people go like crazy. I was really keen and he recommended that I take an auditioning workshop or some kind of thing that he ended up being at, running the camera, and liked the work that I did."

The following week, Parker's name came up when the agency had a meeting to decide which actors would be dropped from its roster. "Nobody knew who I was. I had never worked, I had been there for three years. And Murray said, 'No, no, no. We should keep her.' When I went in to see him, he said: 'Why don't you go study? There's this new place called the Gastown Actors Studio. There's this guy Mel Tuck who just moved out here from back east and you know he taught at Ryerson, he taught at a bunch of schools, he's a really good teacher.'

"So, I went 'round there. It was summertime, I had just graduated from high school. Mel was away for the summer but Brent Stait, this actor in town, had taken over the classes. And I took two months of classes from Brent and it was like that Pollyanna-esque kind of epiphany. It was like, 'I want to be an actress forever.' It was so exciting, it was so fun to come into this class and do this work and learn about acting.

"When Mel came back after the summertime I got slotted into his class and it was the most extraordinary time in my life. It was a class with me and Nick Lea and Martin Cummins and John Cassini and John Pyper-Ferguson and Kim Restell. Ben Ratner was there.

"I saw better work in that class than I have seen since. There were twenty-five students at that time, for the first couple of years. And it was very exciting, people were doing really good work, Mel was a great teacher, people were really excited and inspired by him. We all really loved each other. It was very intimate kind of work and we were all so young and working through it. It just worked, you know. For me, as Gastown went on, it became bigger and bigger and sort of lost that focus that it had, but in the beginning it was a really, really great place to be."

For Ben Ratner, who went on to star in *Dirty* and *Last Wedding*, the scene selection at Gastown distinguished it from other acting schools. "Mel introduced us to it all, from Neil Simon to Greek tragedy to Shakespeare. Not too many scene-study classes are doing Greek tragedy. He gave us a taste of the whole gamut. Molly and I did a scene from Shakespeare's *Cymbeline*. And we walked out of that place thespians."

§

Martin Cummins was born in Fort Smith in the former Northwest Territories where his dad was teaching. The family settled in the Vancouver area when Cummins was six and he went to high school in suburban Delta. He seemed to spend as much time in boats as in class, a deckhand at age nine for his fisherman father. "I skippered the boat for him from sixteen till twenty-three. The only things I've really done are fishing and acting."

Cummins started acting when he was sixteen on *Fifteen*, a Canadian teen soap opera. "We did thirteen episodes in thirteen days or something like that. It was great. I made $3,200. It could have gone either way, right. I could have been a fisherman. I was probably better at the fishing than I've ever really been at the acting. I was a pretty good fisherman."

After high school, Cummins was already getting work in episodic television. "Just the gig in Vancouver where you do guest spots on TV – the same stuff everybody was doing," he recalls. "It's the shows that were in town, like *Danger Bay* and *21 Jump Street*. There were also all these different shows that of course aren't around now and nobody remembers, like *J.J. Starbuck*. There was a pile of them. Vancouver was so much at that point, and still is to a great degree, a TV town. So, everybody made their living playing bad guys on TV. Then it was cop shows – *Street Justice*, *The Commish*, *21 Jump Street*. People were working all the time and everybody was making a living at it. I didn't need much as a twenty-year-old guy. It only took a couple of guest starring roles to make your year. You could do two or three guest stars and make $35,000."

There was also the occasional Canadian independent film made in the Vancouver of the early '90s, including Fred Frame's *Home Movie*, Richard Lewis's *Whale Music*, and Richard Martin's *North of Pittsburgh*.

Cummins heard about the Gastown Actors Studio from John Cassini (*Home Movie, North of Pittsburgh*) and John Pyper-Ferguson (*Hard Core Logo*, which was partially shot in Vancouver). "They were talking about this guy who was teaching in Gastown, Mel Tuck – that he was really good," he says. "I liked these guys, and I thought they were good actors and they were going to this place so I thought, 'Okay, well, I'll go down there.'

"I've had two really fantastic acting teachers in my life. One was Mel Tuck and the other one was this Native guy in the Kasi Band, up on the Fraser River. I remember him saying to me one day, 'If you're fishing, fish, and if you're towing, tow.' And it sounds really stupid, but it made total sense to me as a fisherman and as an actor. And that was: make your choices and then don't fuck around with it. Just let it ride.

"You can't act while you're fucking around with it and while you're up in your head and trying to make it perfect. Make your choices, set it up, and then roll the dice. And do it as naturally as you can. That made total sense to me. He was the guy that if everyone else was getting 200 fish, he was getting 800. And that's just the way it was. I mean, he knows how to fish. So, I learned a lot about fishing from him and I could fish that area pretty well."

§

Although Gastown had the longest list of working alumni, Vancouver's strong acting base came out of a variety of stages and schools, from Langara's Studio 58 (grads include Jillian Fargey who was nominated for a Genie for *Protection*) to the Vancouver Playhouse Acting School (*The New Addams Family*'s Ellie Harvie) to UBC (*Last Wedding*'s Tom Scholte and Marya Delver). As well, many actors made their way to Vancouver after training in other cities such as Edmonton (*Last Wedding*'s Nancy Sivak and Vincent Gale) and Winnipeg (*Live Bait*'s Jay Brazeau, *Da Vinci's Inquest*'s Donnelly Rhodes).

Da Vinci's Sue Mathew, who grew up on the city's west side, studied briefly at Gastown but more with Peter Breck, the star of TV's *Big Valley* and grade-B films such as *Shock Corridor*.

"Peter's a wealth of information. He's like really, really old Hollywood," Mathew says of Breck, who relocated to Vancouver to teach acting. "I learned more about the business and heard so many stories. He's a really good acting coach. I studied there for about a year and then was approached by an agent who said, 'I'd like to represent you.'"

It didn't take long for links to form between the new actors and filmmakers of the 1990s. One early connector was the Cold Reading Series, organized by actor Kathleen Duborg and *Kissed* co-writer Angus Fraser in the summer of 1993.

"There were so many scripts that started at the Cold Reading series: John Meadows' *Wisegirls* that was in Sundance, *Kissed* was read there, Reg Harkema's stuff, Bruce Sweeney's film," says Duborg.

"I was doing plays, sort of dabbling, getting auditions for little TV gigs and that kind of thing. And Angus and I had this idea to do the Cold Reading series, which was a place for scripts to be read. He was writing scripts, I knew about play-building and that kind of thing – that it's really good to hear your words out loud. Angus knew that very much – he was in the process of writing scripts himself, so we got together with [screenwriting school] Praxis and asked them if we could use their space."

The series, which would inspire similar undertakings (particularly the Alibi Unplugged series founded by actor Anita Adams), has featured many of the city's better actors, including Jennifer Clement, Callum Keith Rennie, Ben Ratner, Nancy Sivak, Tom Scholte, Babz Chula, Ian Tracey, Sue Mathew, Venus Terzo, Vincent Gale, Jillian Fargey, and Molly Parker.

"The whole point of the Cold Reading series was to bring actors and writers together in a room to exchange ideas," Duborg says. "There was a need for it. This was the first thing that brought the theatre community and the film community and merged them."

§

Not all of the local actors who began working in the '90s have remained in Vancouver. Unlike earlier generations of actors, however, they had their start in film in the city and have, in large part, maintained a working relationship with the Canadian film community. They either move between work in Canada and elsewhere (the Molly Parker model) or remain in Canada without actively seeking work in Hollywood or the service industry (the Tom Scholte model).

There are also those who happily disappear into the American studio system, never to work in Canada again (the Michael J. Fox model).

Of these, Mike Myers asks the strangest questions. "I love being from Canada, I love Canadian things. Why don't we have more movies that are distinctly Canadian?" Myers asked students during a speech at Toronto's Humber College, seemingly oblivious to the many set-in-Canada films that filmmakers struggle to cobble together. Particularly puzzling, considering this is the man who turned his home suburb, Scarborough, Ontario, into American suburbia in *Wayne's World*. Although he hasn't shown a lot of interest in doing so, Myers is one of only a handful of Canadians who could likely secure a $50-million-plus budget for a set-in-Canada movie.

So, despite the swell of filmmaking in Canada, the lure of Hollywood remains enticing, and some Vancouver-based actors still regularly relocate to L.A. for TV pilot-audition season.

Carrie-Anne Moss is somewhat of a throwback to an era long before Vancouver was Hollywood North, when local actors such as

Yvonne De Carlo dreamed of Hollywood South. "I always knew that I wanted to live in California," she says. "If you watch television and you watch films, America's certainly tantalizing to a youngster."

She has become a familiar face on movie screens and magazine covers since costarring in the 1999 cyber-action movie *The Matrix*. "Well, it transformed my life, actually. I feel

Carrie-Anne Moss. *photo by Jon Murray, courtesy* The Province really blessed and lucky to have the career that I have. I think it's incredible that I even make a living as an actor because it's so difficult. Making *The Matrix* was and is a total joy for me. Before *The Matrix* I was doing TV, you know."

Moss lived in Burnaby until she was fifteen, when she moved with her mother to a condo in Vancouver's False Creek area, attending Magee high school because of its drama and music departments. "Magee had one of the best choirs in Canada and we travelled all over Europe singing." Her first performance outside school was a *Fiddler on the Roof* production at Burnaby's James Cowan Theatre. She left Vancouver at nineteen, modelled in Toronto and soon landed a role in *Dark Justice*, a syndicated TV series. Then she moved to Los Angeles. "I was very, 'I'm going to Hollywood and I don't know anyone and I have no money and I don't have a green card but it's my dream and I'm going.' And I did it."

Slowly the work came and now she's starring in *The Matrix* sequels. "It takes six months to train to just deal with the work because there's so much physical stuff," she says. She won a best-supporting actress Independent Spirt Award for *Memento* and has appeared in *The Crew*, *Red Planet*, and *Chocolat*. Although Moss has remained in L.A., over the years she's "come to see that I'm a Canadian girl all the way and love Canada so much. I just find that Canadians are a little different, in a good way – optimistic, kind." She's one of Canada's best-known actors, but has never appeared in a Canadian film, noting that the country's movie industry was far less developed when she lived in Vancouver. "I was never an actor who lived in Canada. And when I first started acting, it was different. So my development of my career has been based out of the States. That's just the way that I've done it." She does, however, often return to visit family. "There's nothing more beautiful than a beautiful day in Vancouver."

Joshua Jackson managed to become a well-known actor in the U.S. without moving to southern California. The popularity of his shot-in-North Carolina TV show, *Dawson's Creek*, made Jackson a teen magazine cover guy and a guest host on *Saturday Night Live*, with roles in movies such as *The Skulls*, *Lone Star State of Mind*, *Cruel Intentions*, and *Urban Legends*.

Jackson grew up around the Vancouver film industry. His mother, Fiona Jackson, is a casting director involved in local productions since the 1970s, including the Vancouver classic *McCabe and Mrs Miller*. Jackson made his debut in the 1991 made-in-Vancouver film *Crooked Hearts* and before *Dawson's Creek* was a regular in the *Mighty Ducks* movies.

"It's a very alluring job, believe me. So I knew right away that it was something that I enjoyed doing. I like working and this was something that I thought that I could do."

When *Dawson's Creek* wasn't shooting, Jackson was anxious to get back to Kitsilano, the Vancouver's neighbourhood where he grew up. "The neighbourhood hasn't changed too much. Now when I go into Blockbusters there's films with my face on them, which is a little bit different, but other than that it's pretty much the same old thing."

There are other current U.S.-based actors from B.C.: Gil Bellows, who costarred on TV's *Ally McBeal*; Rachel Roberts, the title character in the film *Simone*; Pamela Anderson, star of movies such as *Raw Justice* and TV's *Baywatch*; Eric McCormack, costar of TV's *Will and Grace* (homes in L.A. and Vancouver); Deborah Unger, who appeared in *The Game* and *The Hurricane*, and occasional Gastown student Barry Pepper, who's been featured in such movies as *Saving Private Ryan*, *The Green Mile*, and, sad truth be told, *Battlefield Earth*. But by the 1990s, the north-south flow for Canadian actors was no longer the only route to go. There was enough work in Canada that some Canadian actors were moving back after sojourns in the U.S. To Ontario: Nicholas Campbell, Wendy Crewson, Nick Mancuso, and Marilyn Kuzyk; to B.C.: Campbell (again), Helen Shaver, Alan Scarfe, and Carly Pope.

Pope moved to L.A. just out of high school, after landing a starring role in the WB TV series *Popular*. Following the series' short run in 1999, she remained in L.A., appearing in studio films (*Orange County*, *The Glass House*) and TV movies (*Trapped in a Purple Haze*). But after a couple of years, Pope returned to Vancouver. "For me it was a very personal decision to move back," she says. "I'm happier up here. I guess the best way to put it is I just feel full here and I didn't down there. I'm around my friends, my family, my support system. It's just a matter of where is home. And home to me is here. I felt very lucky to go down there and experience it but I felt luckier to come home." Canada's film scene made coming home more inviting and she quickly landed a starring role in the shot-in-Vancouver indie *Various Positions*. "I'm always, always, always looking to work from home. It's really a blessing. I feel very lucky to have the opportunity to be auditioning and reading and have any sort of involvement in anything Canadian because I do think it's important to support. And necessary to produce."

Shaver, from St Thomas, Ontario, had studied acting in Vancouver in her early twenties, then moved to Los Angeles and lead roles in U.S. (*The Color of Money, Desert Hearts*) and Canadian (*In Praise of Older Women, Bethune*) films. Shaver would return to Vancouver with her son and husband to star in tv's *Poltergeist* because producers had promised her the chance to direct episodes. After *Poltergeist* disappeared, she stayed, working as an actor and director between Vancouver and L.A. Shaver quickly developing a reputation as a fine director, with an Emmy nomination for the Showtime movie *Summer's End*.

§

Along with the Canadian film scene, a couple of Vancouver-shot television shows have made particular contributions to the development of the local film-acting pool – Fox's *The X-Files* and cbc's *Da Vinci's Inquest*.

In the late 1990s, *Da Vinci's Inquest*, about a Vancouver-based investigative coroner, became the television program of choice for Vancouver indie actors who don't often watch episodic tv. "The pride that people take in that show, you feel it from the lead actors to the wardrobe trailer," says Tom Scholte, who won a 2001 Gemini award for a guest performance on the program.

Da Vinci's regular Donnelly Rhodes says standard tv writing often leaves actors trying to rescue a project from itself. "I mean, how to make it not embarrassing. But when you have something like *Da Vinci's*, you don't have to use tricks – you can actually just go with the material. It's exciting. It's fun to do. It's like attending an intensive actors' workshop. Because of the writing everybody has something to look forward to as opposed to the usual level that you get on television, which is actually a lot of work on knowing what not to do, on how to save it."

The series is one of those instances when popular taste is in sync with artists' tastes. It has a huge audience, regularly wins the Gemini as Canada's top tv drama, and Vancouver's best actors love working on it. "If the actors want to do your show, it raises your standards," says *Da Vinci's* creator-producer Chris Haddock, who also writes the show with Alan DiFiore and Frank Borg. "The actors here in Vancouver can handle any material so I say, 'Let's create tougher, challenging stuff.'"

Da Vinci's Inquest does for television what Vancouver independent filmmakers such as Bruce Sweeney and Lynne Stopkewich do for movies – provide a quality alternative to the schlock produced by Vancouver's U.S.-based film and TV industry. And the series has more links with the indie film scene than anything else on North American television. Stopkewich and Keith Behrman have directed episodes and many in the cast of Sweeney's *Last Wedding*, for instance, have also appeared on *Da Vinci's*: Scholte, Ben Ratner, Nancy Sivak, Frida Betrani, Jillian Fargey, Vincent Gale, and Jennifer Clement. Betrani played a street prostitute on one *Da Vinci's* episode. "The writing on that show is so good it's like you're eating it off the page. It's delicious," she says, adding that its depiction of women is uniquely respectful for television.

And just as the Sweeney group is comfortable on Haddock's show, you get the impression Haddock's regulars, such as Rhodes, Nicholas Campbell, Ian Tracey, Venus Terzo, and Sue Mathew, would be at home on a Sweeney set. Haddock places *Da Vinci's* squarely in the same camp as the indie directors who emerged in Vancouver during the 1990s.

"They've realized the answer is to make films about what you know and where you are, which is what I've learned and I do with *Da Vinci's*," he says. "Simultaneous with their arrival on the scene was the boon in Vancouver actors' confidence in portraying themselves as Vancouverites after the years of being asked to change their accents for bland American television. That's almost like taking the language away from an indigenous people.

"It's great for actors to know their wardrobe is right for Main and Hastings because they've been to Main and Hastings."

The show's costume designer, Siobhan Gray, elaborates: "The beauty of the show is that I'm representing Vancouver. My job's to show people what Vancouver really looks like. Most shows you're trying to make someone look really good, look cool, and on ours it's not about glamour. I think most actors are quite comfortable with not looking their best all the time."

Sometimes Haddock keeps an actor in mind for years until a part fits their talent. Gina Chiarelli auditioned repeatedly without landing a role before a recurring prison-activist character was developed for her. "It is the most creative environment I have experienced in television, by far," Chiarelli says. "The reason is Chris Haddock, because he is a true artist and a person who values good acting. He's not interested in formula. He hires people who look like real people. His respect for actors is so high and you feel that in that audition room."

§

"I have a very different perspective from a lot of other people," Haddock says, looking out his office window at rain falling on city rooftops. It's a *Da Vinci's Inquest* kind of day. Vancouver's gritty downtown streets are under a big grey sky. Inside the old Dominion Building on Hastings, a wooden banister spirals to the top of what was, for a long-ago moment, the tallest structure in the British Empire. Now, its marble floors are cracked.

Haddock didn't make a living in TV or movies until he was thirty-six. "I kicked around. I was one of those guys at thirty who thought I'd never have a straight job. I know a lot of different jobs, I know what it is to grind and eke out a living, I've been in contact with thousands of interesting people. It can't help but rub off."

He grew up in a large family near the gates of UBC, where his dad was a forestry professor. After graduating from Lord Byng high school in 1970, he worked a number of jobs: cleaned animal cages at the physiology lab at UBC, unloaded boxcars, was a janitor at the Jewish Community Centre, broke rock at the False Creek seawall, worked at Octopus Books, played street fiddle, played bass in a country rock band, travelled cross-country in a troupe called the Breadbakers Theatre.

Haddock didn't do time in film school. But he always loved movies and when he decided to write one, he simply went to a library and looked at a copy of a screenplay. The result was *Success Without College*, which he optioned for $2,000, "more money than I'd ever seen." Nothing happened with the movie, but he was hooked on screenwriting and his talent was quickly recognized, and he got work on several Canadian-based TV series before creating *Mom, PI*, a CBC sitcom which established him as a producer-writer.

Now, he's one of Canadian television's top show runners, a producer-writer-creator-director with a variety of major projects on the go, including moves into feature films and U.S. network TV (the CBS pilot *Street Boss*). In 1996, 20th Century Fox won a six-figure studio bidding war for a Haddock script called *The Man Inside*. Haddock also bought the rights to *Run Man Run*, a novel about racial conflict, which he wants to direct. And he's planning a feature-film version of *Da Vinci's Inquest*.

More significant than *Da Vinci's* popularity, Haddock has redefined Canadian television, injecting a dose of high-grade reality, with scripts such as the two-parter about the disappearance of prostitutes in Vancouver. *Da Vinci's Inquest's* sensibility is closer to a tautly written 1930s' Warner Brothers' movie than it is to other current TV crime dramas. Coroner Dominic Da Vinci, as played to perfection by Nicholas Campbell, is a worldly, weary anti-hero reminiscent of Humphrey Bogart, John Garfield, and Warners' other tough city guys.

"I imagine that character of Dominic was born a block away from the PNE grounds and hung around Little Italy," Haddock says.

Haddock is a "child of '60s politics," who hung out in the leftie political milieu on Commercial Drive and performed street theatre. "I've always been driven to express. *Da Vinci's Inquest* is a hugely gratifying thing to create and I get to write about things that go on in Vancouver."

Along with hiring feature directors such as Stopkewich and Anne Wheeler, Haddock is known for giving unknowns their shot, and crews and actors are eager to work with him. "I'm drawn to people who have a creative impulse and urge to create. I'm drawn to people who have the courage and need the courage. The crews are technically as skilled as anybody in the world and have a great attitude. People here are eager. That's distinctly Canadian."

He expects Haddock Entertainment will be operating pretty much the same way a decade from now. "I think I'll still be talking about a dozen different projects, running a creative home for artists." Will he still be in Vancouver? "Yep. I'm going to be here till I croak."

Da Vinci's regular Ian Tracey says working on the show keeps getting better. "The crew's always mellow. Nobody has an ego. Chris doesn't have an ego. No one would put up with it. I'm loving it. We all love it. Everyone's so cool and so proud to be working on it."

Another series regular, Sarah-Jane Redmond, concurs: "There's just no attitudes there at all. If I watched TV, that would be the show that I would watch."

§

The X-Files, the popular Fox series, was the other 1990s' made-in-Vancouver TV series to heavily impact local actors. "I think it showed everybody that we can do it," says Nick Lea. "[Producer] Chris Carter, say what you will about him, was the guy who took a real chance. And he hired a lot of Vancouver actors to play big parts on that show."

Lea, like other Gastown students, had started on Vancouver television long before *The X-Files* or *Da Vinci's Inquest*. "I think the first professional thing I ever did was *Secret Lives*, with Dr Don Dutton. I was a young guy whose mother was going through sort of a rebirth of her younger years and she was sleeping with all these men and my

Nicholas Lea. *photo by Chris Relke, courtesy* The Province

126

character just couldn't handle it. I walked out after shooting and – I'll never forget this – one of the lighting guys, he pulled me aside and said, 'Hey, you know, you're pretty good.'"

It was the first time Lea's work had been acknowledged outside an acting class but, like Cummins and Parker, he would soon break out of bit roles on local television. On set for a small role in an episode of *The X-Files* during its first season, Lea met Rob Bowman, who would go on to coproduce and direct the American service-industry series. "I always come to the set with tons of ideas and he was somebody who listened. And so we used a lot of the things that I was thinking about and we just really kind of hit it off and became friends."

In the second season, about twenty-five L.A. actors read for a new role, that of Alex Krycek, but producers still weren't satisfied. "Then Rob Bowman said, 'You've got to go to Vancouver and read that guy that we used in the first season, you've got to go up there. He's perfect for it,'" says Lea. "And so they finally acquiesced and they came up to Vancouver and I was the only guy they read and I got the job. So every time I see him I give him a buck."

The show would become a television phenomenon and Lea was asked to do press in Europe and the across the U.S. "People would go absolutely ape shit, like we were the Beatles," he says. "We did the Virgin megastore on the Champs Elysees in Paris. It was fucking packed, thousands of people came out to see us and get our autographs, to watch us talk. We were in Atlanta and Washington, where I did one of these conventions, and somebody paid $500 for the seat that I was sitting on. And it was just like a folding plastic chair. Because I was sitting on it.

"I've become pretty adept at standing back and looking at it and realizing it's got very little to do with me or my ability or who I am. Like when I was in Dublin, we were doing a thing in a Virgin megastore and all of a sudden people started crying and passing out in lineups, so they stopped it because they didn't want anybody to get hurt. And we couldn't leave the building because these people had blocked the front and back exits, so we waited for about an hour. We weren't allowed to leave because they felt we were going to be hurt. And finally they walked us next door, up to the catwalk and to the building and down through their building and out their delivery door in the back. The guy said: 'Okay, the door's going to open, just keep your head down. You're going to be on the street, take a left, take another left. There's going to be a red Mercedes with a door open, so get in and just keep your head down and go. We did that, we opened the door, we were walking with our heads down, and I saw the car with the door open out of the corner of my eye, we got there, we were just closing the door. And around the corner came hundreds and hundreds of screaming people. Kids, adults, they were shaking the car and crying and trying to jam things in through the window to us, and the car was going back and forth. We had to drive around Dublin for half an hour to lose them. It was like we were rock stars."

That same day in Dublin, a child approached Lea, causing him to reassess the calling he decided to pursue years earlier in Vancouver.

"I've got the thing at home. This little boy walked up to the front and he pushed this note in front of me and said, 'Please deliver to them.' And I looked at it and it said, 'Dear Mulder and Scully – There's evil in Ireland and the government can't do anything and the police aren't able to stop it. I wrote the Power Rangers but they didn't write me back. Can you please come to Ireland and save us?'

"I got really choked up, you know, but that's the power of film or television. That was the moment when I kind of realized, 'Wow, this is huge. It's such a huge influence that's it's got over people and it's unfortunate that it's as irresponsible as it is.'"

A TALE OF TWO FILM CITIES

The home-grown actors who emerged from the Gastown Actors' Studio and elsewhere in the Vancouver of the 1990s weren't the only actors in the city. Vancouver had become one of four North American cities – along with L.A., New York, and Toronto – where actors go to be in films and TV, and the service-industry boom resulted in a generation of Hollywood actors who knew their way around Canadian cities.

"I like Toronto and Vancouver quite a bit," Rachael Lee Cook said on the Vancouver set of *Josie and the Pussycats*. "It's where the film industry is now. Whenever something says 'exterior New York street,' it's like I know I'm going to Toronto. That's the way it is. And honestly, I really don't mind at all. I'm starting to learn my way around. I know people here, I have friends who live here now."

The 1990s were a tale of two film communities in Vancouver. While the booming American industry dined at the Sutton Place Hotel and rented homes on the West Vancouver waterfront, the fledgling independent scene ate at the Alibi Room and lived in West End flats. While indie filmmakers could be found editing their features in cramped offices at 23rd and Oak, American filmmakers could be found contemplating their movies of the week over drinks at, well, the Sutton Place.

"It's a Hollywood away from Hollywood. If Hollywood existed on the moon it would look like the bar at the Sutton Place," says Benicio Del Toro, who shot *Excess Baggage* (with Alicia Silverstone) and *The Pledge* (with Jack Nicholson, directed by Sean Penn) in B.C. "I went there one night, it was like, 'Wait a second, everybody's here.'"

Through the U.S. service industry, the most elaborate infrastructure this side of Hollywood had entrenched itself in Vancouver. In 1996, CDN$557 million was spent on production, a twenty-four percent increase over the previous record – 1995's $432 million. In 1998, Vancouver edged Toronto in dollars spent on film production ($808 million), staking its claim as the third film centre in North America, behind L.A. and New York. The following year, the industry passed the billion-dollar mark. "It's a billion, baby," the provincial government's movie minister Ian Waddell effused at a press conference.

§

Ken Olin's experience in Vancouver was fairly commonplace for a visiting American actor. Olin, who starred in TV's *thirtysomething*, was fortysomething when Vancouver began to play a recurring role in his life. After the series went off the air, he starred in a string of the made-in-Vancouver-but-set-somewhere-else TV movies that were at the heart of the city's U.S. industry in the 1990s. He lived at the Sutton Place Hotel when he worked in Vancouver but his life, along with actor wife Patricia Wettig and two children, was in Santa Monica, California.

"My family's not here. I live in a hotel. Basically my day is I work out and go to work, come home and order room service."

In some ways, Olin's life in Vancouver was not so different than it was on the west side of Los Angeles. He went to Chapters, which is pretty much like Barnes and Noble; went to the Virgin megastore, which is pretty much like Tower Records; went to Starbucks, which is pretty much like Starbucks. "I'm pretty comfortable coming here because I know the people at the Sutton Place and I have kind of a routine. I go get coffee, I go to Chapters, maybe I'll go to the record store. But it's still limited and I come here primarily to work.

"I look forward to coming up . . . I like the air here. I like the mountains and the water. I find it generally to be a very pleasant place to work. I assume when I sign up to do a television movie it's going to be shooting in Vancouver."

By the mid-'90s, Vancouver residents were as blasé about most movie actors as they were about film shoots on their streets. "Most people I think recognize me from *thirtysomething*," Olin says. "And I get recognized a lot. People here are very polite. I think they're somewhat used to it – not like Los Angeles in terms of how many . . . but there are certainly a number of celebrities in Vancouver."

Neighbourhoods throughout the Vancouver area were taking on the appearance of trailer parks as production circuses showed up overnight. New sound stages were being built and the infrastructure could barely keep up with the demand or the changing technology. For instance,

North Vancouver's Pinewood Sound constructed a fully digital sound-mixing studio theatre, in which a gunfight could be heard from both sides of a room. "Producers will be able to not just shoot here but to finish here as well," noted Pinewood's Geoff Turner. "This will be the latest thing in Canada but only for a day or two. That's just the way this industry goes." The steady production meant a labour force that by 1997 had grown to 12,000 full-time jobs and 19,000 indirect jobs. The largest union of film workers, IATSE, had grown from forty members at its founding in 1962 to more than 4,000 by the end of the century.

Every visiting actor's routine does not revolve around the Sutton Place. Gwyneth Paltrow and her family went through a personal ordeal while shooting *Duets*. "I think the biggest challenge making the film was struggling with the fact that my father was so sick and just trying to be strong for him," she says of her dad, Bruce, who learned he had cancer shortly before coming to Vancouver to direct the film.

"You know, our whole family was up there," she says. "We were all there to support him. But it was very difficult. He was very, very sick and not himself. And so my biggest challenge was to try to just be a professional and a grownup and not be a scared daughter. And to try to make his life as easy as possible."

Paltrow was at the peak of her popularity when she came to Vancouver to star in *Duets* (its message: singing drecky songs to each other will set us free) for her father. But many of the "stars" who came were on downward trajectories when they signed on to service-industry productions.

Case in point: Sylvester Stallone. He would spend time in the city in the 1990s, making the unwatchable *Get Carter* and the unreleaseable *I See You*. The latter's original name, *D-Tox*, was changed because cast members would arrive at the Vancouver airport to be greeted by drivers holding the sign, D-TOX. Observers would approach cast members to express their sympathies, noted Stallone, adding: "Kris Kristofferson said, 'I'm not walking over there [to the sign].'"

Not all U.S. actors came to Vancouver to stay at the Sutton Place. Travolta had already gone home but several others moved to B.C., with Molly Parker's home-town Maple Ridge, of all places, becoming something of an actors' colony, though it'll never be mistaken for Malibu. The town in Vancouver's outer limits had long been known as an athletic spawning ground (baseball's Larry Walker, hockey's Cam Neeley, among the many) but since the 1990s its residents have included Michael Moriarty (*Law and Order*), Judy Norton (*The Waltons*), Meg Tilly (*Agnes of God*), and Colin Firth (*Bridget Jones's Diary*). Jennifer Beals, of *Flashdance* and an array of American independent films, often spends time there, too. The ranks of American expat actors elsewhere in the Vancouver area include Rob Labelle (*The Burial Society*), Colin Cunningham (*Zacharia Farted*), Kim Hawthorne (*Da Vinci's Inquest*), and Brian Markinson (*Sweet and Lowdown*).

"If I'm lucky enough to have kids I would raise my kids up there," says Beals, whose husband is from Maple Ridge. "I don't think I would raise my kids in Los Angeles. What I was thinking about this year was applying for landed immigrancy 'cause I am up there so often. My in-laws are there and my stepkids are there and besides, it's beautiful. We actually have a little cabin kind of place in Maple Ridge."

Maybe Moriarty made Vancouver his latest stop because the script inside his head belongs to a damp, dark *X-Files*' episode. Moriarty came to Canada, he says, determined to expose a worldwide liberal conspiracy, believing then-U.S. attorney general Janet Reno was determined to crush him because he didn't believe in television censorship. After being run out of Halifax and Toronto for unhinged, drunken episodes, Moriarty wound up in Vancouver's West End neighbourhood. (Odd place for to go for someone trying to escape liberals – at the time, the federal government was Liberal, the provincial government was liberal social-democrats, the provincial opposition was conservative Liberals, and his urban neighbourhood would have voted for Hillary Clinton were it given half the chance.) "It's called Hollywood

TEN MEMORABLE U.S. SHOOTS IN B.C. DURING THE 1990s

Bird on a Wire (1990). Comedy meets action with Goldie Hawn and Mel Gibson. Goldie Hawn, along with Kurt Russell and family, would return to live in Vancouver in 2002.

The Crush (1993) and *Excess Baggage* (1997). Alicia Silverstone double bill.

Intersection (1994). Vancouver finally gets to play Vancouver, with Sharon Stone, Richard Gere, Lolita Davidovich.

Legends of the Fall (1994). Greek tragedy meets soap opera with Brad Pitt, Anthony Hopkins.

Little Women (1994). Among the best of the service-industry, with Winona Ryder, Susan Sarandon, Claire Danes.

Jumanji (1995). The relentless computerized action overwhelms

North," Moriarty says. "The future of film in North America, I think, is in Vancouver. It's a young city, it's not afraid of growth. It's got a great police force." Not great enough, apparently, to prevent Moriarty's involvement in a series of late-night confrontations. He moved to Maple Ridge, where he was hospitalized after a severe beating outside a bar.

In an earlier incarnation, Moriarty was one of the best actors of his generation (*Bang the Drum Slowly*, *The Last Detail*) and in Vancouver he's done some bits in service-industry productions, including *Along Came a Spider*. (In 2002, he had a comeback of sorts when he won an Emmy for the TV movie *James Dean*.)

A Tale of Two Film Cities

Vancouver has played the U.S. often enough now that visitors such as *Along Came a Spider* director Lee Tamahori quickly hear how badly things can go wrong. *Rumble in the Bronx*, for instance, has become part of local movie lore. The 1997 Jackie Chan action movie should have been called *Mountain in the Bronx* – there was apparently no attempt by filmmakers to avoid shooting the west coast scenery and several supposedly New York sequences have spectacular mountain backgrounds.

"You've got to be very careful – I can't look towards mountains, I can't do this, I can't do that," Tamahori noted on the set of *Along Came a Spider*. "This won't be like *Rumble in the Bronx*, you know, this will be more accurate. [With *Rumble*, it was] 'we will shoot this anywhere in the world and then we'll call it *Rumble in the Bronx*'. . . . There's mountains, and this stuff, and you go, 'This is insane.'"

Along Came a Spider – your basic crime story with Morgan Freeman and Monica Potter – was slightly better than *Rumble in the Bronx Mountains*. "It's a funny thing," Tamahori

Robin Williams, Kirsten Dunst, and anyone who tries to sit through this.

Mr Magoo (1997) and *Wrongfully Accused* (1998). Leslie Nielsen film festival.

Double Jeopardy (1999). Local actors played a big role in this box-office hit that had Ashley Judd hunting down her sleazy "dead" husband played by Bruce Greenwood.

The *Air Bud* movies also arrived in the 1990s (this series and the later MVP (most valuable primate) movies are Disney-style Canadian-American productions often directed or produced by Vancouver's Robert Vince).

Also: *The Hitman* (1991), *Timecop* (1994), *Big Bully* (1995), *Carpool* (1996), *Happy Gilmore* (1996), *Unforgettable* (1996), *Seven Years in Tibet* (1997), *Snow Falling on Cedars*, (1999), *Dudley Do-Right* (1999), *Reindeer Games* (1999).

said between shots. "I was kind of like told to come up here, you know. I wouldn't have chosen to come up here because I don't think this looks anything like Washington. I would have chosen another city, perhaps Toronto, perhaps somewhere else.

"I said, 'This is ridiculous, Vancouver looks nothing like Washington.' But then we looked at the movie and most of it was interior anyway. It's a very interior movie. Fifty percent of it's inside, so we knew we could deal with that. The rest of it you can hunt around all over Vancouver and you could always find places."

Along with the service industry's somewhat memorable films such as *Along Came a Spider* and *Rumble in the Bronx*, there are its many forgotten features (*Bordello of Blood*, *Thor*, *The Hunted*, *Gold Diggers*) and movies of the week you only wish you could forget.

§

While all these shenanigans were going on, the West Coast Wave was about to launch its first post-*The Grocer's Wife* feature. *Double Happiness* premiered at the 1994 Toronto International Film Festival to a staggering response – director Mina Shum was heralded as a great new director, the film's star Sandra Oh was showered with offers, and U.S. distributors came knocking. All this for a funny, introspective, semi-autobiographical movie about an immigrant Chinese family in Vancouver, focusing on a rebellious, artistic young woman navigating through two cultures

"I was shocked, actually," Shum says. "I thought it was going to be one of these arty, independent Canadian films that people just liked, and that was it. But people really liked it. And then the U.S. market jumped on board. Fine Line released it. I couldn't believe it. In my mind, I always sort of prescribed to the Spike Lee code which is the more specific, the more universal. But I never thought it would pay off the way it did with this story, because it's the story about a girl moving out. And yet people gravitated toward it. I had people at various festivals standing up telling me they were Jade, the lead character. Like, I'd be looking at a sixty-five-year-old Russian Jewish man and he'd go, 'This story happened to me.'"

For Shum, the success of *Double Happiness* was an affirmation of her punk rock roots. "Putting a band together, being in a band that no one really wants to see and there's no record deal and you're just doing it for the fun of it, that prepares you for making your feature film," says Shum.

"And I think part of my training was from that punk rock movement when I was younger. Never say never. I mean, *The Grocer's Wife* thing was a punk rock experience. Do it yourself. Do it. By any means necessary. And that comes from that music scene background, I think."

§

One of the distinctive characteristics of Vancouver's independent film scene is its links with music. Directors Shum and Lynne Stopkewich were punk rockers, director Blaine Thurier performs with the band the New Pornographers, producer-director Chris Haddock was a street musician. Vancouver actors who perform musically include Tom Scholte, Nicholas Lea, Ben Ratner, Babz Chula, and Barbara Williams; musicians who act include Bif Naked, Sook-Yin Lee, Kinnie Starr, and Joe "Shithead" Keithley (the Vancouver punk rock legend's daughter, Georgia Keithley, was one of the featured children in John Travolta's *Look Who's Talking Now*).

Mina Shum on vocals for Out of Proportion, playing Shindig at The Savoy. *courtesy Mina Shum*

Stopkewich, who directed the documentary about the Lilith Fair women's music tour (*Lilith on Top*), asked tour organizer Sarah McLachlan to act in a film.

"Lynne asked me to be in one of her films [*Suspicious River*], a little side role as a stripper," says McLachlan. "For many reasons I said 'no.' I didn't want to bare my ass to the world. It would have been a very brief scene because I don't act and I don't know how to act and so I probably would have been horrific."

"No," Stopkewich says,

"It probably would have been a featured part of the movie."

Shum sees a parallel between alternative music and independent movie-making. After spending much of her childhood watching musicals on TV, Shum traded in Gershwin for Johnny Rotten when she realized she could be in the musical by attending punk shows. She became a regular at the all-ages hall gigs often starring D.O.A. or The Subhumans, and soon was the lead singer of Playdoh Republic.

"It was everything, from the time I was about fifteen till nineteen or twenty," Shum says. "Having the punk rock thing gave me a place to be a freak and it was okay."

When "alternative bands" began distributing their music without major label support in the late 1970s, it created a Vancouver independent ethos embraced by directors who would make films without input from major studios. Later, Scott Smith, Joshua Hamlin, and other local directors would distribute their own films, circumventing the powerful distributors much like local punk bands had earlier bypassed major record labels. "I think partly we always feel like we're the other big city in Canada so there has to be a DIY attitude in order to get things done," says Shum. "It's partly because we are a little marginalized."

∫

Shum was the first of the West Coast Wave out of the gate after *The Grocer's Wife*. "I applied to the Canada Council for an Explorations grant to do a short and I actually got the money before I graduated so I knew I was going to graduate from school and go and make a short.

"I applied for another grant to write *Double Happiness*. I didn't get the money the first round, but I got it the second round. I had to wait four or five months. When I got the money, I immediately started writing.

"I'm very fortunate that the Canadian funding bodies were focusing on people of colour in the early '90s. The film board had money, especially to develop women of colour filmmakers," she says. "It's partly trying to balance everything. And then I went to the Canadian Film Centre in 1991."

Since UBC had provided her with the basic filmmaking stills, at the Toronto's Canadian Film Centre she focused on perfecting her *Double Happiness* script. Back in Vancouver, everything fell into place and it became a joint production of the National Film Board, B.C. Film, and Telefilm.

Shum had been encouraged by the success of *The Grocer's Wife*. "It's not the most straightforward movie, it's not *Men With Brooms*. It's an arty film. There's art all over it. And that did well and it was recognized. As a little Canadian film that I worked on it gave me the confidence that I could tell my little story and that maybe it might reach somebody some day." She was also encouraged by the experimental filmmaking of Ann Marie Fleming, whom she befriended and worked with shortly after *The Grocer's Wife*. "Meeting Ann Marie Fleming, seeing that she had already had a body of work – whimsical little shorts, very witty and philosophical.

"For my own personal growth, having seen that there was a scene of people making really, really strange movies, not narrative, gave me the strength and the courage," she says. "I love those kinds of films to watch but I would not make them myself. But knowing that there was funding for them. . . ."

Mina Shum makes an invaluable contribution to more than Vancouver filmmaking. Chinese immigrants have been a huge part of the B.C. fabric since they built the railroad and established Chinatowns across the province. With the lifting of anti-Asian immigration laws in 1967, they've also become an increasing part of the demographic. In a city with a huge Chinese community, it's vital that someone put their stories on screen in theatrical feature films. And Shum has been that someone. "You write about what you know," Shum says. "Actually, it's funny. In film school I was trying to be David Lynch. I was doing this satire on the American family and my teacher turned to me and said, 'The most interesting character in the entire script is the Chinese drummer you have in here. Why don't you write about her?' And I was like, 'I don't know.' I actually said, 'I don't think anybody's interested in my Chinese drummer.' And he said, 'You wouldn't believe how many people. Do you think Shakespeare wrote about anybody else other than people in England?'"

Shum's films are nuanced with the sort of detailed cultural specifics that give them a reality and universality. In *Long Life, Happiness & Prosperity*, for instance, there is a moment where two women in the background argue over a bill in a restaurant. "For most people that just goes by as background but in the Vancouver Chinese-Canadian audience they were laughing at that because it's something we grew up with," says Shum. "We would fight to the death to pay the bill because if I pay the bill then you're my guest and I'm treating you well on earth, then there'll be a good place for me on earth because I've done this. It's funny, when I saw the screening here at the film festival, there was the first laughter, which was like everybody's laughter, everybody got the joke. Then, with some of the jokes, you know this joke's for you if you grew up Chinese. So there's these trickles of different laughters in the crowd, depending on what cultural background that person came from. And that was so cool."

Before film, she studied theatre, with thoughts of becoming an actor, and was particularly drawn to the 1960s Theatre of the Absurd movement. "Just crazy juxtapositions would happen on stage all the time, between the absolute comedic and the absolute sadness of life. I think being an immigrant has got to be one of the funniest and saddest things at the same time. We're always confronted with absolutely absurd situations and juxtapositions because of the two languages, because of the two cultures. And I grew up laughing at that and gaining a lot of strength from the humour that came out of those juxtapositions, which is probably why I write comedies."

Shum followed *Double Happiness* with the less magical *Drive, She*

Mina Shum in costume on the set of *Drive, She Said. photo by Theresa Marshall, courtesy Mina Shum*

Said and television work, but her first movie showed her undeniable potential and 2003 marked the release of her third film, *Long Life, Happiness & Prosperity*, an ambitious project weaving three separate storylines into one movie set in Vancouver's Chinese community.

The film costars Shum's close friend Sandra Oh, the lead from *Double Happiness*. "I wanted to work with Mina again," says Oh, stepping under cover as rain pours on to the make-believe Chinatown that's been constructed at the movie's Commercial Street location. "Mina and I have a very good working relationship and basically anything that she does if there's a part for me in it I'm sure that she'll ask me. I'm so happy to do it."

The Canadian actor has roles on the HBO series *Arli$$* and CBS's *Judging Amy*, and has appeared in such movies as *Dancing at the Blue Iguana* and *Last Night*. Oh met Shum in Vancouver in 1993 when she was starring in *The Diary of Evelyn Lau* and the future director was playing her social worker. "She has like one or two lines," says Oh. "That's it. But we met and she goes, 'Hey, you aren't really fourteen are you?' And I wasn't. I was like twenty. She goes, 'Here's my script.' And I hooked up with her at the end of that project. We just kind of kept in touch. She was cool and then the next year, '94, she called me in January. She goes, 'We got our money.'"

Oh won a best actress Genie for *Double Happiness*. The smart, engaging story about a young Asian woman didn't only apply to Shum. "Hopefully, your heart shows in every project but this was literally both of our lives," says Oh.

On the set of *Long Life*, Shum pauses in a make-believe Chinese market to note that working with Oh again was as pleasant as she anticipated. "Literally, she'll finish a take and I'll look at her and I'll raise an eyebrow and she'll pinch her nose and we know exactly what was wrong or right with the take."

Oh's often assumed to be a Vancouver actor because so much of her work has been shot in the city. But she has never lived in Vancouver, having grown up in Ottawa, and living in Montreal and Toronto before moving to Los Angeles in 1996. "If I could stay in Canada and work my entire life I would. I can't. I would starve to death. I'm telling you right now. Canadian filmmakers who elect to work with me, they call me at home and they call me every four years.

"That's just for me. I mean, Sarah [Polley] is doing it, Molly

[Parker] just moved to L.A. . . . . But I can't do it because I'm not as cast-able as them for some crazy reason. Everything in, let's say television, is all about things that happened in the past where somehow there are no people who look like me there. And that's what's produced here."

Shum is looking to diversify her filmmaking but she won't be forgetting the way people in the past actually did look. "There are the Mina movies, which are my own personal obsession – the ones that I write and direct, which may or may not have to do with the cultural me but probably, just because my obsessions have to do with partly who I am. And who I am is the dual cultures. And then there's going to be the other ones where I just direct and that may explore the side of me that wants to be Steve Soderbergh or it might explore the Coppola side of me, the Italian male director or whatever.

"My work is about trying to find some truth, whether it's in your story that I'm directing or whether it's my own personal Chinese-Canadian drama that I'm making.

"I can live in those two worlds. But if we're talking about specifically the films I'd make, that are mine, that get generated from my head, like my next film that I'm writing myself is a period piece set in China. So it happens to be the subject I'm interested in today. It doesn't necessarily mean it's always going to be like that. I have a romantic comedy I'm trying to write. Does it have anything to do with being Chinese? Not really. But I'd like Sandra Oh to be the lead. So right away there's that. You know, she's a person of colour on screen as opposed to casting a non-person of colour. Because I like her as an actor. It's just it's Sandra, you know, and there's something that she brings to the movie because of who she is."

∫

By the time Shum jumped into the mosh pit, the city's music scene was developing a worldwide reputation. Now, it is film's turn.

"I just like the idea that you persevere because the only person that can define your voice is you and the only way it can get better is by making movies. And so now, with the advent of digital video, anyone can do it. That goes back to my punk roots. Anyone can do it."

Double Happiness, about a young Asian woman torn between two cultures, premiered as Vancouver was dividing into two film cultures:

the U.S. service industry and the independent, home-grown scene. Shum's instant indie classic served notice that the West Coast Wave out of UBC had arrived.

"The thing that's cool about the UBC group is we're still all young," says Shum. "We were really young when we first came out, now we're still fairly young. So what are we going to do? We're all continuing. Nobody's letting up. It will be interesting to see where this group is, the group I graduated with, what kind of films we'll be making in ten years."

THE SWEENEY GROUP

10

The future of Vancouver filmmaking has convened for a dinner party in a condo in suburban Burnaby.

"We're all from here," actor Ben Ratner's character is saying as cameras roll on this party scene for Bruce Sweeney's *Last Wedding*. Ratner, who grew up in the city's Dunbar neighbourhood, has come home from L.A. for this. Maple Ridge's Molly Parker, who lives in L.A., has come back, too. And there are other actors who came and never left – Nancy Sivak, Tom Scholte, Vincent Gale, and Frida Betrani.

They've assembled at this condo to shoot the anti-romantic comedy that would be selected to open the 2001 Toronto International Film Festival. This day, though, festival accolades are a year away and these actors are just happy to be home together.

"That's how they do it in France," explains Scholte's character, talking architecture at the dinner table.

"We're not," says Parker, "in France."

No, this is clearly Vancouver, with Sweeney's characters in a lively dinner debate about the state of the city's Expo 86 site. Like Sweeney's earlier, envelope-pushing features (*Live Bait, Dirty*) there is no mistaking this film for a TV movie-of-the-week made for a U.S. network. This director and these actors are among the best of Vancouver independent film, the ones creating a made-in-Vancouver, set-in-Vancouver film scene. They are also friends, so when Sweeney shouts "cut" on the dinner party, the scene evolves into an actual dinner party, with the actors talking about movies, their work, their lives.

∫

Bruce Sweeney examines the plate before him at a Vancouver sushi restaurant. "I have no quail egg on here," he says finally, disappointed. "I like to have a quail egg. You heard me say quail egg, didn't you?"

Spend any time with Sweeney and his friends and you quickly learn about their predilection for sushi. They put sushi scenes in movies, discuss their projects while munching sushi, meet the press and everyone else at sushi restaurants.

"Quail egg," Sweeney tells the waitress, "on top."

"Oh yeah, I forgot, that's right," she says, sweeping his plate back to the kitchen.

∫

A year after Mina Shum arrived with *Double Happiness*, Sweeney became the second of the UBC group to release a post-*The Grocer's Wife* feature. *Live Bait*, his master's thesis/feature film, is a witty coming-of-age-on-the-west-side-of-Vancouver story.

Nancy Sivak was in *Live Bait* . . . barely. She and a friend went to the Royal Centre theatre in 1995 to see the movie; her friend bent down to pick up his popcorn and when he sat up Sivak said, "You missed me." But Sivak went from that bit part in *Live Bait* to a costarring role in Sweeney's next movie, *Dirty*, about dysfunctional, interlocking lives in Vancouver's east end. And Sivak was back again for *Last Wedding*.

Sivak is part of Sweeney's ensemble not only because she is a fine actor but because she loves honest, tough movies with genuine characters, especially Canadian ones. "I was talking with Tom Scholte after we finished shooting today," Sivak said after a day spent shooting the dinner-party scene, "and I was saying how years ago back in Edmonton I'd loved slipping into a theatre to watch Canadian movies. We both said that to be making a movie like *Last Wedding* is a dream come true."

Although they haven't all been in every movie, an extended ensemble of actors, defined even more by their tastes and values than their abundant talent, have moved with Sweeney from *Live Bait* to *Dirty* to *Last Wedding* and, next, *American Venus*.

If there's any truth to the old saying that you can judge someone by the company they keep, Sweeney is in good standing. The actors and crew he assembles have nothing to do with the artificial glitz and contrived "product" that characterizes so much of the film industry.

"The fact is that indies are a certain type of thing," says Scholte, who's appeared in every Sweeney feature. "Someone like Bruce gets put off by someone who says, 'You know, I'm available to do indies.' It's not just another type of work. You can't just be going, 'Put me out for that stuff, too.' It's not: commercials, features, MOWS [movies of the week], and indies. It's as much about the sensibility as it is the talent. And he's not in any way out to be exclusionary, but it's been an organic process – a bunch of people finding each other in what's kind of a wasteland in a certain way. We love each other."

Alongside Scholte and Sivak, there is Vincent Gale, who started as a child actor in the Canadian classic *Bye Bye Blues* and wound up winning a Genie for the quiet anguish he distilled in *Last Wedding*; Ben Ratner, who moves easily between comedy and drama, going as ballistic on a computer in *Dirty* as Dustin Hoffman did on the hood of a cab in *Midnight Cowboy*; Marya Delver, who mixes innocence with brashness to light up any screen; Frida Betrani, who in *Last Wedding* delivers a riveting portrayal of a woman surviving the worst marriage this side of *Who's Afraid of Virginia Woolf?*; Babz Chula, whose Angie in *Dirty* is one of the best performances in Canadian film. And there are others: Jay Brazeau, Kevin McNulty, Kathleen Duborg, Micki Maunsell, Jennifer Clement, Rebecca Harker, Jillian Fargey.

Chula calls Sweeney's loose ensemble *the family*. "They're my favourite people to work with," she says.

(l–r) Actors David Lovgren, Molly Parker, and Vincent Gale are watched by Dave Pelletier and Bruce Sweeney on the set of *Last Wedding*. *courtesy Bruce Sweeney*

Scholte and Chula were largely responsible for introducing Sweeney to the best of Vancouver acting. "I got to know a bunch of people
in theatre through Tom," Sweeney says. "And I got to know about acting through seeing tons of plays and talking to him and then meeting
Babz Chula. It's through actors I learned about acting and how to
direct actors. Casting, in a lot of ways, is everything, because you have
your script but the fact is they're the people that are saying your words
and they're the people, in an exact sense, that are representing the
film. To have it miscast, which you see so often, really takes you out."

Sweeney is loyal to his acting ensemble and won't be bound by the
casting dictates of big-money producers. "If that's what you have to do
then I'm just not the right person. If they said you can't make *Dirty* unless
you get Cybill Shepherd instead of Babz, then it just falls apart. And then
I do it on a lower scale, shoot it on digital, whatever. But it's just unaccept-
able to me to have Cybill Shepherd. End of story. Not gonna happen."

§

"You actually have to eat the food, which could be disappointing,"
Sweeney tells the cast before the dinner-party scene gets under way. In
front of them are plates of lasagna, salad, and garlic bread. "But it's my
way of getting back at you guys."

"For what?" says Molly Parker. "I just got here." It's her first day on
Last Wedding, in the role of a conservative young architect that would
eventually garner her a supporting-actress Genie Award. "I'm really
excited to be here," she says. "Bruce makes movies about people. He
makes moves about people in Vancouver. I'm interested in the process of how he works." Parker was pleased to be part of the Sweeney
ensemble. "They're artists, they really are, and they're friends of mine,
and they're great actors. To be asked to be included in Bruce's company this time around, I felt really honoured."

Parker got to know Sweeney when she was an actor and he was a
boom operator on their friend Lynne Stopkewich's *Kissed*. "Being the
boom man you just really get attuned to people's voices and her voice
is such a complete knockout," Sweeney says. " You know, I just loved
listening to her say her lines."

Stopkewich recalls the day shooting began on *Kissed*. Sweeney
called her aside. "He had this whole commentary about my script and

how this stuff in it wasn't really working for him," says Stopkewich. "And I was already shooting it. It was so overwhelming for me. I was shitting bricks, thinking, 'I have to shoot this movie now, what if I don't know what the fuck I'm doing?' And there's Bruce going into this thing. I told him, 'Dude, not now, man. It's too late, it's too late.'" At the end of the shooting day, though, she would pull her friend aside to hear to his ideas. And Sweeney has nothing but fond memories of *Kissed*: "It was such a tremendous shoot because it was about those things a film should be about. Independent of corporate investment, just an idea-based film, everyone pulling together and chatting together and hanging out together. It was just truly a great experience."

§

Directors have found their place in North America's increasingly celebrity-driven popular culture. The Oscars are usually the second most-watched television show in any given year (after the Super Bowl), half of North America has an opinion on the weekend box-office champion, and first-time directors are regularly feted by *Premiere* and *Entertainment Tonight*. So it's not surprising there are directors who seem to

Bruce Sweeney. *courtesy Bruce Sweeney*

have nothing in mind other than being cool filmmakers who get to dress hip and travel to festivals with their derivative films.

Sweeney, though, is a refreshing throwback to an earlier time when directors were people in love with the movies, who worked their way into their calling almost by chance, starting with any job they could find on a set just because they wanted to be close to filmmaking.

While studying art at SFU, Sweeney was a regular at the Van East Cinema, which screened foreign films, and the Pacific Cinémathèque, an unadorned, New

York-style art house in downtown Vancouver. "I was heavily into European films. I wasn't thinking, 'Wow, I want to be a director.' That was the farthest thing from my mind. I was thinking, 'I love the movies.' I would watch them and be transported to another place. I would just think about the stories but I would never think about being a director. It didn't seem like an option that was very viable."

After Sweeney's experience on *The Grocer's Wife*, he started thinking about directing a feature and in 1992 began work on *Live Bait*.

§

Scholte and Sweeney met at UBC in 1991. "Bruce was doing his masters in film and I was doing my undergrad in acting. They take the undergrad actors who are in their final year and the first-year film directors and put them together in a film-acting class. And that's where we met.

"My first memory of Bruce is of him not wanting to answer the teachers' questions. A type of university student loves to say, 'I think it's this way, this way, and that way.' But not Bruce. He would make some smart-ass joke and I thought, 'Who the fuck is this guy? Clearly he's an intelligent guy and he will not offer his opinions.' As I got to know him over the years, I understand some of that as his suspicion of absolute statements. You look at *Live Bait* and that character, and that's

Tom Scholte. *courtesy Bruce Sweeney*

an exploration of that sort of psyche, that very defensive, protective, cynical psyche. Now, he's much more out front."

Scholte grew up in a middle-class home in Scarborough in suburban Toronto. Drawn to acting at an early age, he immersed himself in theatre and old movies and, after completing high school at the Etobicoke School of the Arts, came to Vancouver to study theatre at UBC. "I wanted to go to university to study acting and I wanted to go away from home. My idea was I would go away for a few years, then go back and work in the Toronto theatre scene or work at Stratford or Shaw or something."

He had come to UBC for theatre, but the beginnings of the West Coast Wave were all around him on campus. "I wasn't thinking about coming here because it had anything to do film," he says. The year Scholte and Sweeney were classmates, they also became friends. "We were having beers on the last day of class and he said, 'I'm going to make this movie.' And he finally sort of floated it past me." Sweeney had put a lot of himself in *Live Bait*, the story of a young, alienated UBC student, struggling with his relationships, his family.

Sweeney had seen Scholte in university productions and directed him in a classroom scene from *The Graduate*. Both raised in southern Ontario, they had remarkably close sensibilities. "I was born in '62, he's '67, but he had a similar upbringing," says Sweeney. "Particularly in *Live Bait* and *Last Wedding* you could definitely say that he was either my alter ego or my surrogate son or whatever he was." He quickly recognized in Scholte an actor "amazingly easy" to write dialogue for. "It just comes off of Tommy. And there's also his voice; I love his deep voice. I think there are similarities in the way we look, too. So, it's all kind of there for him. It's uncanny. Unnerving, maybe."

Scholte says he and Sweeney didn't realize how fully they were in sync until they started work on *Live Bait*. "We literally would discover that our favourite albums were the same, our favourite tracks were the same. One thing after another."

Soon Scholte was also hanging out with John Pozer and Ross Weber and staying up all night watching UBC film student Erik Whittaker's movie *Airport In*. "Bruce had this great, really long director's cut of *Airport In*. Just bizarre. So I started, very early, to get the sense that there was an interesting, crazy little ensemble of people here that are starting to break out. It felt like a real exciting little group of artists that were fermenting something."

That feeling was confirmed when Scholte attended a screening during a visit to Scarborough. "I was this theatre guy suddenly surrounded by all these film people and then suddenly *Double Happiness* was happening, too. And then, when I was home for Christmas, I went with my parents to see *Double Happiness* in the theatre and went, 'Whoa! Okay, this is pretty cool.' My folks loved it. And to be at a Canadian film with my parents and have us all walk out satisfied was a great moment, and again it made me feel like I was hooking into something.'"

§

Chula met Sweeney while shooting Michael Holboom's *Valentine's Day* in Toronto in 1992. "It was a sequel to a movie called *Kanada* and it was, you know, real low-budget alternative filmmaking. It wasn't even independent. It was beyond independent. I was playing a junkie tough gal. And we're shooting in a house and there are absolutely no amenities. You work with Michael knowing when he says cut and you've got to change, you've got to find a corner to do it in. But the work is so exciting that it's worth that. Gabrielle Rose and I were the actors; there was also Steve Sanguedolce, who is Michael's partner and director of photography and key grip and everything, and Bruce Sweeney, who was a student who knew Mike's films and volunteered to be the sound and boom person."

Babz Chula was born Barbara Zuckerman (Chula is leftover from a youthful marriage). Her childhood in a working-class Jewish neighbourhood in Queens, with a grandmother next door, aunts and uncles down the block, came to a sudden end when her father Larry, a mechanic and stock-car driver, was killed in a race when he was twenty-seven. "I was six years old. My mother was a twenty-four-year-old widow. His parents were absolutely devastated. You cannot know the suffering. My aunts . . . these people never recovered. It left me empty . . . and lot's of questions to this day I still seek answers to."

Her mother, Abby, who had been an aspiring actor, took Chula and her younger brother to Hawaii. "She said, 'We're going to live on the beach and we're going to cry a lot.'" They eventually settled in Los Angeles, where during the 1960s Chula was more Dylan than Beach Boys. ("I wasn't a grab your surf board and hit the beach kind of kid.") She moved between coasts, heading to New York to be a folk singer, returning to the west coast counter-culture, moving to the Kootenays in the B.C. Interior, raising children, singing in rock bands. In the early '80s, Chula relocated to Vancouver where her talents were quickly recognized, singing with an *a cappella* group, acting on stage (first play: replacing Barbara Williams in the original production of John Gray's *Rock 'n' Roll*). The film industry was new to Vancouver when Chula took a role in 1983's *My American Cousin*, but by the time she met Sweeney she had a long list of theatre, film, and television credits.

Chula had barely noticed Sweeney before he approached her on the last day of shooting on *Valentine's Day*. "He came up to me and said, 'Look, I'm doing a film for my thesis and I'd really like to know if you're interested in being in it. Could I call you?' I gave him my phone number, I said, 'Yeah, kid, give me a call.'

"About a year later, he called me and had to remind me who he was. He said, 'I'm ready to shoot my film. Can I meet you?' So I met him at some place on Robson Street, where I sat outside and this kind of rumpled guy, who looked vaguely familiar, came up to me and handed me a couple of wrinkled, soiled notebook pages with handwriting on them. I said, 'What is this?' You know, they're all earmarked and smudged. He said, 'Well, it's not a whole script, it's just your sides.' I said, 'Yeah, but what is this?' And he said, "Well, I don't

Babz Chula. *courtesy Bruce Sweeney*

want you to know anything about the other characters. I just worked with Mike Leigh and I'm going to try this, I'm experimenting with this idea that you come to this as a full character without any knowledge of the script or anyone else; just aware of your own journey.' And I was already in.

"I talked to him for like, really, it was five minutes. And I just said, 'I'll do this with you,' because I liked him and I liked how certain he was of what he wanted to do."

The next thing Chula knew, she and Kevin McNulty were playing the alienated parents of the alienated student portrayed by Scholte. "Bruce and I established a rapport immediately. I took the time to find out what he was asking me to do. You can't always ask [U.S. director] Jonathan Kaplan to be more articulate. You just have to go, 'Okay, I think this is what he means.' I didn't have to do that with Bruce. He was fifteen years younger than me, was absolutely, totally inexperienced, and he was asking me to work for him. So I got to say to him, 'Look, if that's what you want me to do, this is how you say it, this is how you get me to do that.' So we established language and that was really illuminating and inspiring for both of us. And we started really working together."

Much of *Live Bait* was shot at the Kerrisdale-area house Scholte shared with Sweeney and some of the director's friends from Sarnia. Scholte says the shoot had a magical ensemble feel from the beginning. "Kevin McNulty at that time was working nonstop on American stuff and I think, even in the midst of that, this seasoned pro had an experience of, 'Wow, these characters are really compelling.' I think everybody had an experience on that film that was so special that it felt like a family right away. It made sense that we would be together again.

"There's a scene in the film where I hold up this salmon as though I caught this big fish. After a day of shooting, everybody was gone, we took that salmon, put it on the barbecue and cooked it up. We took the lights from the film, set them up on the front lawn and me, [cinematographer Dave] Pelletier, and Bruce just ate salmon and played badminton till well into the morning, with these film lights flooding the front yard. It was really one of the most magical nights of my life. It's never that fun making movies. That was it."

Scholte was working on his masters degree at UBC while Sweeney was finishing *Live Bait* on campus. "Whenever I wasn't in class,

152

I would go over to Brock Hall and just sit in the editing room and I literally watched Ross [Weber] and Bruce edit almost that entire film. Whenever Bruce needed a break, we would go stroll around campus, then he'd go back to work and I'd go back to class."

Chula wasn't so close to the post-production process, and *Live Bait* slipped to the recesses of her mind after the shoot. "I went home and I didn't hear anything again about it. I didn't run into anybody who said to me, 'Oh, my god, I saw *Live Bait*, it was so great.' Nothing."

She still wasn't giving the movie much thought when it premiered at the 1995 Toronto International Film Festival. "I didn't even go to Toronto to be a part of the *Live Bait* scene. I ended up going to Toronto because Michael Holboom's film was in the festival. I went to stay with Mike and I kind of forgot about *Live Bait*. 'Oh yeah, I'm in that movie,' I thought, you know. And I ran into Bruce somewhere. He said, 'You're coming tonight?' And I went, 'Oh, yeah, I should come and see the movie.' Then I saw it. And people rose to their feet.

"It was the best first movie I had ever seen. There wasn't a sound in the audience. People got it. I was stunned at Bruce's skill because in the working with Bruce it was just another little student film that I was doing, really."

Scholte wasn't nearly so surprised. "I told myself that I was surprised but, in fact, I wasn't. I believed we were doing something that was going to be significant. I never said it out loud. Bruce loves to be cynical and pessimistic. The night they showed *Live Bait*, of course, they played the trailer in front of it that says: 'This film is eligible for the Citytv Award.' And Bruce went 'Yeah, like that's gonna happen.' And I sort of snickered along with him. I used to take on his cynicism because I didn't want him to think that I was naïve, but I actually believed we could win that prize. In my heart of hearts from the beginning of making the film I believed that we were doing something special that was going to break something open. I can say that now but I haven't been able to even admit that for years."

Live Bait would win the Citytv Award for best Canadian film at the festival.

"And then," says Chula, "we were on the map, the front page, you know."

§

As Sweeney's acting ensemble came together, a like-minded crew assembled too, including cinematographer Dave Pelletier, production designer Tony Devenyi, and editor Ross Weber.

"They're perfect for low-budget filmmaking," says Scholte. "Dave will hang out of a window with a camera. He'll do whatever it takes. Bruce ended up choosing him as much for his personality as for who he was as a shooter. Dave is a true maverick. John Pozer was sort of the spiritual leader in the sense that he showed us that anything was possible and really showed Bruce that you can do this: 'Get the fucking equipment and start shooting. Make a fucking movie. Why not? They can't stop me.' Pelletier's been a huge factor that way too. Whenever there's any kind of setback, it's just Pelletier saying, 'They told you you couldn't do it. Fuck that.'

"Ross is really the unsung mentor of Bruce in a way. Esthetically, Ross was a big influence on Bruce. When we shot *Live Bait*, Ross had no official title on the film. He was there every day, though. Ross was there just to talk in Bruce's ear."

Weber had never edited before, but Sweeney knew he would be right for *Live Bait* because, like Scholte, he was kind of like Sweeney. Sweeney figures that if he has a crew and actors who like what he likes, he'll wind up with a movie that he likes. "I don't think we've ever argued about anything," says Weber. "We have the same esthetic taste right down the line. That's why it works. I mean, it's like we're totally in tune when it comes to cinema.

"I like cutting Bruce's movies. Well, they're good, for one thing. The other thing is he leaves me alone. He goes, 'Go cut the movie. See you in a month.' He's not precious about anything, not precious about his words, not precious about scenes – very unusual as an editor to work with somebody like that. He wants to make the best movie possible and he's not attached to anything. He sees the thing as a whole. This is why he's so great to work for. So I'll show him kind of a rough fine cut and then he'll come in and go, 'I think we should cut that down. Why don't we cut ten seconds out of here.' And then he'll get more specific, sort of like ten or fifteen things to say. He'll go, 'Is that the best that can happen here? Don't we have something else?' And I'll go, 'No, that's as good as that's going to get.' And he'll go, 'Okay.' We won't have to spend a day pulling film out and looking at it.

"He picks people who have same esthetic. It's more important than their skill, as long as they're bright enough to develop it. He's uncanny at picking people to work with him. Sometimes, you know, he would pick an actor I wasn't sure about, and they turn out great."

Chula was surprised that Sweeney saw her as the middle-class housewife and mother of Sweeney's alter ego (Scholte) in *Live Bait*. "I loved the character and I loved that Bruce had offered me a character no one would have offered me. No one would have offered me a repressed, perverted housewife. And I kept saying to Bruce, 'Why me? I play bikers, I play junkies, I don't get it.' He said, 'I want that in there. I want to know there's something in there that she knows, that she's pretending she doesn't know about.' And I loved that he said that to me because right there, I thought, 'Okay, this guy knows what he wants.' That's all you have to do: know what you want. The guy who's trying to please an audience doesn't even fucking know what he wants.

"Bruce makes the movie he wants to make. If there's anything, it's that that makes him so good. I don't think that it's always going to mean that he doesn't make mistakes or he doesn't have weaker moments and stronger moments within the same film, or that he doesn't fail at some point. But he knows what he wants. That's his gift. So, I'd drop everything to work with Bruce. I respect him because he's asking himself questions and he never puts himself above anybody. I always find it interesting that people will sometimes say – because Bruce is not a comfortably verbal person, although he's getting way better – that 'I find Bruce a little odd' or 'He's rude.'"

Sweeney is affable with those he respects, but he won't pretend. He does have an impatience with the nonsense of everyday life, an attitude augmented by a sudden illness shortly after the release of *Live Bait*. Things were going well, he thought, following the film's debut in September 1995, but eight months later, in April 1996, he was on an operating table to remove a blood clot.

"If you're going to die, it just doesn't look good, particularly when things are just starting to go well," he says. "Basically, I was completely losing it and having massive headaches and it got to the point where I was losing feeling in my left side. I was misdiagnosed with migraines. I'd go to the hospital and they would send me home and I would go to the hospital and they would send me home. That went on for a couple weeks.

"Another thing that didn't help was the fact that I don't like hospitals. I've always prided myself, incorrectly, as being that guy who's just tough and doesn't need to go to the hospital. So I was abusive, just wanting to go home. I was out of my mind. I can't remember what I said but apparently I was just a big idiot. If I was diagnosed correctly, then I would have had surgery. In the end, everything was fine but we cut it close to the wire, I think, because I was losing it completely, you know, slurring my speech. As soon as they did the CAT scan I was on the operating table in an hour, this big golfball-sized thing in my head."

"That was certainly a life-changing occurrence. I was always quite uncompromising in terms of what I was doing with my life, but certainly that entrenched my feelings of being an uncompromising filmmaker. I think it really solidified my view of the necessity of making strong work here in Canada and holding on to what you want to do. I think your patience with idiots evaporates."

Sweeney lives with his wife, writer Caroline Adderson, and their son Patrick, in the west side's Mackenzie Heights. ("I found the perfect mix. She reads books and talks about books and I watch films and talk about films.")

∫

Shooting *Live Bait*. courtesy Bruce Sweeney

As *Live Bait* made its way through the 1995–96 festival circuit, Sweeney was thinking about his next project, *Dirty*, which started with a play, *The Bingo Sweethearts*, written by Scholte. "Around the same time I gave Bruce a copy of it to read, I asked Babz if she would read it. And they both read it and both really liked it and then I did this rehearsed reading with Babz and Callum Keith Rennie, because Babz was actually involved with Callum at that time. So we did a reading of it at Secret Space Theatre at Main and 30th."

Ultimately, the script would be revamped with Scholte receiving a "story by" credit. Character development was a drawn-out process between Sweeney and the actors. "We went to Rotterdam with *Live Bait* – Tom, Bruce, and I," Chula recalls. "We got very, very close. Tommy went back and Bruce and I just stayed in Amsterdam and worked on [her *Dirty* character] Angie D'Pasquali. It took a lot of talking about things, sharing things about oneself. We would spend a day together and an evening together and then we would not spend a day together so we could both think about it. Then we would come back with new ideas. We started to build her because she was the centrepiece of the film. And we did that for three years.

"Once we knew who Angie was, we started improving scenes with other people: Tom and I, Nancy and I, Benny and I, Benny and Tom. Bruce kind of orchestrated the development of the script that way. He orchestrated these sessions with us, then he would go away and write."

Inspired by improv techniques he'd picked up during the Vancouver filmfest forum with British director Mike Leigh, Sweeney developed a video-workshopping procedure which involved the actors working through scenes and constructing back-stories. Through this process, Sweeney wrote the script.

"In the midst of all this, my mother came to visit me," says Chula. "I remember the moment, being in the kitchen with my mother, and Bruce is over. 'Mom, this is Bruce. Bruce, this is my mother.' I remember him sitting there and there was a look on his face and I thought, 'No, wait a second.' He wanted my mother in the movie. And I remember him asking me if it would be difficult, and me knowing what I was going to basically do here was agree to let Bruce exploit my relationship with my mother in the name of art. And I did. For the rest of my life I will be indebted. He gave my mother something she wanted her whole life. And I know that when the producers had difficulty with the budget and it was going to end up costing an extra $18,000 to get a work visa for the American actor, the producers came to Bruce and said, we have to lose this actor. And he said, 'No, I'd rather not have craft services than lose this actor. This actor has to be.'"

Dirty was an underground success story after premiering at the Sundance Film Festival in 1998. The story of desperate interlocking lives in Vancouver's east side resonated with audiences at major festivals and opened in theatres across Canada.

For Sweeney's next movie, *Last Wedding*, he wrote a script, then applied his video-workshopping process to shape the final screenplay. "I shoot it on digital and then go back and then tweak it and rewrite it and then give it to them [the actors] again," he explained. "And then we do the same thing. It's just a process of do it and then write and then do it and then write until you get to the point where it starts to sing."

There were starts and stops with film-funding agencies, but actors such as Scholte and Sivak said they'd work for nothing to get *Last Wedding* made. Sweeney's father kicked in $100,000, and ultimately enough money materialized. "I really admire Bruce, who just doesn't give a shit," says Weber. "He's an admirable guy because he really is a doer. And if some huge obstacle gets in the way he puts his fist through the wall and continues on."

The determination paid off. *Last Wedding* was the fruition of the filmmaking talents that had emerged in Vancouver and it became the first Western Canadian movie to open the Toronto International Film Festival. Festival director Piers Handling said: "We think this is an important work of international stature. He is beginning to arrive as a greatly skilled filmmaker at that level." *Last Wedding* is a masterful mixture of comedy and drama, cutting between three combustible relationships, each suffering a universal malady – different world views, spiralling abasement, indifferent passions – expressed through everyday behaviour. "You want to show that Nancy and I have settled into a kind of domestic thing, it's her making pickles," says Scholte. "There's no scene where anyone's complaining, 'Oh, the fire's gone out.' We see her making pickles and I'm on my way out the door."

Last Wedding was selected as best Canadian film by Vancouver and Toronto film critics' groups, and it had long runs in the two cities. Sweeney has received offers from U.S. producers ("They're just so bad it's frightening.") but he doesn't want to shoot anyone else's script. "It would screw up my equilibrium. I can't see it going well, first of all. I just feel very motivated to work on my projects and to live here. I don't want to start frittering away my time on projects that are useless, just to make money."

No matter how international its stature, Sweeney's sushi-eating, movie-making troupe will continue to make its stand in Vancouver. "For me, a film has a lot more truthfulness and validity if it's actually set somewhere," Sweeney says. "I'm interested in stories that come from people who live in Vancouver. I mean, there are scenes at sushi restaurants, there's leaky condos. If you're from here and you're setting your film in Seattle but shooting it here, then I just think that is reprehensible behaviour. I can't get around that – that's just complete, untruthful sellout." Sweeney understands that people from a particular time and place are unique and to set something in a place that the writer, the director, and the actors don't know results in senseless characters. "It's easy for me. I don't even have a debate in my head about that. I just think, 'Well, I'll just set it in Vancouver.' And that comes into the text of it and that comes into the visual sensibility of it, too. And that will make it stronger. I don't think you can make it somewhere else.

"I just think your sense of place is so intricate to your sense of story. The two in many ways are inseparable, even if one is sublimated throughout the film. It still has to be there."

Scholte says he could feel the interest in Canadian film as the Sweeney group squired *Last Wedding* around the country. "People in the audiences that stick around for the Q&As are as fired up about the importance of Canadian cinema as we are. Someone at the Calgary film festival asked Bruce, 'Are you worried this film won't sell in the U.S. because all the references are local?' Are you worried, this, that and the other? And Bruce said – he wasn't grandstanding or trying to get some big response – he said, 'I honestly didn't think about it when I was making this film.'

"And there was this burst of spontaneous applause, just for saying, I actually wasn't thinking about selling this in the States when I made it. There is a grassroots, ferocious Canadian interest in our cultural sovereignty, for lack of a better term. People are looking for spokespeople in the face of all this globalization. We think of Canadians as having to be dragged to Canadian cinema or convinced that it's worth watching but there are people out there, and not just young people – I see a lot of women in their fifties and sixties who love Canadian cinema. They've just gotten to that point in their lives where they're really tired of what's out there and they're hungry. And to see them react like that and to see the real, genuine passion in the room. They're having the same conversations that we're having, you know, and they're our audience members.

"I love the fact that we've done something and that Bruce has done something that's true to his vision and that is penetrating the mainstream at the same time. To find out that they're adding screenings in [Vancouver suburbs] Coquitlam and Abbotsford – that to me is thrilling. That to me is more thrilling in some ways than playing in New York, as thrilling as that would be. If the film makes it to a screen in Scarborough, then I'm really going to feel like it's a triumph."

Sweeney lives on the west side of Vancouver – attending galleries, the theatre, and especially movies – and is determined to reflect that urbane side of Canada in his movies. "It makes it easier for me to write dialogue. You know I can't write dialogue if I'm supposed to sort of inhabit the mind of a fisherman. I don't know what they say. I mean, I'm not the person to write that dialogue."

His city movies break with the Canadian tradition of beachcombers and wheat fields. Before his first shoot, Sweeney made a list of items to avoid. "I can't remember all the things on it but I had a top ten things I would refuse to do in cinema. The top one was, 'No fields of blowing wheat.' The fourth one was, 'Nothing else can blow in the wind either.' I also had, 'No candles around the bathtub.' And this just went on and on. You know, you strive for a certain kind of purity."

§

"At the heart of it – as misanthropic as Bruce's work might seem to some people – is a tremendous compassion, because he sees everyone as basically a fool, and everyone is floundering in a way, and if they don't look like they're floundering, it's usually because they're putting up a good front," says Scholte. "It was obvious that he knew what makes people tick. And about the way his actors tick. He knows what to feed you to get you going, starting with casting. His intrigue in

160

having a scenario in which I have an affair with Marya Delver [in *Last Wedding*] comes out of having known us both when we had a relationship. He met her because I had a relationship with her."

More than any other actor in the Sweeney group, Delver combines a Canadian indie sensibility with a hankering for Hollywood mainstream glitz. Having moved with her mother from the Prairies to Vancouver at sixteen, she met Scholte while studying theatre at UBC. "He was passionate, he knew everything about everything, and he was a great storyteller. We fell in love and then we went out together and it was great. And then it was over. You know how things like that happen."

Shortly after the breakup, Sweeney called to offer a role in *Dirty*. "He saw everything that I did at UBC. Bruce was up on things, he was always checking things out, he was interested in what's new that's happening. And he liked using people from UBC." Although Delver's a fine actor, who followed *Dirty* with *waydowntown* and a Genie-nominated performance in *Last Wedding*, her self-confidence wasn't cresting when Sweeney called.

"I didn't know that I could act anymore after leaving UBC and I knew that Bruce only picked people who could really act. So, when he called me I was like, 'I don't think I fit in there.' When he's interested in people, it's because of their essence or their quality, not necessarily their performance. So, I go over there and I get the scenes. I looked at it and I was like, 'Okay, I'll call you tomorrow and let you know.' I wanted to play it cool, you know. I just thought I'm not going to be a geek about it. I was too proud. I got on the bus and went back home and then I called Bruce the next day and said, 'Yeah, let's do it.' I loved it. I read it and it was amazing.

"When you're working with Bruce, when you're on set, it's 'cause he believes in you and what you're doing. That's true in any capacity. Like Tony Devenyi, the set designer, he believes in Tony. Diamond Dave – he believes in Diamond Dave as a cinematographer. He completely trusts you, so you become much more liberated in doing what you want to do. He wants you to do your job the way you want to do it, under his vision. He has a very clear vision of what he wants."

Delver has a lead role in Sweeney's next movie, *American Venus*. "We were having sushi and he said, 'This is the next movie.'" *American Venus* follows the tribulations of young actors in Vancouver. Although

Sweeney has involved actors in workshopping *American Venus*, like *Last Wedding* it's not as improvisational as his first films. "It's got gigantic holes and problems and everything but still it starts as a written piece," he explains. "It doesn't have what I consider to be some problems of improv-genesis films in that they don't have the strong trueline in terms of plot. *Dirty*, for example, became very much about elemental, human, obsessive tendencies. The question of the plot is in many ways irrelevant, whereas I think it's somewhat more important in *Last Wedding* and certainly more important in *American Venus*."

§

"You heard about the boat sinking?" says Scholte, leaning forward to tell a remarkable story about filmmaking tenacity. It starts when a paperwork glitch left *Last Wedding* without anticipated government funding, but Sweeney decided to proceed anyway.

"Bruce said, 'We've just got to shoot or I'm going to lose my mind.' The other quality Bruce has is he gets people to do shit that they wouldn't do for anybody else. Vince Gale and Ben Ratner are both very fussy men. These are not guys who want to go up to a cabin and sleep five guys in a room in sleeping bags to shoot a film. And that's what we did.

"So, we're shooting nighttime hot-tub scenes. It was a skeleton crew, it's pitch black, we're going all night, and we're on the deck where the hot tub is. It's a twelve-foot drop off the edge. [Director of photography] Dave Pelletier says, 'Trevor, bring me that lens.' Trevor Flory falls into the blackness, twelve feet or more on to the rocks. He could have easily died. It was sickening. We all just froze. All we hear is this moaning, like he could be paralyzed. It was awful. And there's Bruce just kind of looking around.

"Trevor's down there and you hear, 'Keep shooting, go ahead, I'm all right. Keep shooting, I'm okay.' So, with him still lying down there, we kept going. And in between takes they helped Trevor hobble up. He's all bruised, he hurt himself badly because as he was falling the main thing he tried to do was save the lens. We were mortified. I thought I was going to throw up. Anyway, we got through that day and Trevor was fine. And we were all going 'never again . . . he could have died up there. My god.' Anyway, Trevor's alive, we go to sleep that night

– jubilation. The next day we were going to go out on the water and shoot the boat scenes.

"We got up, and just when we think we've dealt with the worst thing we could have on this no-budget shoot, we discover the little tug boat has sunk, was swamped over night. The dock was just too low. We had to shoot that day. Pelletier led the charge, he stripped all his clothes off and jumped in the water. Someone had to go under the thing and try to hoist the boat. All of the actors and whatever crew there was had buckets and a pump – the entire cast and crew, led by a naked Dave Pelletier.

"So, you've got a stark-naked director of photography. And there's Bruce sort of standing in the background with this old Montreal Expos hat on. And his dad was there because he paid for that part of the shoot. It was surreal. We bailed the boat out, cleaned all the salt water out of the engine, got the thing going, and went out on the water and made our day that day. The image we all remember most is Pelletier, stark-naked, furiously bailing in this boat. It's what galvanized us. I loved it."

The Sweeney Group

THE OTHER HOLLYWOOD NORTH

11

There was an instant when West met East on a Toronto red carpet. The night Bruce Sweeney's *Last Wedding* opened the 2001 Toronto International Film Festival, he stood at one end of the opening-night carpet, about to enter the theatre, when he glanced up and saw another filmmaker standing at the other end of the carpet. Instead of welcoming the Vancouver director to his city, Atom Egoyan walked past Sweeney and didn't acknowledge him the entire evening.

It may be that Egoyan didn't want to draw attention from another filmmaker, or was shy. Or, as happens at social gatherings, planned to approach Sweeney later but never got around to it. Or maybe he did snub Sweeney.

As accounts of the incident circulated on the west coast, however, the nature of the Vancouver-Toronto relationship prompted much of the film scene to conclude that some ego/jealousy/challenge-to-his-status-on-his-turf could explain Egoyan's behaviour.

The "Did-you-hear-Egoyan-snubbed-Sweeney?" incident would say as much about Vancouver as it did about Toronto and, fittingly for this somewhat dysfunctional relationship between English Canada's largest cities, the filmmaker who is the heart and soul of the Vancouver scene grew up in Ontario (Sweeney is from Sarnia) and the filmmaker who is the heart and soul of the Toronto scene grew up in B.C. (Egoyan is from Victoria).

Some of the Vancouver-Toronto hostility is misplaced regional prejudice, largely from people ignorant of the other city. But within the west coast's film community there is also a real concern, even among those who love Toronto, that the funding apparatus has traditionally favoured eastern filmmakers. And there are those who feel Vancouver is ignored by Toronto, and not just at film festivals.

West coast filmmaker Scott Smith, who made *rollercoaster*, says Vancouver's role in increasing Canada's movie profile internationally hasn't been acknowledged in Toronto.

"If you look at the Toronto International Film Festival as a festival, *Last Wedding* opening was a huge thing. But in the last five years, a lot of the really strong films came from Vancouver and, in fact, if you talk about the Canadian film industry in the last ten years and its growth outside of its own borders, you have to give credit to films like *Kissed* and *Double Happiness* as much as [Atom Egoyan's] *The Sweet Hereafter* for helping do that, I think. And yet if you go to Toronto, it's not mentioned at all. So, it's just like being an ignored kid and it's as much about Vancouver's insecurity as it is about Toronto. We'd be much better off if we actually joined forces."

Dreaming in the Rain

Toronto actor Nicholas Campbell, who divides his time between the two cities since landing the title role in *Da Vinci's Inquest*, says the animosity is almost entirely one way. "When you're in Toronto and someone says, 'Where are you from?' and you say Vancouver, they go, 'Great, that's cool, mountains, beautiful city.' But if you're in Vancouver and someone says, 'Where are you from?' and you say Toronto, they go, 'Fuck you.'"

(l–r) Actors Vincent Gale, Tom Scholte, and Ben Ratner stroll down the red carpet on the opening night of the 2001 Toronto International Film Festival, for the premiere of *Last Wedding*. *courtesy Bruce Sweeney*

166

Molly Parker agrees. "It's true and it's ridiculous and I have to tell you that it's ingrained. And it's the same kind of thinking that goes into electing the Reform Party. I think it's regional crazy thinking. And I think it's limiting. But what I do know is also, because I've worked all over the country – Newfoundland, Montreal, Winnipeg – there is no question that the west coast got ignored.

"You know, it's funny because I did spend time living in Toronto and I have to tell you that what's odd to me is that my experience with Toronto was not ever that people were anti-Vancouver. They just didn't know what was going on there. That's all. Whereas people in Vancouver hate Toronto. It is stupid. Work together."

Others suggest that while Toronto may not share the hostility, it has a condescending attitude that inspires the hostility. Leonard Schein, the founder of the Vancouver International Film Festival, recalls an interview with an eastern reporter the year he was director of Toronto's film festival. "He said, 'How does it feel to finally live in a place like Toronto? I mean, isn't it great to be out of Vancouver?' And I said, 'Well, actually, you know, I enjoyed Vancouver.' He just was so condescending, as though Vancouver was a wilderness. He thought anything north of Eglinton was living in the bush.

"In Toronto, they honestly think that there's two major cultural cities in North America – New York and Toronto. They even leave Los Angeles out. Toronto's next to New York, that's how they view the world. They agree New York is bigger and better than Toronto but only New York. And they consider Montreal to be beneath them as well. They don't even consider Vancouver. They just say, 'Oh Vancouver, that's where everybody goes rollerblading and it rains all the time and they're all granola freaks.' They don't take it as serious competition.

"I grew up in Los Angeles and there was a sort of thing between Los Angeles and New York. I mean, it wasn't Los Angeles versus San Francisco. Woody Allen expresses that quite well, the L.A. mentality versus the New York mentality."

As for the Toronto mentality versus the Vancouver mentality, Sweeney, having spent considerable time in both cities, notes: "I like the fact that in this town people celebrate the idea that you can get away. They don't really celebrate the city. You don't come here and think, 'Oh, great, I can experience the night life of Vancouver.' You'd be disappointed, right? It doesn't exist in a big way. Toronto celebrates the idea that 'we're a big city.'

"I like the idea that there's this something that just hangs in the air which makes Vancouver kind of easy-going and not stuffy. It's sort of a rootsy sophistication. There is sophistication but there's also a strong sense of casualness. I mean, you don't have the same dress codes as they do in Toronto. We've got a place – actually you can see it in *Last Wedding* – out at Pender Harbour. It's a little cabin on an island. Growing up in Ontario, when you drive north to your parents' cottage, if you have one, it's very crowded. People are clamouring and competing to get their little piece of recreation, whereas out here you take one or two ferries and you have a sense of openness that you do not have in Toronto at all. And with the ocean tides going up and down fifteen feet, it seems volatile and moving. There's a kind of an old, established quality back east that you just don't find here. You have new cities, kind of like Prince George or something, that are quite hellish, or Powell River, little pulp towns, but you don't have old stone buildings. You don't have a sense of the old here."

Toronto, too, has distinctive advantages, from vibrant neighbourhood street life to beautiful brick Victorian houses. And from a film vantage, it has Canadian distributors.

By the 1990s, Vancouver and Toronto each had a base of talented actors, directors, and crews. Unlike its eastern counterpart, though, Vancouver didn't have film distributors. To access federal funding, Canadian filmmakers have been required to have a distributor, but attempts to form a Vancouver-based company failed. Schein formed the distribution company, Festival Films, in the late 1980s. "The way the system worked at that time, unless you had a distributor you couldn't access your funding from Telefilm, and the Toronto distributors gave, of course, preference to the Toronto filmmakers. By us being here and being able to green light a number of Vancouver productions, they were able to be made."

Festival Films' Vancouver movies included *Angel Square*, *The Legend of Kootenai Brown*, and *Terminal City Ricochet*, but the city's film scene was slight and the company's pockets weren't deep enough to continue competing for films with U.S. and Toronto distributors. "At that time, Vancouver-made films weren't as good as the Vancouver-made films are today," says Schein. "We were distributing films of much less quality, which meant less money theatrically, less money from television, less money from video. So it was harder to survive. In one sense it would be easier today with the Vancouver-based films because they are better."

There is talk of Vancouver filmmakers forming a western distribution company but, for now, they have to fly to Toronto to secure a distributor. An eastern company will back established directors such as Lynne Stopkewich or Anne Wheeler, but is more likely to support first-time Toronto filmmakers than first-time Vancouver filmmakers. "They're not there for social contact. It just will be harder for them," says Schein. "It would be a lot easier if they had a Vancouver film-distribution company."

While a local distributor might make filmmakers' lives easier in some ways, it's no guarantee that a good film would receive a wide release. Although Toronto's film scene includes several distributors, it's still fumbling around in search of the route to the large Canadian audience that lines up to watch the studio-dominated screens of the Famous Players and Odeon theatre chains.

These days, Telefilm's priority is to increase the domestic share of the Canadian box office to five percent. Rather than reimburse distributors who acquire Canadian producers' films as it did when Festival Films was operating, Telefilm is now funding producers directly and providing distributors with marketing monies contingent on their promotional efforts.

About ten percent of the North American box-office take announced every weekend is Canadian. Thus, Canada's moviegoers regularly contribute upwards of US$10 million to studio blockbusters (Canadians doled out $53.3 million to see the first installment of *Lord of the Rings*), while spending a small fraction of that on the most popular English-Canadian films (2002's *Men With Brooms* drew a record $4 million). French-Canadian films fare better, with about nine percent of the Quebec box office going to domestic films (it's only one percent in English Canada). Still, many of the most accomplished Montreal filmmakers have recently directed English-language films in an attempt to break beyond their limited audience, including Denys Arcand (*Stardom*), Robert Lepage (*Possible Worlds*), and Leah Pool (*Lost and Delirious*).

Federal funding for features has been relatively equitable across the country the past few years. For instance, of fifty-one films Telefilm funded in 2001, ten were made in B.C. (*Last Wedding, Lola, Low Self Esteem Girl, Lunch With Charles, Mile Zero, On the Nose, Protection, The Rhino Brothers, Sister Blue,* and *Suddenly Naked*): almost twenty percent in a province with thirteen percent of the country's population.

Television production, though, is more eastern-based. "I think Toronto gets the bulk of the money and the press," says *Da Vinci's Inquest's* producer Chris Haddock. When Haddock was in Toronto for the 2001 Gemini Awards, he experienced his own odd East-West incident, starting with an interview with a *Toronto Sun* reporter.

"He says, 'What about the competition between you and [Toronto series] *Blue Murder* and [Vancouver series] *Cold Squad*? And I said, 'Oh, there's no competition there, I'll wipe them out in the first round.' And I'm just sort of laughing.

"Sunday night's the big night for the first writing and directing awards and stuff. I'm up for both of those. Well, that Sunday morning it [*The Sun*] has published a headline that we're going to kick the shit out of *Blue Murder*. I did not see it, but I walk into this thing in the evening and there's a couple of actors from *Blue Murder* who are giving me the nasty stink-eye. I'm going, 'What the fuck is the matter with these guys?' I walk right up to them and say, 'Hey guys, I'm Chris Haddock.' 'Yeah, we know.' And they're like really fucking glum. I'm going, 'Man, these guys are glum, what's their fuckin' problem?' They've bought out the front row seats so at the front of the auditorium – the entire front, middle thing – it's all *Blue Murder* people. Well, we win the writing award and I go up and I see them sitting there in the front, all glum and snarly, and I'm going, 'They still got a problem. What's the matter with these guys?' Then I win the directing award, and it's like they're just squirming now. No happiness. The next day I said, 'Those guys had some bad attitude.' And someone said, 'Well, did you read the fucking press here?' That's how I found out."

Acrimonious anecdotes aside, there is also an increasingly productive connection between the two cities, with a parade of Vancouver filmmakers attending Toronto's Canadian Film Centre and the Toronto International Film Festival playing a major role in introducing West Coast Wave directors to the larger film world. "I just think the programmers at the Toronto festival have been extremely good," says Sweeney.

Scratch Haddock, even, and you'll find someone who's spent long, and not entirely unenjoyable, stretches of his life in Toronto. "I came to kind of dig Toronto, actually. I love the joint, I just can't handle the weather," he says.

Vancouver and Toronto have more in common than some might want to admit, and it's not just their trendy restaurants, obsession with hockey, large alternative communities, and relatively clean streets. Just contrast any L.A. award show with Toronto's Genies, where Canadian "stars" park their cars in the concrete bowels of a hotel convention centre, then climb dank stairwells in search of the auditorium, without an autograph hound in sight. Both cities have film scenes resolutely independent and Canadian, operating outside the studio system in a constant state of cobbling together their movies.

"I love Toronto even more after this Genie trip," said lapsed Torontonian Tom Scholte, after attending the Genies as a nominee for *Last Wedding*. "It was so thriving and I had a great time. I'm going to make a film back there. I'm going to make a Scarborough homecoming film."

As for the Toronto-Vancouver hostility, Scholte says: "I'm allowed to make those jokes because I'm from there. I feel like I can slag Toronto like you can slag your own mother but other people aren't allowed to."

As for Toronto feeling it's more of a cultural hub than L.A., ask another Genie nominee, Marya Delver, who moved between the two cities in 2001: "It's funny, once you're in America, Toronto doesn't even exist."

§

Why does every Toronto indie film look like *Eyes Wide Shut*?

The cold stylings of Stanley Kubrick (it was no coincidence that his most famous character was a computer) have often found their way into the Toronto films of David Cronenberg and Atom Egoyan and, more recently, younger filmmakers such as Jeremy Podeswa (*The Five Senses*) and Colleen Murphy (*Desire*).

If Toronto's mentor is Kubrick, Vancouver's is, oddly enough, Woody Allen. Vancouver films, from *Double Happiness* to *Live Bait* to *A Girl is a Girl* to *No More Monkeys Jumpin' on the Bed*, have an oddly Woody Allen-esque sensibility. These are anti-romantic comedies that chronicle the love lives of urbane, intellectual, neurotic characters. And the filmmakers often have a passion for the city of Vancouver that's as strong as Allen's love affair with New York. Even those who are already working directors when they move to Vancouver from other cities seem compelled to try their hand at anti-romantic comedies (see Anne Wheeler's Vancouver movies). West coast filmmakers, of course, point to many other influences, from John Cassavetes to Mike Leigh to David Lynch, but none seems to show up in Vancouver as often as Allen.

"I think that's very true. I think what's encouraging is that people aren't afraid to use humour," says Bruce Sweeney. "Somewhere at some point people don't want to take themselves oh so seriously, which is different from Toronto, where the seriousness level goes up a huge notch."

Allen has been as consistent as anyone during the past thirty-five years, making a movie a year, almost all of them entertaining, a few of them great. And Allen has had a huge influence on film, giving a new kind of cool to New York, intellectual conversations, Gershwin music, Bergman movies, and, yes, even neurotic behaviour. Nowhere has Allen's influence on the next generation of filmmakers been more evident than the west coast of Canada.

Vancouver director-editor Ross Weber recounts his days with Bruce, Woody, and a stopwatch. "I met Bruce and he wanted to make a movie. He wasn't just talking about it. He was studying how to do a cheap 16-mill movie and so we were watching a lot of Woody Allen. And Bruce would be sitting there with a stopwatch, going, 'You see, no scene's over a minute long, right.' That was his big thing. And he was right. I mean, you watch Woody Allen movies, he's in and out, tells a couple of jokes, moves the narrative. And it just moves those films. It just moves them along. And we got into Bergman and I'm a huge Bergman fan."

Scott Smith is drawn to the technical side of Woody. "Woody Allen's rhythms are similar to mine," he says. "I associate a lot to music and I think when you find filmmakers that have a similar rhythm you connect to them and you start watching them.

"I like the psychology of Woody Allen's blocking, I like when he moves actors, why he moves actors. I like the nature of the movement in his scenes, the movement of the camera grows organically from the nature of the content in that scene. And it's all rooted in the sort of semi-neurotic kind of, you know, if you step closer to me I'm going to step farther away from you. I think of all the filmmakers and the way they block, his really points to subtext in the scene. *Crimes and Misdemeanors* coincided with my interest in film and it was the first time I saw something outside what I was used to seeing and yet something I connected to and ever since, he's the guy I sort of go back to once in a while and study."

Like Allen and other New York directors such as Martin Scorsese and Spike Lee, Vancouver's Mina Shum tells her own stories and sets them in her ethnic milieu.

"One of the biggest compliments I've ever gotten was on the video box for *Double Happiness*. It says, '*Joy Luck Club* meets Woody Allen.' And I was like, 'Awesome. Great.'

"The only box set of DVDs I own is Woody Allen's work," she says. "I just watched *Crimes and Misdemeanors* again. To me, it's brilliant. It's funny and it's deep. Two days later I was talking about the movie, having seen it for the nineteenth time.

"I think in terms of subject matter where he and I have an affinity is we laugh at the pain. It's really strange when I think about my existence, which will be far too short, as Woody Allen always says. 'The food is horrible and there's not enough of it.' *Annie Hall* starts that way. It gives me great comfort just to hear him say it's far too short and there's not enough of it. It's true."

Sweeney says Allen had a "huge" influence on his filmmaking. "Stylistically. I mean, I could see in his work a synthesis of the past masters and then what he would do with it would be a lot funnier.

"I love Woody Allen. Watched *Manhattan* a million times. I loved all his films, but I like *Manhattan* in the sense that you could see in that film that he was drawing upon influences that he loved. The longer takes, I mean, all the shots in *Manhattan* are beautifully composed, and it's Bergman and it's funny. I wanted to take some of that kind of sensibility and apply it to west coast living out here and what's it's like, just be specific about it."

Why does Vancouver, of all places, have this connection with Allen? It's not as urban as Montreal, doesn't have the diversity of Toronto. I mean, who among us hasn't watched a Woody Allen movie in Vancouver and been the only one laughing in the theatre?

But there is a line that runs through Bergman, Allen, and Vancouver: the city is the perfect grey, rainy setting for a Bergman film, but it also evokes a unique comic sense brought on from having witnessed one too many rock climbers in Spandex shorts rollerblading alongside the sea in a cold February drizzle.

Even the earliest Vancouver directors, 1960s indie filmmakers Larry Kent and Jack Darcus, became Woody fans ("*Manhattan* is the perfect movie," says Darcus), after being Bergman fans.

"We're already marginalized," says Shum. "We're Vancouver, not Toronto. If you think of Toronto, it's sort of set the mainstream in indie cinema for us. We're the marginalized so of course we're going to do something completely opposite. You either laugh or cry and I think we've chosen to laugh. We're not going to try to be cool.

"I guess a lot of people here on the west coast want to be like Bruce Sweeney and a lot of people there want to be like Atom Egoyan. How do you be like anyone, really? I don't think Bruce wanted to be like Woody Allen. I think he just saw that there were people making movies about their own experiences."

Tom Scholte, who has starred in Sweeney's and Weber's movies, is perfect to play the neurotic, urban Canadian everyman.

"What else do people do in this city but hang around and talk about their relationships, and have coffee and argue with each other?" says Scholte. "What else do they do here? I've watched *Manhattan* at least thirty-five times. *Manhattan* was a huge influence on *Live Bait*, for sure. It's like the twelfth monkey or something, it shows up everywhere. So many of us as kids in North America discovered European cinema through Woody Allen. We fell in love with Woody and he kept talking about these other guys and so we started watching them.

"I got into Woody Allen at a really young age. Like, I was watching *Annie Hall* when I was thirteen. I knew I wasn't Clint Eastwood, I knew I wasn't John Wayne, I knew I wasn't any of the big swaggering heroes. I loved them but because I knew that wasn't me or would never be me they faded from my mind very quickly. When I saw that you could make money being clumsy, anxious, and overwhelmed, I thought, well, this is definitely the right profession for me."

MOLLY AND LYNNE

12

Molly Parker is the first Vancouver movie star. There have been other movie stars *from* Vancouver. But Yvonne De Carlo, Michael J. Fox, and the rest rarely gave the city a backward glance after going Hollywood. Parker, though, continues to work in Canada, and some of her best work has been shot in Vancouver. "It's never been a difficult choice for me to continue to work in Canada or in Vancouver because there are people there that I really want to work with more than anywhere else," says Parker. "I am in a really fortunate position because a community is starting to exist where I am able to consistently do films in Canada.

"It's there. It exists. For a lot of actors who came before me, who are ten years older than me, there was no independent film, certainly in Vancouver or really even much of it in Toronto. And I would not have the career that I have internationally if I hadn't come out of Canadian cinema."

She has followed a route that's new for a Canadian actor but has long been tread by Europeans, from Greta Garbo to Penelope Cruz: establish themselves at home before trying Hollywood. Before the emergence of a Canadian film scene, actors had to look elsewhere for breakout roles, but Parker's was in the Vancouver-made *Kissed*, which resulted in a best-actress Genie Award and all sorts of Hollywood offers after it debuted at the 1996 Toronto International Film Festival.

§

Parker isn't the only Vancouver actor whose career outside Canada has been impacted by the rise of Canadian film. Bruce Greenwood credits his role in Atom Egoyan's shot-in-B.C. *The Sweet Hereafter* for changing the way he was perceived in Hollywood, ultimately leading to major roles in studio films such as *Thirteen Days*. "It [*The Sweet Hereafter*] was nominated for best screenplay [and director], a lot of people saw it. There were strong performances in it. People saw me in a way they had never seen me before – quite unrecognizable from the normal kind of fare I had been doing up till that time, mostly television." And Sonja Bennett, another Maple Ridge native ("Molly Parker and I had the same high school drama teacher," she notes), was signed to a contract with Fox television because of her performance as a relentlessly malevolent teenager in the Vancouver independent film *Punch*, directed by her father, Guy Bennett.

When Greenwood moved to L.A. in 1984 the TV roles came (including the series *Legmen*, *St Elsewhere*, and *Knots Landing*). While he continued working in L.A. television, something was stirring back in Vancouver. First, the development of the big American service industry that would call him back for the feature *Double Jeopardy*. "It was the first biggie I did back here. Great locations, over to Bowen Island all the time." Another thing that happened while Greenwood lived in L.A.: the growth of a Canadian independent scene. "You get down there and you get a bit of a profile, so Canadians are willing to hire you and you can help them market their movies to some degree, I guess," he says. "Once you get down there and you've done a bit of work it's easier to come back here."

(l–r) Bruce Greenwood, director Lynne Stopkewich, and Brian Markinson on the set of the tentatively titled film *The Life*. photo by Ric Ernst, courtesy The Province

Greenwood has developed an ongoing working relationship with Toronto's Egoyan (*The Sweet Hereafter*, *Exotica*, *Ararat*), appears in Deepa Mehta's forthcoming shot-in-Toronto adaptation of Carol Shields' novel *The Republic of Love*, and was happy to return to Vancouver for Lynne Stopkewich's CTV movie tentatively titled *The Life*. Now that a film scene exists in Vancouver, Greenwood has considered a full-time return to his home town. "I think about it all the time but I've still got to be down there for meetings. If I had a family I'd be more inclined to move back here but it's just my wife and I," he says. "When I have the time and something Canadian comes up and it's good, I'm there."

Bennett is excited about acting but refreshingly nonplussed by the film industry's procedures. After *Punch* premiered at the 2002 Toronto filmfest, she was approached by card-wielding agents and film reps but didn't take the attention seriously. "I thought it was like a joke," Bennett says. "I thought it was just shmoozie, like just handing cards around." So, the card handed Bennett by a Fox executive just sat in her wallet. "My agent phoned me a month later and said, 'This woman from Fox said she saw *Punch* at the Toronto filmfest and she hasn't been able to get you out of her head and she wants to meet you down in L.A. She said she gave you her card. Why didn't you tell me?'"

§

Parker's life in L.A. just wouldn't have been the same had she arrived unknown by bus the way the Canadian hopeful did in David Lynch's *Mulholland Drive*. "I arrived here in this really fortunate way, having a hit film that was in Cannes, that went all over the world, and being signed to these agencies. So my experience here has been completely different than all my friends who came down and struggled for years and years and years.

"I wouldn't have this career had I just gone down to L.A. and done pilot season every year and tried to break in – like every other girl from Iowa or Cleveland or wherever. To be able to stay and work in Canada was a way that I could be seen internationally and still is, you know. We make Canadian films that may not been seen in Canada but in Europe lots of people really care about Canadian film."

Parker's Canadian films since the late 1990s include *Marion*

Bridge, Rare Birds, Last Wedding, The Five Senses, Sunshine, The War Bride, Looking for Leonard, and *Men With Brooms.* Her strongest bond in the Canadian film scene is with her friend, Vancouver's Lynne Stopkewich, who directed her in *Kissed* and *Suspicious River.*

"My relationship with Lynne is the most important creative relationship that I've had in my life because there's a continuity to it and we grow together and learn together," Parker says.

"I have a kind of loyalty, certainly to Lynne and to Bruce [Sweeney], because I've known them for a long time and I really care about what they're doing. But also I feel so fortunate to be able to work on these films. The kind of work that I've been allowed to do because I continue to pursue work in Canada is infinitely more interesting to me than the kind of work I see most actors that I know living in L.A. pursuing. I have been afforded the opportunity to play leads in feature films, female-driven films often."

While Parker often works in Canada, she lives in L.A. and has appeared in strong British (*Wonderland*) and American (*Waking the Dead, The Centre of the World,* the HBO series *Deadwood*) productions, which have made the movie world increasingly aware of the unique intelligence and poise she brings to a role.

Parker has a singular dignity – whether entering a room at a party or portraying a prostitute on screen – that can't be taught at the Gastown Actors Studio or anywhere else. The Studio's founder Mel Tuck

Molly Parker as Sandra Larson in *Kissed*, 1995. *photo by Kharen Hill, courtesy Lynne Stopkewich*

178

remembers the moment in class when he recognized Parker's distinctive, luminescent quality. "She did a scene from *Burn This*. She was playing Anna and she was much too young for the part. He [the "Pale" character] says to her, we can go on a vacation, or something like that. And she had a line which was, 'Really, Pale, really.' And the way she said it at that moment embodied that kind of cool and poetic quality she has and that intelligence she brings to a role. It was a complete understanding of something that was out of her range of knowledge because she was so young. But she just nailed it. Nobody else could do that. It was uniquely her. It was just so clear."

She also has an assuredness that comes with having known what she's wanted to do since she was a novice actor in Gastown. "I studied with the intent of working in films. I have never done much theatre. When I started ten years ago, there was just starting to be all this work in film and TV and I really wanted to do film. That's really what was most interesting to me, always."

§

Molly Parker was born in New Westminster in 1972 and spent her earliest years living in Afghanistan and other far-flung spots along the counter-cultural trail her parents were travelling. Following the *Hideous Kinky* years, Parker's parents returned to B.C., operating a fish store in Maple Ridge, on the outskirts of Vancouver.

Parker started ballet at three and used her grandparents' bed in Quesnel Lake, B.C. as a stage to perform shows for her family. There is an acting pedigree in the family: her great-grandmother directed community theatre in New Westminster in the 1930s and her uncle, Mark Wilson, was a working actor.

"He had come to me and said, 'You're doing all this drama in high school, you're good, and you like it, do you want to come meet these agents?' And I knew nothing about anything. I was like, 'Sure, fine.' They ended up signing me six months later but I never worked. I would go to the odd audition. I didn't get a job, time went on, and when I graduated from high school I was going to go to SFU and study biology."

But acting burseries Parker had won in high school would instead lead her to the Gastown studio and work in television through the early 1990s. "I did a lot of TV in those years. There weren't a lot of films. And there were no Canadian films. The only Canadian stuff that I even auditioned for at that time was the odd CBC thing. I remember auditioning for *The Story of Evelyn Lau* that Sandy Oh did and not getting it. And the perception at that time as a Vancouver actor was that CBC was Toronto. You couldn't get a job doing it. At that time I didn't have any concept of what film was happening in Toronto. It was just so far away. They weren't coming out to Vancouver to audition, so it just didn't exist in our world. So the only work was doing shitty American television."

She did find enough work to make a living acting in Vancouver. "There wasn't that much competition because it was new that Vancouver was a service industry. Every year it was like, 'Oh, there's more work here than the year before.' And there was sort of this thing: 'It's starting to be like there's as much work here as there is in Toronto.' And that was a new thing."

There was the occasional Canadian-made project to audition for, including a TV-movie remake of *Playboy of the Western World* called *Paris in Summer*. "It was going to be shot in Regina and Callum Rennie and I got the leads in it. And Callum and I sort of went and fell in love and had this great time.

"I came back to Vancouver after being in Regina. It was really fun to do this show and again there was sort of like crappy work, you know. All this stuff that I just didn't care about."

If working in the service industry wasn't satisfying, joining friends in their annual migration to L.A. during pilot season had even less appeal. "It sounded totally scary to me and I didn't understand what's the point of going down and doing pilot season to do more crappy television. I remember at that time saying, 'If I have to keep doing this kind of work I'm just going to quit, I'm going to go do something else because it's not interesting to me any more.' And then [cinematographer] Greg Middleton called me up and said, 'Look, I'm doing a film with this woman, Lynne Stopkewich. It's totally weird, I'm not allowed to tell you anything about it because she's made me sign a confidentiality agreement, but I think you'd be great for it, so why don't you go down and check out the script and read it?'

"So, I go down to the production office, meet Lynne. Within a minute and a half we're swapping childhood masturbation fantasies, like some kind of weird craziness immediate connection. And she tells me a little bit about what the script is about and I take it home and I read it in half an hour."

The story of an all-Canadian "girl next door" who's having sex with corpses was, well, different than the TV-movie scripts Parker had grown accustomed to reading.

"And I am so excited. Here is the potential to be a lead in a film, to play a character who is not somebody's sister or daughter or girlfriend. It's like this really self-possessed character. I was so excited about Lynne, I really trusted Greg, and I really wanted to do this movie.

"I auditioned for Lynne twice and then I got the part. And then we shot it almost immediately. It was like a whole new world. I couldn't believe that I could work with somebody, this woman, who actually asked me what I thought about the character, what I thought about how the scenes should play, what I thought about the script and what worked and what didn't. It was mind-blowing to me. I remember the first time we sat down and she said to me, 'Well, what do you think about how this should go or who this person is?' And me feeling that I couldn't even speak because nobody had ever asked me what I thought. I just felt like I was a prop. I was like somebody you put clothes on and walked in the door.

"So that was really exciting. I moved into the production office because Callum and I had broken up and I didn't have a place to live. We were starting shooting in two days, so they built me a bedroom in the production office which was in a building at 11th and Boundary. And I lived there for the six weeks that we worked. And Bruce Sweeney was the boom operator and we'd talk and it was just this great thing.

"When the movie finished, all I wanted was to work in little independent films with people like this because it was so fun and so exciting. But there was nothing – no films being made. I couldn't get an audition for any films being made in Toronto, couldn't even get seen by Atom Egoyan or any of these people. They didn't know who I was, they didn't want to know, they weren't interested in Vancouver.

"It took Lynne a year and a half [to finish the film] in which time I just shrivel up and die. At this point, I hated working in this TV shit so much I couldn't believe it. I was also thinking at this point about moving to Toronto just because I'd heard that at least there are films. So at this point, Vancouver sucked. I hated it. All I wanted was to either quit and do something better with my life or move to another place because

I couldn't believe how fun it was to make *Kissed* and then nothing for two years except this crappy American TV.

"I had this vague hope that when *Kissed* was finished maybe it would be good enough to get into the Toronto Film Festival, and other Canadian filmmakers will see my work and think 'Oh, okay we'll hire her to do some of our movies.' That was my highest hope for *Kissed* at that point. But time went on and none of this happened. In the meantime I lived next door to Lynne and it was all I can do to not just bang on her door every day going, 'Isn't the movie finished?' And then months went by when she couldn't even look at me, she was so embarrassed that it wasn't done yet. But we became really good friends. I met all these other filmmaker friends of hers and Pozer's. By that time, I knew most of them; it was such a small scene, half of them worked on *Kissed*. But still, nobody was making any films. Maybe Bruce was at this time, but he wasn't hiring me.

"When the film finally got into the Toronto Film Festival it had been so long and so weird it was sort of shocking. I had a year where I didn't make any money doing the regular TV. I hadn't worked for eight months. I took a job, one line on this TV miniseries about the Titanic starring Catherine Zeta-Jones. It was one line but it was ten days work, which meant I would make $10,000 and afford to go to Toronto for the screening. And then everything changed."

Parker and Stopkewich flew into Toronto dreading the reception awaiting *Kissed*. "We were worried that the film was maybe no good, that people would hate it, that people would be offended by it, that it just wouldn't do anything. And some kind of miracle happened. Within days I had offers from everybody, from William Morris in L.A., from all the major agencies to sign with them. I had never even been to L.A. as an actor. I mean, I hadn't even considered it as an option, ever. Bruce McDonald wanted me to do this thing called *Twitch City*. That all happened that week. Yves Siminau cast me as the lead in this Fox miniseries. I met Matt [Bissonnette] when I was out in Toronto and we fell in love."

Parker, in the wake of *Kissed*, moved from Vancouver, following work to Toronto, then L.A., where she's in the novel situation of being in demand for starring roles in another country. Parker's career has become something of a role model for actors in Vancouver: taking on projects that don't exploit her or anyone else, mentioned often as an ideal synthesis of Canadian film and world cinema. "I have auditioned for big Hollywoody kind of things that I just don't get," she says. "I think I don't get them because I don't care about them, you know, in the way that I care to do the stuff that I end up doing."

Vancouver's Genie-nominated actor Marya Delver, while spending the 2002 TV pilot season in L.A., noted: "Back home, I'm like a real actor and people respect me, but here no one has any idea who I am. I would love to have the kind of career Molly has. She has a great career. I'm here for pilot season and I'm checking all that stuff out, but I don't really want to do a series. What I really want to do is feature films."

Parker is not the sort of star attraction who draws long lineups on opening weekends, but she is one of a handful of Canadian actors whose name will help a project land film-agency funding. "That's why I do press. If I can get a certain amount of recognition, then I can bring some money to projects I care about. That's so important to me. If there's anything I can do with whatever this is that's happening to me that helps people I think are talented get to make films, I'm right there.

"When I moved to Toronto, I quickly figured out what the deal was. And I go back. I fly myself back [to Canada] and I work for people for no money all the time. It doesn't make my agents here very happy, but it makes me happy. I make sure that I stay connected to the people in that scene and let them know that I'm willing to come and work because I like it, because it's fun for me, and because I want to see us make great films. And if I can get to a place where I can bring money to the table to help do that, all the better.

"Do you know what's weird is that people assume that I've been doing it because they're Canadian and friends of mine, but it's about the quality of the work.

"I worked with Lynne or I worked with Bruce because I think they're fantastic directors, because I really like the movies that they're making. Those scripts and those movies are totally as valid to me as anything that is happening anywhere. You know, it's like a pleasure, it's an honour to work on that stuff."

When *Rare Birds*, which was shot in Newfoundland, screened at the 2001 Toronto Film Festival, there was laughter when the audience learned Parker's character was trying to get into architecture school. Her character in *Last Wedding*, which opened that year's festival, is an architect, too. "It's so strange how things like that happen," Parker says. "Three years ago I did *Sunshine, Wonderland,* and *The Five Senses* all in a row. In all three of those films I played a mother and in two of them my character was a teacher. Then, the next year I did *Suspicious River* and *The Centre of the World,* both about prostitutes."

Along with her quality choices, Parker is savvy about the industry, having coproduced *Looking for Leonard,* cowritten and directed by her husband Matt Bissonnette. "Distribution is a problem. Basically, Canadian distributors buy Canadian films because they can make money from the television licensing. They know the Canadian TV networks have to show a certain number of Canadian films, therefore if a film is halfway good they're going to buy it because they have to for their

Molly Parker. *photo by David Clark, courtesy* The Province

Canadian content. That, combined with money they get from Telefilm, is the only reason they buy Canadian film. I mean, I have had a major Canadian distributor tell me, 'We're not in the business of distributing Canadian film. That is not what we do.' They can't make money doing it and that's why they don't do it, or they haven't figured out a way yet."

The decentralization of film production has made vagabonds of actors, many with agents and homes in two or three cities. Even before the release of *Kissed*, Parker spent a couple of years travelling between Vancouver and Toronto, "making sure I had representation in Toronto, going out and meeting people, making myself known to that industry. And that's what I did in terms of coming to L.A. I mean, it's an investment that you put into your career. I will be a Canadian actress who lives here, who lives there, who works everywhere. I fly to London all the time, even still, on my own dime, to audition for films there because I want to work there." *Molly and Lynne*

Wherever Parker's acting takes her, she will continue to make courageous choices, from *Kissed* to *Max*, in which she portrays the wife of a Jewish gallery owner who interacts with struggling young artist Adolf Hitler in between-the-wars Austria. Director Wayne Wang's *The Centre of the World* also inspired controversy, including one enraged film exhibitor in Ohio who took it upon himself to personally edit the movie before screening it. Parker's performance, as a stripper/rock musician who's offered $10,000 to spend a Las Vegas weekend with a computer programmer, drew an Independent Spirit best-actress nomination but, says Parker: "To be totally honest, I was really unhappy with the way they marketed that movie.

"It was like, 'Come see the sex film.' And it's an art film. The film is certainly about these people's sexual relationship, but it's not a sexy film. Although I was unhappy with the marketing, I think it's kind of interesting because you look at this film and you go, 'Here are these people who go into this situation wanting money, power, and sex, all in different kinds of ways, and none of them get what they want out of it.' And here this film's being marketed as, 'Hey, come see this. This is a sexy film.' And nobody's going to get what they want out of that, if that's what they're looking for."

§

It's fitting that the actress who works outside the Hollywood mainstream would live outside of it too. Climb the stairs to the top floor of the old house in L.A.'s Echo Park neighbourhood and you're transported to a rustic residence on Hornby Island, the kind of a house where a west coast fisherman might feel at home.

Martin Cummins had taken his directorial debut, *We All Fall Down*, to the 2000 Toronto Film Festival when he ran into Parker, who was there for *Suspicious River*. "Whenever I see somebody from that [Gastown Actors Studio] time period, it's just like yesterday," says Cummins. "I hadn't seen Molly in ages and ages before we did the festival circuit. But seeing Molly again it was like only a minute ago, you know? It was like I walked out the door and I forgot my wallet and I came back. So I see her in Toronto and she knows I'm going to L.A. and she says, 'If you need a place to stay, why don't you stay at my house?'"

The next thing you know, Cummins, who was in the midst of a marriage breakup, finds himself driving around the Echo Park area looking for Parker's house. "I was in a bad spot, having a lot of trouble. I went down to L.A. and I opened up the door to Molly's house and there was all her stuff, you know, *Molly's stuff*. I was out of my mind but I was comforted by Molly's stuff, even though she wasn't there. And she left me a little note and told me about the neighbourhood being where Charlie Chaplin had lived. And I haven't, I mean, I think I've seen her once since. That's the way it is with a lot of the people who were in that class."

§

The first major filmmaker from B.C. was Nell Shipman, one of the first women to direct movies in the U.S. She also wrote and starred in the 1919 feature *Back to God's Country*, the most popular Canadian film of its day. Shipman was just the first of a long line of renowned women directors from B.C. It's not that Vancouver has more female filmmakers than other movie-making cities, but what distinguishes it from Toronto, L.A., or New York is that most ot its benchmark films have been directed by women. The first movie directed by a woman in Canada was Sylvia Spring's made-in-Vancouver *Madeleine Is. . .* (1971). Sandy Wilson's *My American Cousin* (1985) was one of the first B.C.

features to reach audiences across North America. The West Coast Wave's early features included Mina Shum's *Double Happiness* (1994), Kathy Garneau's *Tokyo Cowboy* (1995), and Lynne Stopkewich's *Kissed* (1996). Vancouver's big box-office movie of the 1990s was Anne Wheeler's *Better Than Chocolate* (1999). And the city's best-known documentary (Nettie Wild) and experimental (Ann Marie Fleming) filmmakers are women.

"The politics of the west coast is a lot softer, a lot more progressive," suggests Spring. "The women's movement is very strong here. I became a feminist while I was living here and working on *Madeleine Is . . .* There's a lot of discussion about women's issues and female politics."

Shum also believes there are a lot of mentors. "I think it helped that Sandy Wilson made *My American Cousin*. It gave us the confidence to do it. Anne Wheeler taught us a workshop. I remember Lynne and I both sat in on that. Women in Film had just been formed when we were in our last year of film school and they had a big directing symposium and they brought all these women in from all over the world. There were L.A. directors and what-not and we just sat through these sessions and learned."

Wheeler began her career working on documentaries in Edmonton in the 1970s. By the time she moved to Vancouver in 1995, she had directed notable narrative features such as *Bye Bye Blues* and *Loyalties*. "Until I moved to Vancouver, I had never been on another director's set. It had all been self-taught," she says. "I was in the business a good twelve years before I made a feature and I knew that being a westerner, being a woman, I better not fail because I probably couldn't get a second chance." In Wheeler's 1999 film *Better Than Chocolate*, she left behind her usual Prairie setting to create a girl-meets-girl love story set in Vancouver's Commercial Drive neighbourhood. And she's continued her feature work in the city (*Marine Life, Suddenly Naked*).

§

In September 2000, Stopkewich's *Suspicious River* made an auspicious debut at the Venice International Film Festival. The *Suspicious River* entourage, including Stopkewich and Parker, drew a rousing ovation as they entered the Venice theatre and when the screening finished, the response was even more emotional. "People were stunned silent," Stopkewich recalls, "and then all these men just started walking up to where we were sitting in the theatre and they were sobbing. It was pretty intense."

In *Suspicious River*, Parker plays the girl-next-door motel receptionist doing tricks on the side, a story that could easily turn exploitive if it fell into the wrong hands. With Stopkewich at the helm, though, the movie has a depth of insight about women's lives that's rarely seen on screen. "Socially it's more acceptable for a woman to take it out on herself than to take it out on the other," Stopkewich says. "Even the strongest women I know will come out with, 'I'm having a bad hair day' or 'I can't eat that cake or I'll weigh too much.' It's all about how we look. That's our currency – your tits and your ass and your youth. Because her [Parker character's] life is so out of control, her measure of control is her body – 'I'm going to do this at this time with my body and I'm going to be paid this.' It's something she controlled."

Vancouver actor Sarah-Jane Redmond, who had a supporting role in *Suspicious River*, recalls an on-set conversation with Stopkewich. "I remember she came into my trailer one day and said she knew how hard it was to keep a career going and to survive in this industry as a

Director Lynne Stopkewich with actors Molly Parker and Callum Keith Rennie on the set of *Suspicious River*. photo by Diyah Perah, courtesy Lynne Stopkewich

Dreaming in the Rain

woman and how she supported me in that. That meant a lot to me. It's something that really hit me hard, just in terms of her respect for actors and that acknowledgment of just how difficult it is – being a female actor and staying in the business and staying sane and grounded and real and honest."

§

Like Parker, Stopkewich made her splash with *Kissed*, a directing debut which led to a stack of offers when it premiered in Toronto. The offers kept coming. But she turned them down. A couple of hundred of them, her pay starting at upwards of us$300,000. *Girl Interrupted* with Winona Ryder. Stopkewich said no. *Ever After* with Drew Barrymore. Nope. Madonna's *The Next Best Thing*. No.

"None of those projects meant anything to me. It's one thing if I can make all of this dough, but it's another thing to be standing in the rain telling an actor what the scene's about. If it doesn't speak to you, how are you going to speak to the actor? I need a connection," she says. "I don't have the personality to say, 'Yeah, give me the money, I'm going to go and direct, you know, *Tits and Ass, Part 2*. That's not who I am.

"I drive my mother's hand-me-down leaky lemon, live in Strathcona, don't own a house, I don't have any of the trappings. That's not what's important to me. What's important is having a place to write."

Stopkewich followed *Kissed* with *Suspicious River* and *Lilith on Top*, a documentary about the final Lilith Fair tour. These days, she's planning her next feature, *People Who Knock on the Door*, based on a novel by Patricia Highsmith (*The Talented Mr Ripley*). For tv, she's directed an episode of *Da Vinci's Inquest*, Bruce Greenwood in what's tentatively titled *The Life*, and *Man from Mars*, based on a short story by Margaret Atwood.

Growing up in East End Montreal, the future director and her childhood best friend, future author Lynn Crosbie, shared imaginations. "I just remember when we'd be walking home from school, the twenty-minute walk every day, we'd tell each other stories."

Stopkewich's eyes were fixed on a North American pop culture world of comic books and *Mad* magazines, *Brady Bunch* and *Partridge Family*, Hollywood musicals and Barbie dolls. "I always would laugh about being a director because directing movies is like Barbie dolls but with real people. You get to dress them, you get to create a story, you get to tell them where to go and what to say and how to say it."

But she soon recognized that the homogenized sitcom universe didn't really exist, at least not in her East End francophone world. "I wanted it so bad," she says, but that split between an unreal surface world and the real world underneath would be reflected in her movies. "You think about the films I make. *Kissed* – this person's the girl next door and she gets it on with dead guys. My favourite movies are *Singin' in the Rain*, *The Wizard of Oz*, and *Blue Velvet*. It all makes sense."

It does, too, when you consider that *Suspicious River* has particles of David Lynch's *Blue Velvet* sensibility and *Lilith on Top*, the musical, is a descendent of *Singin' in the Rain*, especially the tour's much-anticipated last concert in an Edmonton downpour.

After UBC, Stopkewich would go on to be a production designer in the film industry, even attracting a Genie nomination for Sandy Wilson's *Harmony Cats*. She was trying to pull together her own film, *Tell Niagara Falls*, when she discovered *Kissed* in Toronto's Pages bookstore. "I walked in, looked up, and there was an anthology and it was edited by my best friend, my bosom buddy of childhood, who I had lost touch with when we were ten years old, when she moved away – Lynn Crosbie." She bought Crosbie's collection of women's erotica, *The Girl That Wants To*. Inside was Barbara Gowdy's *We So Seldom Look On Love*, the short story that inspired *Kissed*. "I start reading it and I'm just completely floored. After page one I realized who this character is, that she's this sort of sweet, unassuming girl-next-door and a full-blown necrophile. I thought that was so great and creepy at the same time. And sort of wonderful. Just polar opposites smashed together."

When she decided to make *Kissed*, the reaction wasn't all positive. "People thought I was crazy, like who would want to make a movie about a necrophile? To me, the interesting thing is if the work can affect you in any way or change the way you see the world in any way," she says. "It's interesting because with *Suspicious River* and even Lilith Fair, that's exactly the same concern. Part of my interest in doing the Lilith Fair documentary was to see what really goes on, to see what's behind the machine. And with *Suspicious River*, I mean the story's about this small-town, married, fresh-faced, polite-looking girl who works in a motel, who is turning tricks and going to hell in a handbasket. So there's that whole thing of appearances, and what you think something is, and then what it really is."

After an arduous two-and-a-half year process, *Tell Niagara Falls* fell through, so Stopkewich went to New York to work on a screenplay for *Kissed* with writing partner Angus Fraser. To finance the film, she sold shares in it to friends and family; a postal worker, cinematographer, parents, artist, lawyer, and editor were among the investors. The big money arrived, however, after the movie's debut at the Toronto's film festival, where distributors got into a bidding war. *Kissed* played Canadian and U.S. theatres and was featured at more than thirty festivals, including Cannes and Sundance. Fifteen talent agencies approached Stopkewich and she signed with William Morris. That's when the scripts started arriving.

She almost said yes to *Severed*, based on L.A.'s Black Dahlia murder case, but eventually turned that down too. It was picked up by David Lynch, who also, ultimately, left the project. Unlike some of her UBC friends, Stopkewich is more David Lynch than Woody Allen. ("I love that ironic humour and the way he sort of pulls you into that dream world.") Her casting agent for *Suspicious River*, Joanna Ray, also works with Lynch, so when Stopkewich was in L.A. she was invited to the set of her favourite director's *Mulholland Drive*. "I was just so nervous. I told him that I had been stalking him for two years. It was like the first thing that came out of my mouth. And he said something like, 'Gee, that's an interesting way to spend your time.'"

What was Stopkewich looking for in a script that the offers were missing? "Content," she says with a laugh. "You know, some interesting character arcs, a good story, some subtext. It got to be a big joke around the office. There would just be this pile in the corner that was getting higher and higher."

After turning down scripts for two years, two L.A. producers who had seen *Kissed* sent her a copy of the novel *Suspicious River*. Stopkewich wound up writing the script as well as directing. "It's incredibly dark material. It makes *Kissed* look like a fairy tale. I read this book and immediately I just think Molly, right, but then I'm thinking, 'Oh god, will she want to do this?' It was hard enough her playing a necrophile; this was even worse" But she sent Parker the script. "She phoned me and said, 'No. Don't ask me to do this.' And then she said, 'Why, why do you want to do this? Why?' And then she turned me down."

In the end, however, the quality of Stopkewich's script proved too much for Parker to resist. "We're really good friends," Parker says. "I think somehow we've developed this really safe and yet challenging creative relationship. I would never have I think done either of these movies if it hadn't been her that was making them. Both *Kissed* and this [*Suspicious River*] deal with darker sexual scenes and it's just not a place you want to go without knowing there's someone there who's telling the story in a respectful way and in a way that respects you and respects the character and respects women. She will not let me get away with anything less than she knows what I can do. I would work with her again in a second. I remember right toward the end of shooting she turned to me and she said, 'Do you think we'll do this again?' And we both laughed."

"Sometimes there's no need for us to even talk," says Stopkewich, "we sort of already know what the other person's thinking. So if I go for another take, I'd look at her and she'd say, 'I know.'"

Stopkewich also remains close to her filmmaking friends from UBC. "It's not like I see these people every day. I mean, I hadn't talked to Mina in a long time, but the day before I went to camera [for *Suspicious River*], there was a message on my answering machine from Mina, a message from Bruce Sweeney. All my friends who are film directors going, 'Hey, tomorrow's your first day on your second show. Good luck.'"

Shum and Stopkewich developed a close bond during their UBC years. "For me, coming out of *The Grocer's Wife*, it was great being in the same group with Lynne because we were both strong women who had certain visions," says Shum. "That's really cool. You don't meet that every day. Lynne was the production designer and I was the AD so we were there every day being equal to all the other people on the set. We were the only two women on the front lines of that show."

The impact of *Kissed* energized another generation of Vancouver filmmakers. Scott Smith, who worked as a grip on *Kissed*, was attending the Canadian Film Centre in Toronto when the film played the city's festival. "I saw what happened when it sort of exploded on to the international scene. If you're a young filmmaker you go, 'Shit, I want that.' It sets the bar higher. That becomes the thing you start to strive for as opposed to just simply getting a film made."

Smith and Stopkewich were among the Vancouver filmmakers

who came together in a building at 3737 Oak Street, a sort of Brill Building for the local indie scene. The building was owned by the parents of Peter Roeck, the location manager on *Live Bait*. His production company was in the office and he was responsible for maintaining the low rents that attracted his friends in the scene.

"That was in some ways another convergence of things," says Smith. "I had just finished a film (*rollercoaster*) and was about to go through the distribution, whatever you want to call that. Lynne was in the process of finishing two films (*Suspicious River*, *Lilith on Top*) and *Mile Zero* was going into production. Bruce was in there while we were editing, then [*Mile Zero* producers] Anagram took his office. You had three separate filmmaking entities at three distinctly different parts of production all in the shit together, basically. I know, from where I was sitting, to do what I had to do in that year and a half with *rollercoaster*, alone in an office in a building somewhere, would be an entirely different thing than being able to look out the door and go, 'Oh yeah, you're in the shit, too. Yeah, I'm in the shit. We'll get out of it.' We'd go down and show posters and say, 'What do you guys think of this?' And Lynne could show edits and *Mile Zero* would come up and say, 'What did you guys do when this came up?' We'd have cocktail parties on Fridays. I think it was a way of keeping up morale."

§

The most moving moment at the 2001 Toronto International Film Festival took place as *Lilith on Top* was ending. Stopkewich's documentary screened at the ornate Elgin Theatre a couple of days after the attacks of September 11. Usually, an audience pours from a theatre during the closing credits but when *Lilith on Top*'s credits rolled alongside an image of Sarah McLachlan singing the hauntingly beautiful song "Angel," the audience stayed in their seats. They sat frozen, quiet, as though McLachlan's song was the affirmation of life they needed at that moment.

"Lilith Fair was about people who came together to sing 'goodness,'" says Jessica Fraser, one of the movie's producers. "It was real. I think people were staying away from fiction after the 11th." Along with Stopkewich and Dean English, Fraser operates Boneyard Productions, which produced *Lilith on Top*. She was among the small group of women who approached Vancouver residents McLachlan and Stopkewich separately before the last Lilith Fair tour in 1999.

"They came to me and said, 'Lynne wants to direct this documentary,'" says McLachlan. "They went to Lynne and said, 'Sarah wants you to direct this documentary.'" Stopkewich says when the two finally met to discuss the project, they said simultaneously, "So you want me to do this." Says McLachlan: "We had a great conversation and we connected 'cause I really didn't know Lynne very well at all previous to that."

With *Lilith on Top*, Stopkewich combined three distinctive characteristics of the Vancouver film scene: music, women filmmakers, and progressive politics. The result was entirely unlike anything a rock-video director would have produced. Stopkewich utilized her skills as a narrative feature filmmaker to turn Lilith Fair into a developing character, who has a tentative beginning, an exhilarating middle, and a melancholic end. Stopkewich had a lot to work with. First, the musical acts on the women's music tour were outstanding, from Sheryl Crow and the Pretenders to Bif Naked and the Indigo Girls. Second, Stopkewich and her small crew joined the tour for forty-two gigs over two months, so they had 400 hours of footage. "It's an amazing experience because you work from seven in the morning till midnight," English says. Then they would go to sleep on the bus and wake up in a new parking lot.

Lilith on Top prompted McLachlan to consider the tour's legacy. Before the tour she had gone about her career quietly. As the festival's organizer, McLachlan was suddenly at the centre of a cultural phenomenon. "The film brings it back for me, it brings back all the flood of emotions, the euphoria and the despair, and all the craziness," McLachlan says. "It was an amazing experience because I really had to find out exactly what it was I believed in, as opposed to having some sort of wishy-washy ideas and ideals about the whole thing. I guess I realized, most important, that no matter what you do you're not going to please everybody. And that was a real epiphany 'cause oh, I thought, 'It's going to be so great, everybody's going to love it.'"

§

One of Stopkewich's fondest moments came the day those who had gambled on *Kissed* were given more than their money back. "Handing those cheques over brought tears to my eyes because these were the very first people who believed in the project, believed in us, and in me, and the film could never have been made without them. So it was really incredibly gratifying to be able to write a cheque back."

Audiences have an instinctive way of knowing whether they're being handed the real deal. Stopkewich's work touches people because it cuts to the bone, through all the pretence, and finds a glimmer of raw truth and, thus, a glimmer of hope. Going under the surface isn't always pleasant, whether it means standing all day in the rain shooting *Suspicious River* or researching *Kissed*.

Molly and Lynne

"I had to go visit a funeral home and saw an actual dead man lying on a slab and tried to imagine what it would be like to. . . . I was totally just sickened. I mean, I almost passed out. I just sat down on the sidewalk and put my head between my knees because I almost puked."

So, plunging the depths to make *Kissed* wasn't particularly appealing.

"No, but what it represented was. Full-on rebellion. I loved the subversion. The fact that it made me uncomfortable I found appealing."

CLASH OF THE HOLLYWOODS

There was an instance during the filming of *The 13th Warrior* when North met South. "Ice niggers," the American director John McTiernan shouted at the Vancouver crew. The director had been riding the Canadians throughout the Vancouver Island shoot, firing entire departments on a whim. Now it blew up, nearly turning into a physical confrontation. *The 13th Warrior*, besides being an unbearable shoot, turned out to be an unwatchable piece of cinematic crud.

The differences between Hollywood North by Northwest (Vancouver) and Hollywood North by Northeast (Toronto) are incidental compared to those between Hollywood South (L.A.) and Canada. Some Canadian crew members have taken to wearing T-shirts that on the front read, "I don't give a fuck," and on the back continue, "how you do it in L.A."

The clash isn't confined to on-set conflicts. In Los Angeles, there is anger at the very existence of Vancouver's American-based film industry. Canadian tax credits, a tumbling dollar, and quality actors and crews with weaker contracts than their U.S. counterparts, all combined, by the turn of the century, to have more than 35,000 B.C. residents drawing pay cheques from an industry that spent more than $1 billion annually on production in the province.

§

Vancouver, like pretty much everywhere in the world, has had a relationship with Los Angeles since the early twentieth century. For the first half of the century, L.A. was some dreamscape to gape at on a giant screen. The city of Los Angeles came of age in the years after the Second World War. Many of the soldiers who, during the war, had gotten a taste of the California winter sun returned with their young families to live there. It wasn't just Americans daydreaming about living in

L.A. during the '50s and '60s. It was the time of "California Dreamin'," and practically everywhere (including Sandy Wilson's Okanagan) there were sun-fun images from beach movies and surf music, *77 Sunset Strip* and Disneyland. Much of L.A's kitschy signage and architecture still reflects that gaudy postwar era. So, L.A. arrived just late for the sort of Tin Pan Alley musical tributes given Chicago or New York. If New York has a Gershwin soundtrack, L.A. has the Beach Boys. It's no coincidence that the best songs about L.A. were written by a '70s punk band (X's "Los Angeles") and a '60s folk singer (Phil Ochs' "The World Began in Eden and Ended in Los Angeles").

Vancouver actor Ben Ratner has returned home to work as an actor-writer-director, but while living in L.A. in 2000 he noted: "There are so many shallow people in L.A. and complaining about shallow people here is like living in Vancouver and complaining about the rain. If it's really getting you down, you got to get out . . . because it's not going to change. It's worse here in some ways. *The Georgia Straight* is full of ads about kayaking, whale watching – what else do people do? – fishing charters. The L.A. papers advertise vaginal laser rejuvenation surgery."

Which brings us to an old sign at the L.A. airport: "Welcome to Los Angeles, city of tomorrow." You have to wonder whether L.A. is really a city of yesterday, whether Hollywoodism was a twentieth-century ideology. The suburban sprawl of the postwar years has not aged well and fewer people swarm in from the rest of America. Studios are running away to shoot elsewhere, no one in town knows where digital technology is taking them, the indie scene has gotten popular enough to stage its own version of the Oscars. And the studios haven't made a good movie since the 1970s. (Okay, the occasional one slips through.)

There was a time when Hollywood studios made great films. Long before there were weekend screenwriting symposiums or doctoral film students, there was a new phenomenon: talking pictures. Following the release of first talkie, *The Jazz Singer*, in 1927, studios scrambled to produce more of the new movies. Since there were no trained screenwriters, the studios collected agit-prop playwrights and other ink-stained New Yorkers and put them on the train to Hollywood. For more than two decades these writers would deliver great screenplays, from *The Wizard of Oz* to *Casablanca* to *High Noon*, from Columbia's screwball comedies to MGM's magic musicals to Warners' downtown dramas.

The history of the Warners studio is, in some ways, a microcosm of the history of Hollywood. Long before there was a WB Network or an AOL Time Warner conglomerate, there were four brothers. They were brash, scrappy children of Polish-Jewish immigrants, determined to make their stand in a new industry in a new country. The Warners created a studio in their own image. They hired streetwise writers – mostly children of immigrants, too, who had been involved in the edgy New York theatre of the 1930s. The actors they hired were smart-talking city boys and girls such as Humphrey Bogart, John Garfield, Barbara Stanwyck, Edward G. Robinson, Bette Davis, Paul Muni, Joan Blondell, Lauren Bacall, Jimmy Cagney, and the Bowery Boys. These actors and writers would create a Warners library of brilliant, tautly written movies about society's outcasts, filled with a snappy patter and a social conscience.

Those who think "Hollywood movie" is a pejorative term should take long look at the movies Warners produced during its prime. It's the finest video collection of any production company – *Casablanca, I Am A Fugitive From a Chain Gang, The Jazz Singer, A Streetcar Named Desire, The Maltese Falcon, Little Caesar, Rebel Without a Cause, The Glass Menagerie, Yankee Doodle Dandy, Four Daughters, Key Largo, The Life of Emile Zola, Dark Victory, The Petrified Forest, A Star is Born, The Sea Wolf, Dodge City, Public Enemy, 42nd Street, They Made Me a Criminal, The Little Foxes, Mildred Pierce, Angels with Dirty Faces, Dead End, Treasure of the Sierra Madre*; the list goes on and on.

For each great movie there were several pedestrian ones. But the entertaining movies came often enough and were good enough to inspire a generation of Hollywood-obsessed European directors, from Jean-Luc Godard to Francois Truffaut, who would, in turn, inspire the next generation of English-language directors. The 1960s and '70s was a time of student activism and student film-going. A cinephile culture emerged on campuses, with the Larry Kents and Jack Darcuses frequenting the Varsity or the Studio or a student auditorium to watch the new European cinema, along with old prints of Bogart and the Marx Brothers.

So why haven't the studios, with any consistency, made good movies since the 1970s?

The old studio system did not fade to its current state overnight. It's a process that's been taking place for decades, becoming more pronounced as the studio system turned increasingly international in scope. There are several dilapidated signposts along the way, including antitrust suits which forced the studios to divest themselves of their movie theatres and end their practice of block booking, a system that forced exhibitors to purchase a studio's films by the group, including movies that might be commercially risky. When each film had to be sold individually, the studios became less likely to take chances.

The anti-Communist witch hunts left their mark, too. Besides being the kind of artists who could make gritty, witty, thoroughly entertaining movies out of the day's headlines, the Warners writers, for instance, were the sort targeted by the McCarthyite blacklist when it hit Hollywood in the late 1940s. So many of these screenwriters would get blacklisted that by the mid-1950s Hollywood was on a downward trajectory it would never recover from. The talent would never be as rich as it was during the pre-blacklist days but, still, there was enough left to continue making some great films, especially during the studios' death spasm of the early 1970s. What happened, though, to the ownership of the "big eight" studios would result in the virtual death of the great studio film:

Columbia (*Mr Smith Goes to Washington, From Here to Eternity, Born Yesterday, His Girl Friday, On the Waterfront*): purchased by Coca-Cola Co in 1982. Acquired by Sony USA in 1989.

United Artists (*The African Queen, High Noon, Some Like It Hot, Scarface, Marty*): became a subsidiary of the TransAmerica Corp in 1967, merged with MGM in 1983, dissolved into MGM – which was owned by the French bank Credit Lyonnais – in 1992.

Metro-Goldwyn-Mayer (*A Night at the Opera, The Wizard of Oz, The Philadelphia Story, Easter Parade, Singin' in the Rain*): purchased by Turner Broadcasting System in 1986. Sold to Credit Lyonnais in 1992. Acquired by a "management group" financed by Kirk Kerkorian in 1996.

Paramount (*Sullivan's Travels, Double Indemnity, Stalag 17, The Heiress, Rear Window*): purchased by Gulf & Western Industries in 1966. Acquired by Viacom Inc in 1994.

RKO (*Swing Time, Citizen Kane, Top Hat, Suspicion*): purchased by General Tire in the 1950s.

Universal (*Spartacus, Frankenstein, Destry Rides Again, Dracula, All Quiet on the Western Front*): became a subsidiary of of MCA Inc in 1962.

Acquired in 1990 by the Matsushita Electrical Industrial Company.

20th Century Fox (*All About Eve, Bus Stop, Gentlemen's Agreement, The Grapes of Wrath, How Green Was My Valley*): became part of Fox Inc, which includes Fox Broadcasting, when acquired by Rupert Murdoch in 1985.

Warner Bros: Purchased by the Kinney National Service conglomerate in 1969. Acquired by Time Inc in 1989 to eventually form AOL Time Warner.

By the latter part of the 1970s, the shift from family owned companies to corporate entities was irreversible and the reconstituted studios had regained their footing. They seldom dealt with the obstinate, counter-culture filmmakers whose success during the first years of the decade had been such a puzzle to them. A new, winning format had emerged – the blockbuster (*Star Wars, Jaws, Superman*). While the studios would occasional dabble in smaller films, as their ownership and their audiences became, in succeeding decades, increasingly global, their strategy was entrenched: mass marketing of mega movies.

The first generation of moguls, like employers in any industry, were certainly at odds with their employees. It was the era when the Screen Actors Guild and the Writers Guild of America were established and actors were locked into restrictive long-term contracts. There is much not to lament about the old studio system, but unlike the studios' current ownership, the moguls at least had a passion for the movies. When Warner Bros was the Warner brothers, they lived in L.A. An irate screenwriter could knock down their office doors, and occasionally they'd make a risky movie on a pitch or a whim.

"The old studio bosses – Jack Warner, Sam Goldwyn, Darryl Zanuck, Harry Cohn – were all friends, or friendly enemies I knew how to deal with. They offered me work," Orson Welles would reflect in *This Is Orson Welles*, which he co-wrote with Peter Bogdanovich. "I was a maverick, but the studios understood what that meant, and if there was a fight, we both enjoyed it. With an annual output of forty pictures per studio, there would probably be room for one Orson Welles picture."

Greg Krizman was SAG's spokesman in 2001 when he noted: "They [the old studio ownership] understood the product. Now, most of the studios are just one income stream in a multinational company that has maybe ten, maybe twelve, and the people at the top of that company don't probably really understand much about making movies or care much about the Southern California economy, much less the Vancouver economy."

By the 1990s, the studios' bottom line was decided by faceless, fearful young executives in Tokyo or Wall Street, with little interest in movies. They continue to scramble to rebottle what seemed to have worked before (though there hasn't been a great sequel since *The Godfather, Part II*) and it has become a purely economic matter. The summer of 2002 was typical: *Men in Black II, Stuart Little 2, Halloween 8* (*Halloween: Resurrection*), *Austin Powers 3* (*Austin Powers in Goldmember*), *Spy Kids 2*. There was also *Spider-Man*, which was really a prequel, having already gotten the go-ahead for two sequels, and the latest awful episode of *Star Wars*, a movie series so convoluted they released *Episode VI* a couple of decades before *Episode II*.

It used to be that a movie would open in one or two theatres in Vancouver and good word of mouth would keep lineups forming for months. At the height of the studio era, the release of a feature required 350 prints. By the 1990s, a new film required 6,000 prints. The rapid expansion of stadium-seat multiplexes in the 1990s has made the heavily promoted studio film practically immune to bad word of mouth because it opens on so many screens that it's made an opening-weekend profit before anyone knows what anyone else thinks of it. And the studios are targeting, with lowest common denominator violence and titillation, an international, teenage male market.

It's no longer unusual for a film's foreign revenues to surpass its domestic revenues, with the international market continuing to expand as countries such as China open their doors to the studios. Since the "product" is no longer aimed primarily at an American audience, the English language has become burdensome, so theatres from Moscow, Idaho, to Moscow, Russia, have the same sound of explosions and car crashes and endless computerized special effects.

The new global studio system affects the quality of the film in other ways. WGA spokesman Michael Seel explains: "These are huge, vertically integrated companies, public companies, whose main financial audience is Wall Street. And what Wall Street likes, even more than five or ten percent more profit, is predictability of profit. They don't like volatility. The nature of these companies now makes everything favour predictability, which gets down to film selection. It's not as much about 'In the third act let's tighten this scene,' or 'Let's get rid of this character.' It happens way back here when they [make their selection]. It's all about Steven Seagal's *Exit Wounds* – no offence to Mr Seagal, but it's a genre picture and you can estimate what that picture's going to do with much greater predictability than *You Can Count on Me*."

The studios, along with the producers who work with them, make the safest, most cost-effective choices possible, making Vancouver increasingly inviting at the beginning of the new millennium – as long as its dollar was still plummeting and its film workers towed the line. There is the rare good service film, such as Christopher Guest's hilarious mockumentary *Best in Show*. But a studio system that seldom makes quality films at home can't be expected to make good movies in Vancouver. Their riskless, artless agenda is what they brought to Vancouver, operating, often in concert with Canadian producers, an industry almost entirely comprised of mind-numbing formulaic theatrical releases and bad movies of the week for networks which are small-screen versions of the mega-studios. It's for and by the numbers too – in the first years of the twenty-first century, the service industry produced such features as *40 Days 40 Nights*, *24 Hours*, *13 Ghosts*, *The Sixth Day*, and *3000 Miles to Graceland*. There were also the immortal *Ballistic: Ecks vs Sever*, *Head Over Heels*, *Scary Movie*, *Life or Something Like It*, *I Spy*, *Freddy Got Fingered*, and *Get Carter*.

The biggest-budgeted service-industry shoot in Vancouver history was also the biggest flop. Not even the most uncritical of Trekkies could bear to watch director Brian De Palma get lost in space in 2000's *Mission to Mars*. The low point, however, in made-in-Vancouver film was the 2001 release *Valentine*, about a group of young women being subjected to a parade of ghastly graphic violence – murder by knife, axe, electric drill, shards of glass.

∫

The response to all this has been the rapid increase of independent filmmaking. It was not, despite popular belief in some quarters, invented by Quentin Tarantino sometime around 1994. In fact, virtually every film made outside the major studios in Hollywood is an independent film – every Italian or British or French film. Even in Hollywood, the independents go back to the beginning, with Welles (along with others such as Charlie Chaplin and Sam Goldwyn), a member of the Society of Independent Motion Picture Producers in the 1930s. Every Canadian film is an independent film because even the country's largest producer, Toronto's Alliance Atlantis, is minuscule in comparison to the major studios.

Although they operate almost entirely autonomously from one another, there is a natural alliance between the Toronto and Vancouver indie scenes, American independents, and the Hollywood unions who say Pasadena should be Pasadena, Vancouver should be Vancouver. The Vancouver filmmakers who bristle at their city being a film surrogate for Seattle are echoed by independent filmmakers such as Mike White, the screenwriter-actor behind *The Good Girl* and *Chuck and Buck*. He also wrote the TV series *Pasadena*, which became controversial when Fox decided to shoot in Vancouver instead of Pasadena. "I was pissed," White said. "I mean, I like Vancouver, I love going up there. The actors were all, 'I don't want to go to Vancouver.' And then they went up there and now some of them want to stay even after we shut down production. It turned out okay but it seemed just so silly. And then all the people who sent us up there are gone now so . . . it's a little bit like, what are we doing here, you know, especially if it's freezing cold? We can't do exteriors, it's supposed to be Pasadena. Everybody's like sitting in the house like trying to figure out who to seduce."

§

Why is this union gathering different from any other union gathering? For one thing, the anguished father from *The Graduate* is hosting the affair. For two more things, Rhoda and Duddy Kravitz are here. So are a medium from *Ghost*, a cop from *Adam 12*, and a passenger on the Titanic.

Having shown up early to talk about the impending actors strike with a SAG spokesman, I was invited to a press conference about the business relationship between actors and agents. Screen Actors Guild president William Daniels (*The Graduate*) was fielding questions, surrounded by a union cast that included Valerie Harper, Richard Dreyfuss, Whoopi Goldberg, Kent McCord, and Frances Fisher.

Although this meeting had other themes, this was 2001, and the strike most everyone thought was about to happen (but didn't) wasn't far from anyone's thoughts. SAG and the WGA seemed about to wage a historic confrontation with the movie studios, with both unions prepared for a worldwide shutdown of U.S. film and TV production. Alongside the economic issues, SAG and the WGA were raising new questions about the very nature of the increasingly global industry.

SAG activist Richard Dreyfuss was eager to talk about this "sea change" in the industry when he bounded to the mike with the irrepressible energy of *The Apprenticeship of Duddy Kravitz*. "It is possible now in this business to make billions of dollars. That's new. You can now make product that goes instantaneously all around the world in technology that we barely understand," he says. "None of the producers do, none of the studios do, we're all making it up as we go along. But we got a membership here that is an incredibly interested party to all of these things – new technology, new financial structures."

The technology is new but even back in the 1940s, Hollywood actors were looking at financial structures and finding avenues outside the studios. "I gotta look myself in the mirror every morning," John Garfield said in Larry Swindell's biography *Body and Soul*. Garfield was a major star of the day who left Warner Bros to work independently. "There's a fear in Hollywood about tackling dangerous subjects, difficult subjects. . . . I owe it to myself to be available when some enterprising people want to try something tough."

Garfield would end up blacklisted, and died at age thirty-nine. His spiritual descendants at this SAG press conference may not realize they also have spirited allies north of the border.

"I want to totally wean myself off auditioning for any U.S. stuff," says Tom Scholte. "Just the act of making a film in Canada is inherently political because we live in a state of cultural occupation. So making a Canadian film is like an act of resistance. Making a film, making a piece of Canadian art, is political, I believe, in and of itself – particularly film because of the political pressure to make sure they keep a stranglehold on our distribution."

At the heart of Vancouver filmmaking is a particularly feisty bunch, with activist backgrounds that would have had the old Hollywood McCarthyites drooling to have at them. There are, for instance, onetime anarchist punk rockers (Lynne Stopkewich), Commercial Drive activists (Chris Haddock), Prairie feminists (Anne Wheeler), draft resisters (Leonard Schein), even children of politicos. "That's sort of the spirit of the place, though," says Molly Parker. "That's certainly the spirit of how I grew up. I mean, I was raised by a bunch of leftie hippies."

Although they may be more likely these days to be on a set than at a protest rally, having done that at one point in their lives has given them an anti-establishment sensibility that sticks. "That's not something that if you're genuine, care about social causes, you can't just kind of shuck that," says Haddock. "That's what art is, right? Engage them. Totally. There's no point otherwise."

Mina Shum was drawn to the anarchic politics of punk. "I was interested in the 'Nobody rules OK,' that whole question authority, never stop questioning, don't settle for the status quo," says Shum. "I would basically side with anybody who wasn't the authority figures. I would go to any of these 'Rock Against' concerts. I was always constantly arguing with my consumer dollars. I would go and I would spend my five bucks on a show and then I'd argue with the rest of the world that their vision of the way it should be is not necessarily the way it has to be. And hence comes the cinema from there. That whole Vancouver sensibility of cinema, not that everybody's rooted there, challenged what was status quo at that time. I mean, we all grew out of that movement in one way or another."

Scholte says there's often a subtlety to Vancouver politics on film. "In terms of a personal political thing, Bruce [Sweeney] is a left-wing guy, and at the same time you'll never find a message in any of his films and one of the things he's repeated over and over again is 'I'm very skeptical of messages.'

"It gets submerged in their work and expressed in different ways. The first thing I said about *Dirty* to Bruce the first time I saw it was, 'It's an indictment.' The first time I saw it I read it that way. The two compulsives in the film, the two addicts, myself and Nancy, both have major scenes where financial transactions are used to try and fill the hole. I've got to try and buy the sex from somebody, Nancy's buying stuff, and then she had to get up in front of a bankruptcy court and because she apologizes to a bankruptcy court, suddenly the slate is wiped clean and these two damaged people, who still haven't gotten any real help, are sent back out there. I saw it as an anti-capitalist film. And I didn't go in looking for that but I got out of it that it was an indictment of a buy-and-sell society.

"My commitment to Canadian film and Canadian culture of all

kinds is very much mindful of the resistance to globalization. I think the act of making a film in Canada is an act of resistance to the studios creating that homogeneous culture. It's subversive to put a real person on screen. That act is subversive because it's so unmediated and it's chaos. A film like *Dirty* is chaotic."

Haddock agrees that the U.S. studio system operates in "an atmosphere of globalization. They haven't succeeded in making very good movies. Why should they? They're good at making profit and popcorn."

§

"You're inviting Americans in at the crassest level," declared Jack De-Govia, an American production designer involved in large Hollywood Boulevard protests against U.S. filmmaking in Canada. Following a major rally in 1999, DeGovia, spokesman for the Film and Television Action Committee, had this to say about American producers running off to Canada: "They don't care about Canada, they don't care about your culture, they don't care about your values, when they get a better deal somewhere else they're going to leave. Canada doesn't look like the U.S. It just doesn't. But there's a process of making motion pictures about America in Canada. They use Canadians as Americans and use Canada as America. Instead of having the guts to fund its own industry, the provincial and federal governments are sucking up a mature industry that took seventy years to create."

At the time, former prime minister Kim Campbell was somewhat of a liaison between Canadian and American producers in her capacity as Canada's consul general in L.A. "We're a huge market for American film and television and it's not unfair that we should have an opportunity to be part of the economic activity," she said. "It's not something to blame Canada about at all." Supporters of the service industry pointed out that while Vancouver had grown into a CDN$1 billion-plus industry, Hollywood's was $30 billion and the work hours of L.A.'s craft unions continued to rise. Also, for most of the century there had been a talent and financial drain the other way, including Canadian networks annually spending US$500 million to obtain rights to U.S. television programs.

DeGovia and other Hollywood workers, however, had their own

numbers and anecdotes about friends throughout the L.A. industry who hadn't been working because a huge portion of movie-of-the-week production had left for Canada. There were L.A. crew members whose families had worked in Hollywood film for three generations, who suddenly found themselves in a vanishing industry. Chris Carter, who produced *The X-Files* in Vancouver, said he sympathized with the protesters – to a point. "There are a lot of people out of work in Los Angeles, Hollywood. And I can see their frustration and even their anger," he said. "But this is simple economics and I think you've got to be competitive as a film producer."

Not every Canadian has been unsympathetic to the Hollywood workers, knowing there would have been a similar outcry among Canadian workers had a collapsing U.S. dollar and American tax incentives drawn an old B.C. industry such as fishing to Washington State. Actor Nick Mancuso, for one, doesn't join the chorus of Canadian producers and politicians who get livid whenever the Screen Actors Guild asks California politicians for the sort of tax incentives Canadian governments provide. "They're totally entitled," says Mancuso, whose Toronto-based Working Actors Group is trying to improve Canadian actors' residuals and working conditions to those of SAG standards. "We're in a situation where government monies are being used to subsidize the industry and in a sense they're subsidizing them in a collusionary manner with big business against the worker."

Much of the northern sympathy disappears, though, when American protesters target Canadian workers instead of the American producers who come to Canada to turn their $3 million into $5 million. Although these producers have little regard for Canadians ("ice nigger" is not an uncommon term for Canadians among Americans involved in the service industry), and contribute nothing culturally to Canada or, for that matter, to America, there are Canadian officials seemingly thrilled at the prospect of hosting their productions, with provincial governments falling over each other trying to outdo the next one's concessions to American producers. (Manitoba recently set the new standard recently with a thirty-five percent tax incentive.)

Subsidizing millionaire film executives apparently has more cachet than subsidizing millionaire hockey-team owners. A recent federal government proposal for tax incentives to save Canada's National Hockey League teams was discarded because of public outcry about handing money to wealthy owners and hockey players (at least most of them were Canadian), but there are Canadians involved in the service industry who stamp their feet whenever anyone suggests it's time to stop providing concessions to millionaire American producers and movie stars and, instead, channel their tax dollars into Canadian film. "Nobody wants to rock the boat because everybody's afraid that the $3.5-billion industry is going to go away," says Mancuso. "Well, it's not going to go away."

What is certainly not going to go away is the increasingly talented bunch determined to make Canadian films, and if the Vancouver industry is to have long-term stability, the focus will shift from pampering the American service industry to building an independent domestic film scene that will persevere regardless of exchange rates. Had the French film industry, or the Italian or British, been based on tax concessions and a bad currency, would anyone know or care about their films?

§

Some sit back and laugh at all the squabbling among Canadian and American politicians and producers. "I think it's hilarious," says Bruce Sweeney. "I heard the term Vancouver South, talking about Hollywood. I thought that was pretty funny."

It's also sad. That the movies could be reduced to an international confrontation over who gets to produce the dregs of the industry is a pathetic victory for commerce in its age-old dispute with art. It's not that anyone finds lost jobs funny, but to be at war over who gets to make *Freddy Got Fingered* is difficult to take seriously in some respects. It represents the ultimate commodification of the great new art form of the twentieth century. At their best, the movies, after all, are something exquisite, and to have governments and businesspeople, Canadian or American, who care nothing about cinema's history or future, quarrelling about the lowest common denominator "product" of their "industry" is barely worth paying attention to.

Fortunately, the battle that matters most isn't the purely economic one. It's the one between studio power and the filmmakers operating in opposition to it. The clash between Canadians and Americans over the spoils of the film industry is far less interesting than the one that pits independents from both countries against the spoilers. Not that every indie film is great. It's just that movies outside the studio box have the potential to surprise, be innovative, and take risks, a concept studio executives are so fearful of.

"I have no relationship with the American scene," says Vancouver director-editor Ross Weber. "I'll tell you right now I'm not a fan of it myself. It's a bit of a pain in the ass. I went to a little place to shoot a scene in the movie (*No More Monkeys Jumpin' on the Bed*) where the character goes to try on a dress or something. And the owner says, 'Well, it will be $2,000.' I went, 'No, you don't understand. I don't have any money, I can pay you $100.' She says, 'No.' And I'm saying, 'Yeah, but you'd be supporting the indigenous film industry.' 'No.' Because people now have expectations. I think *Dirty* had to pay $5,000 for one day at a lumber yard. The guy said, 'You guys have money.' 'Well, we don't actually.' 'Well, I know you have money because there's a whole industry here.' So, American productions have kind of destroyed that part of it.

"And then you have the minister of so-and-so saying, 'We have a billion-dollar film industry here and boy it's going great.' I'm thinking, 'What are you talking about?' It's not Canadian film. I hate it when they say 'Canadian film.' It's actually amazing we have any kind of Canadian film industry at all."

Weber, Sweeney, and other Canadian independent filmmakers question the very foundation of the U.S. service industry in Vancouver.

"I think that my films and a lot of other independent films exist in opposition to the dominant Hollywood mainstream, and my dislike for the Americans coming up here and shooting their crap has remained a constant," Sweeney says. "Out of a hundred pictures that are being made, you know eighty percent are MOWs that you'll never see. They're just terrible. And we're supposed to bow down. Well, 'fuck you.' I'm not interested in that.

"We were mixing *Live Bait* and Stallone was doing ADR [automated

VANCOUVER ACTORS IN HOLLYWOOD FILMS

The best of Vancouver's acting community can be spotted, albeit briefly, in all manner of service-industry TV movies and big-budget, shot-in-B.C. studio films.

Some examples: *The Accused* (Babz Chula), *Insomnia* (Ian Tracey), *Timecop* (Kevin McNulty), *Firestorm* (Barry Pepper), *Double Jeopardy* (Gabriel Rose), *First Blood* (Bruce Greenwood), *The Sixth Day* (Ellie Harvie), *Stakeout* (Jackson Davies), dialogue replacement] on that awful movie *Judge Dredd* at the same sound house up here. And he was just an asshole. You think when people see him they're going to think, 'Oh, what a great moment, I get to see Stallone.' When I see him, I just look contemptuous at him and he just looks contemptuous back."

Babz Chula says Vancouver actors are often forced to choose between the independent scene and the service industry. "We tend to think it's our industry and that's the thing that becomes a real danger for the artist because then you figure if you get two days on *Stargate* playing an alien in unrecognizable makeup that you're doing your work. You have to make choices here and if you choose to do independent film, you choose to do original material, and material that's indigenous to Canada, with local people, then you give up money.

"You're constantly choosing content over money. If I choose to work with Bruce Sweeney I may lose a week on *The X-Files*. You lose a week on *The X-Files* that's going to support you for nine months but you're doing what you love. And it's not to say you can't do work you love when you're working for the Americans or on a television series but you've got to know from the very beginning that you're not featured. I mean, those are lucky breaks and they really live in the realm of economics, you know, they have nothing to do with art.

"If someone calls you because, you know, they want you to play Donna Mills' best friend in a movie of the week and you're working on something you love, you're faced with a choice that I think is really unique to our situation here. Am I going to go work for the Americans as an anonymous person or maybe even with a crumb of a promise something else may happen from this? There's always that little possibility – something else may come from this. Oh, someone's going to see you playing Donna Mills' best friend and really going to want you, you know. Whoever's best friend you're playing it's always: 'I'm worried about you, Rachel . . . I'm worried about you,

Leaving Normal (Ben Ratner), *Dudley Do-Right* (Jennifer Clement), *Cousins* (Anthony Holland), *Happy Gilmore* (Kim Restell), *Prozac Nation* (Frida Betrani), *Look Who's Talking Too* (Suzy Joachim), *Look Who's Talking Now* (Gina Chiarelli), *Friday the 13th – Part VIII* (Martin Cummins), *Life or Something Like It* (Veena Sood), *Mission to Mars* (Jill Teed), *Crooked Hearts* (Vincent Gale), *Best in Show* (Colin Cunningham), *Bird on a Wire* (John Pyper-Ferguson), *Little Women* (Jay Brazeau), *Snow Falling on Cedars* (Tom Scholte).

Katherine . . . I'm worried about you, Margaret.'"

Vancouver actors, directors, and crews are increasingly willing to choose the domestic route. Says Sweeney: "The idea that you can have filmmakers who live and work in Vancouver and shoot their films in Vancouver and have Canadian themes or at least Canadian settings is, I think, quite a fantastic thing."

Stopkewich adds: "I want to shoot at home because I want to hire my friends, bring some money back into the community at an indigenous film level. I love the idea of making a Canadian film with Canadian actors."

§

This is not a state of affairs entirely lost on the more attuned Americans who work in Vancouver. The differences between Canadian indies and U.S. studios reflects a similar internal Hollywood conflict and, like Mike White, many of the actors who come to Vancouver for service-industry jobs also work in American independents.

Something about Parker Posey makes it difficult for her to even audition for studio schlock. "When I auditioned for *Speed*, I had a paper plate and pretended it was a steering wheel for the boat, you know, and I think the director saw that as me being kind of defiant. 'What are you going to do?' I was just trying to have fun, you know. Looking back on it I think, god, what's the big deal?"

Posey, who's appeared in a slew of indie films such as *The House of Yes* and *Party Girl*, shot a Universal Pictures feature, *Josie and the Pussycats*, in Vancouver. But Posey wasn't spending time fantasizing about the studio movie's potential box-office numbers. "I don't care. I really don't. I'm not in marketing," she said during the shoot. "But it's interesting that there's fifteen-year-old kids who know how much money a movie makes – it's on the news. It's really kind of scary. They're more interested in that than the actual movie."

Another American actor, Jennifer Beals, had a hit, *Flashdance*, at a young age, but spurned L.A. offers, instead finishing her degree in American literature at Yale, then moving to Greenwich Village and acting in a string of independent films such as *In the Soup*. "I didn't enjoy being in L.A. It's a very lonely experience. And I wasn't reading a lot of scripts that I was excited about that were coming out of Hollywood, so

I thought, 'What's the point of being there?'" But she's also kept a foot in the mainstream industry, which brought her to Vancouver, where she met and married Canadian prop man Ken Dixon.

Beals is also interested in the Vancouver film scene and has made a point to see some of the movies. "No matter what city you're in or what film scene it is, it's nice to meet people who are fully committed to what they're doing. That's what's so exciting and invigorating. I have to say largely the films I've done in Vancouver are so forgettable. They're mostly American productions that are going up there to try to save money. I don't remember the first one."

She points out that the problems on service-industry shoots aren't always American versus Canadian. "What's really fascinating is that you'll get the American actor on the set and the first assistant director, who is Canadian, is being really nice and really helpful and very respectful. And then they'll call in the Canadian actors and they're treated like shit. The Canadian first AD is treating the Canadian actors like crap and treating the American actors like they're gods. Maybe they don't have the exact same billing that I do but this is your countryman who is excited to be on this film and talented and amazing and they're treated like they're nothing. I mean, it's just terrible. And that's not just on one movie. That's pretty much across the board when I've worked in Canada. Unless it's an all-Canadian production. It's like this weird little self-hatred moment that happens."

Beal's assessment is seconded by Canadian actor Jay Brazeau, who's seemingly appeared in every movie shot within a 100-mile radius of Vancouver, from Sweeney and Stopkewich's films to American features such as *Insomnia* and *Double Jeopardy*. "When I was doing *We're No Angels* – 'Mr De Niro's mat is wet!' Oh no, it's the end of the world. But, you know, we do that to ourselves. That's the worst thing of all. We treat ourselves like dirt," Brazeau says. "It's getting better as people know you, but I see it constantly. I don't know if they have to go to asshole school or what."

The U.S. work Beals has done outside the studio system has similarities with Vancouver independents. Beals could be describing *The Grocer's Wife* shoot, for instance, when she talks about *The Anniversary Party*, which was directed by her friends Jennifer Jason Leigh and Alan Cumming. "It was just such an amazing experience," Beals says. "Nobody had trailers. We all sat out on the lawn and hung out together at all hours, telling stories and jokes. You were always together. And before you knew it, we were all at Cannes. It was great."

Although innovative American filmmaking persists, the Coen brothers, David Lynch, John Sayles, Todd Haynes, Woody Allen, and Darren Arnonofsky are not the American directors who come to Vancouver. It's a service-industry town better known for its *Freddy Got*

Fingered or *3000 Miles to Graceland* than *Insomnia*, the 2002 suspense thriller (a remake of a Norwegian/ Sweden film) starring Al Pacino, Hilary Swank, and Robin Williams, directed by Christopher Nolan, and produced by Steven Soderbergh and George Clooney.

Despite the odds, there is the occasional exception (as Beals says: "Not every American film that's made in Vancouver is a piece of crap and not every Canadian film made in Canada is fantastic"), and *Insomnia* is one of the better U.S. films shot in Canada. That's because the filmmakers' main incentive in shooting in B.C. was the look of the film, not a cheap dollar or tax breaks. Nolan, who lives in Los Angeles, is acutely aware of the controversy back home over losing jobs to "runaway" Hollywood productions being drawn to Canada. "It kind of wasn't relevant to us, which was nice," Nolan says, "'because you don't get glaciers in L.A."

Insomnia is set in small-town Alaska, a look approximated by the town of Squamish and other B.C. locales. "I actually scouted Alaska," Nolan says. "I didn't feel that I was

ON LOCATION IN VANCOUVER

It was a dogumentary-day afternoon at Vancouver's Pacific Coliseum. The old hockey rink was filled with canines and trainers and a banner heralding the Mayflower Club Dog Show. Unlike a real dog show, however, there were also movie trailers and crew members and the Christopher Guest mockumentary ensemble.

That day, the coliseum was the setting for an American dog show. And *Dog Show* was the working title for the movie that would eventually be renamed *Best in Show*.

These days, the curious can see more of Vancouver just spending an evening watching service-industry fare on television than they could on a guided bus tour of the city. They could, for starters, see Lighthouse Park (*Wrongfully Accused*), the Vancouver Public Library (*The Sixth Day*), Gastown's Blood Alley (*Double Jeopardy*), city hall (*Underworld*), the Lions Gate Bridge (*Life or Something Like It*), UBC library (*Agent Cody Banks*), Granville Island market (*Cousins*), the Agrodome (*Rocky IV*), the Museum of Anthropology (*Intersection*), and Versatile Pacific Shipyards (*Another Stakeout*).

going to get as much on screen, not because of the cost of things but because having everybody at a remote location, you know, instead of having studio space. Vancouver's wonderful for this film because you've got great studio space within spitting distance of mountains and water and everything."

Nolan says the Oscar-winning cast fell into place once Pacino agreed to star. "Once Al signed on, the world opens up to you casting-wise because, frankly, he's an actor's actor that every actor wants to work with. So suddenly it's like, you know, 'What's your dream cast?'" Pacino says he wasn't aware of any issues about shooting in Canada. "I was unaware of the controversy," he says. "Of course, I'd like the shoot to come to my house. I'd like to shoot the picture there. But there is so much to say for going to the location. Every time I've been to Canada, you know, Toronto and in Vancouver, it's been swell, although I was popping down on the weekends all the time to see the babes [his newborn twins]."

At the time of *Insomnia*'s release, acting B.C. film commissioner Lindsay Allen suggested that in 2002 that Vancouver was attracting its share of quality films, noting *I Spy*, *X-Men 2*, *Dreamcatcher*, and *Santa Clause 2*. "It's financial, it's exchange rate . . . and we've got the locations, crews, talent here," he says, recalling that great directors such as Robert Altman have worked in Vancouver. "I'd love for him to come back here and do something like *Gosford Park*."

After a while, this stay-at-home tour of Vancouver could become disorienting because things are almost never what they appear to be. For instance, in a case of life imitating something, the Vancouver Art Gallery, which used to be a courthouse, plays a courthouse in movies (*The Accused*). There are Delta's Boundary Bay airport in a cameo as the Beirut airport in *Spy Game* and Richmond's Sand Dunes as Mars in *Mission to Mars*.

Other B.C. locales have portrayed slightly less far-flung places: a Washington town (Hope in *First Blood*), a Montana town (Gastown in *Legends of the Fall*), a Colorado town (North Vancouver's Edgemont Villiage in *Double Jeopardy*), a Michigan town (Prince George in *Reindeer Games*), and an Alaskan town (Squamish in *Insomnia*).

In perhaps the most elaborate shoot, an entire Depression-era U.S. town was constructed in Stave Lake for *We're No Angels*.

Then there are those surprising occasions when Vancouver is actually Vancouver and we catch sight of, say, George Segal climbing the rooftop of the Hotel Vancouver (*Russian Roulette*).

Altman, though, shot *Gosford Park* in England because it was set there, and he chose Vancouver for his early movies for more reasons than making a fast U.S. buck. It was a time when Canada's dollar didn't come cheap and there were no tax incentives. Altman's *That Cold Day in the Park* was shot in Vancouver largely because the city's look fit the film. It's an attitude echoed by Nolan: "We were looking for this type of scenery that we needed to get."

There has been the occasional good U.S. movie shot in Vancouver since Altman showed up, but the Coen brothers, John Sayles, and other great American filmmakers shoot their movies where the script takes them. So quality U.S. productions will remain an anomaly in B.C. but, thankfully, there will be an occasional Altman or Nolan, plus all those Canadian directors whose scripts bring them to Vancouver.

DREAMING IN THE RAIN

Martin Cummins knew he had to do more than bad TV. "*Poltergeist* made me crazy. After about six months on the show I was ready to snap," he says. "It was crap TV. But I knew why I was there."

Cummins had come home from L.A. with a plan but, still, getting up in the morning for an unfulfilling acting job had become increasingly difficult. "That gets tiring after a while. It takes a lot out of you. When I took *Poltergeist*, I made a promise to myself: 'Okay, if I'm going to take this job for money, I'm going to make a movie. (There were other things involved too; my son was going to be born and it took me home, back to Vancouver.) I'm going to save some money and I'm going to make a movie.' And that's what I did. Saved some money and I wrote the thing and I made a movie."

He started to regard the set of *Poltergeist* as a kind of film school. "We got all the toys from the Americans and I was able to learn." *We All Fall Down* is Cummins' semi-autobiographical story of a young actor coping with the death of his mother. Cummins assembled a crew from *Poltergeist*, and cast Barry Pepper, Nick Campbell, Francois Robertson, and Darcy Belsher. He knew Helen Shaver was looking for a reprieve from *Poltergeist* as much as he was. "I wanted to write something for Shaver that was going to be really different from what she had been doing on *Poltergeist* for so long and give her an opportunity to do something that was really out there and wacky. And so I gave it to her and she said, 'Well, this is great. Yes, I'll do it.' I did some more rewrites and talked with her about it and then she kicked money in, too."

Shaver would win a Genie Award for her performance as a Vancouver prostitute in *We All Fall Down*. Her choices, such as *Desert Hearts* (about a lesbian relationship) and *In Praise of Older Women* (censored in Ontario), have not been without controversy. "I love our humanity, I love our flaws," she says. "Like that woman in *We All Fall Down* – a broken mess of a woman, but she's whole. She's broken but

I just don't play her brokenness. I bring a whole person there so that you can't write her off, you have to be moved by her."

Cummins is developing another script, *Tie the Knot*, a black comedy set in Vancouver. "It takes place at the Broadway Rooms on Main and Broadway, and Acme Barbershop will be in it again, and the Main Street Gym. It takes place in that little corner right there. It's great to be able to do that, too, because I drive by there every day, so I can see my character walking out of the Broadway Rooms and going up the street and passing the bank, going by the Goh Ballet, smoking a cigarette, and going to the store. You know, I can see all that. That's my neighbourhood. It's so much less work for me. I already know it. I feel it."

The commitment of Cummins, Shaver, and the rest of the *We All Fall Down* ensemble is an indicator of the breadth of Vancouver's film scene. Similar autonomous productions are not uncommon in the city, arriving by hook or by crook or by Telefilm funding.

∫

In 2002, the service industry slumped, local actors' incomes fell thirty percent and there were unemployment levels of fifty percent in some film professions. A 2001 industry shutdown by producers fearful of an impending strike, along with a generally depressed economy and competition from other locales, had for the first time since 1998 resulted in

Martin Cummins. *photo by Les Bazso, courtesy* The Province

the industry spending less than $1 billion on productions. While costly features continued (*X-Men 2* in 2002, Will Smith's *I, Robot* and Ben Affleck's *Paycheck* set for 2003), there were fewer TV movies of the week, long a major component of the service industry. In response to the industry downturn, producers called on Vancouver unions to allow them to bring in an unlimited number of U.S. crew members, a move that would leave the industry so-called "Canadian" but with American workers. That wasn't accepted but a virtual wage freeze was. Meanwhile, Canadian service-industry representatives lobbied governments for even more tax breaks. In the 2003 federal budget, foreign producers' tax credits were increased (to sixteen percent from eleven percent of Canadian labour costs) while funding for Canadian TV production was reduced by twenty-five percent.

So, the service industry's same old questions ("Will the film industry survive? Are we giving enough to the American producers? Is the rain-infested sky falling?") seemed more real than ever, but in a way they actually mattered less than before. Now, when producers talk about the end of the industry in Vancouver, they are no longer talking about the end of filmmaking. The independent scene is developing a look of permanence.

By 2001, the U.S. magazine *Movie Maker* had named Vancouver the number one independent film scene in North America, edging out New York, L.A., and Toronto. "It's much bigger now. Everything has a curve to it. It's now in its early expansion growth," says Scott Smith. "As well as the established filmmakers making their third and fourth films, you have new filmmakers. Because of the successful indies that came out of here, you're getting Telefilm and B.C. Film taking risks on newer filmmakers, which is really cool. There's a whole other wave coming of work that we haven't seen yet."

Smith's *rollercoaster* was selected best feature at Austin's South by Southwest festival in 2000. Vancouver filmmaker Blaine Thurier's *Low Self Esteem Girl* won the award the following year. The core UBC group continues to produce outstanding work and they've been joined by directors from across the city and other parts of Canada, whose recent Vancouver releases or features in the works include: *Lunch with Charles* (Michael Turner), *Protection* (Bruce Spangler), *Red Deer* (Anthony Couture), *Mile Zero* (Andrew Currie), *Eve and the Fire Horse* (Julia Kwan), *The Delicate Art of Parking* (Trent Carlson), *Flower & Garnet* (Keith

Behrman), *When It Rains* (Claudia Morgado Escanilla), *On the Corner* (Nathaniel Geary), *Shanghai Follies* (Ann Marie Fleming), *Eighteen* (Richard Bell), *Walk Backwards* (Laurie Baranyay), *The Take Out Girl* (Allison Beda), *Emile* (Carl Bessai), *Various Positions* (Ori Kowarsky), *The Rhino Brothers* (Dwayne Beaver), *The Barber* (Michael Bafaro), *Desolation Sound* (Scott Weber), *The Burial Society* (Nicholas Racz), *Touched* (Mort Ransen), *tideline* (Katherine Surridge), *See Grace Fly* (Pete McCormack), *Late Night Sessions* (Josh Hamlin), *The Telescope* (Jessica Bradford), *Noroc* (Marc Retailleau), *My Father's Angel* (Davor Marjanovic), *Little War* (Damon Vignale), *Punch* (Guy Bennett), *Take Two* (Luke Carroll), and *A History of Forgetting* (Coreen Mayrs).

"We're just sort of playing hunches," says Tom Scholte. "Some guy's made a short film and he's got a feature and it's 'Okay, let's go.' Everyone's a pioneer at this point. There is no old guard to lean on. And a success for one of us is a success for all of us."

Actors such as Scholte, Martin Cummins, Jacqueline Samuda, Helen Shaver, Ben Ratner, and Bruce Greenwood are developing their own projects, too. "I'm also starting to produce stuff here," says Greenwood. "I've optioned *Stanley Park*, the novel written by Tim Taylor. It's a great novel. We're into the second draft of it now and hopefully be shooting if not this summer [2003], next summer. It's a whole lot easier to be a hired gun, just come in and do the acting. But I just loved the book and I just thought, 'Ah, what the hell, see what happens.'"

Bruce Sweeney's next film, *American Venus*, is about the actors who, at the start of the new century, see Vancouver as a place where dreams come true. "The funny thing about it is that these girls grew up in Surrey and then they've come to Vancouver," says Sweeney. "For them, making it is getting work on mows. They're not talking about features, they're not talking about being the next Meg Ryan. They're talking about working with Morgan Fairchild. Her agent asks the new girl from America, 'Why did you come here? Why not L.A.?' And she says, 'Well, I like it here and I wanted to start small.'"

Sweeney and friends could be characters in *American Venus* because, more than they might realize, they have given actors and other dreamers new reasons to come to Vancouver. "Every Vancouver actor's dream is to be in a Bruce Sweeney or Lynne Stopkewich movie," notes Christine Chatelain, a young actor who has appeared in TV and movies such as *3000 Miles to Graceland*.

Chris Haddock's *Da Vinci's Inquest* changed the city in a more direct way in 2002. The series was popular enough to catapult Larry Campbell, the real coroner the character Dominic Da Vinci is based on, to the Vancouver mayoralty, leading the civic left, the Committee of Progressive Electors, to its first electoral sweep. "It's like Martin Sheen running for president," complained losing-candidate Jennifer Clarke.

§

Despite its breakthroughs, Vancouver independent film is still a struggling, fledgling scene. There is talk of directors forming a "united artists" western-based distribution company. In the meantime, Josh Hamlin and Scott Smith used old-fashioned punk do-it-yourself ingenuity when they couldn't find distributors for their films. "I'm kind of mixed about the whole thing," said Smith, after renting theatres, booking ads, and assembling press kits for *rollercoaster.*" We went up on the second weekend – our Saturday and Sunday numbers went up but then Schwarzenegger and *Rugrats* came in." Distribution difficulties are not unique to Vancouver. Despite new, inexpensive digital equipment and 2002 indie hits such as *My Big Fat Greek Wedding* and *Monsoon Wedding*, American independent film companies are shutting down or being bought out by conglomerates. *The Hollywood Reporter* estimated that less than four percent of the 2002 U.S. box office would be derived from independent film, with access to theatres so difficult that even U.S. films that draw raves at Sundance are having difficulty finding that elusive American distribution.

Still, Vancouver is breaking out to find links with independents in eastern Canada. Actors such as Cummins, Ratner, Marya Delver, and Babz Chula work east and west. Directors Smith, Anne Wheeler, and Lynne Stopkewich work across Canada. Stopkewich, Keith Behrman, and Toronto filmmakers direct episodes of *Da Vinci's Inquest*, while series creator Chris Haddock prepares to direct an indie feature (*Run Man Run*) in Toronto or Montreal. Vancouver filmmakers (Smith, Mina Shum) have studied at Toronto's Canadian Film Centre, while Torontonians study at the Vancouver Film School. The Vancouver and Toronto film festivals continue to feature each other's film scenes.

There is also an emerging cross-fertilization between the local scene and independent Americans. Molly Parker works east, west, north, and south. Elizabeth Berkley appears with Chula, Jay Brazeau, and other Vancouver indie stalwarts in *Moving Malcolm*, a movie directed by and costarring Ratner. Vancouver actors Frank and John Cassini wrote and appeared in *Break a Leg*, an indie shot in L.A. with a cast of Americans (Jennifer Beals, Eric Roberts) and Canadians (Parker, the Cassinis, Eric McCormack, Sandra Oh).

Hilary Swank's husband Chad Lowe, an aspiring director-writer, started work on *The Space Between*, a short aimed at the festival circuit, while Swank was shooting the sci-fi thriller *The Core* in Vancouver. "He was there and he was saying that he was really wanting to direct something," Swank says. "And I really obviously am supportive of that because Chad's a really enormously talented writer and I said, 'Okay, great, well, write it here and film it here.' I mean, there's an amazing array of talent up here and crews and everything. So he wrote it and we just filmed it up there."

Swank spends a lot of time in Vancouver – seven months of 2001 shooting *The Space Between* and the features *Insomnia* and *The Core*. And that isn't her only connection to Vancouver. Swank, who won an Oscar for *Boys Don't Cry*, grew up in Vancouver's favourite day trip – Bellingham, Washington – venturing north for everything from daycare field trips to teenage drinking excursions. To cast *The Space Between*, Lowe plugged into the local scene and found Ian Tracey, who plays a cop, and Vincent Gale, who plays Swank's husband. "He [Chad] had a casting director and they came in and they met with him and he came home and said, 'I found these great actors. They've done some amazing work,'" says Swank. "Working with him [Gale] was spectacular – very giving. I mean, I only worked a day on the movie, so that little amount of time that I had with him was wonderful."

Gale was just as impressed with Swank and Lowe. "I found both of them real down to earth. No pretension. I would draw the analogy between Bruce Sweeney and Tom Scholte and Ben Ratner and Nancy Sivak. They just instantly put you at ease the way those guys do. It was made instantly comfortable. And beyond that – Chad wrote a great little script."

Vancouver's current film scene isn't only linked with other places, it's also connected to its own past. Patricia Gage, who starred in Larry Kent's *When Tomorrow Dies*, was Molly Parker's mother-in-law thirty-five years later in the American independent film *Waking the Dead*.

Morrie Ruvinsky, Jack Darcus, and Sandy Wilson have projects they'd like to shoot in B.C. "It's tough making movies," Wilson says. "I keep thinking, 'Oh, god, do I have the energy to fight and fight and fight and fight?' But, you know, I've got another idea now and I'm mad keen to do it." Kent is planning to return to B.C. to shoot the feature *Hamster Cage*, with a cast that crosses the generations of Vancouver indie actors, possibly including Alan Scarfe and Tom Scholte. And in February 2003, when Kent was in town for his Pacific Cinémathèque retrospective, Sweeney took him out for sushi.

Carol Pastinsky, who costarred in the second independent film shot in Vancouver, Kent's *Sweet Substitute*, lives with her husband Harvey McCracken in Gibsons, B.C., where they make a point of ordering Canadian movies at the local video outlet. "We asked for *Last Wedding*. Canadian movies are very important and I think they're good. And I really get annoyed that people don't recognize that more. I loved *Last Wedding*. It was witty and it was very cutting but it was not hitting you in the face. We loved *Kissed*. It had a certain edge to it that I found unexpected. And I also thought it was audacious. I thought *Suspicious River* was an even better film. For me, anyway, I thought she had evolved somewhat and the feminist thing just talked to me, from my point of view. Also there was a stillness in that film that you don't find very often in films. And then you listen. I really liked it."

So, it comes full circle, from Kent and Darcus to Sweeney and Stopkewich, Patricia Gage to Molly Parker, Carol Pastinsky to Tom Scholte. They and their friends have blazed a singularly uncompromising, veracious Vancouver film legacy. A Vancouver director, an activist in younger days, told me, "A filmmaker isn't going to change the world." But a movie might change one person's world and, collectively, the movies and other art of the past century have changed how much of the world sees race, sexuality, gender. And it needn't be a Norma Rae clenched first. It could be a Margaret Laurence novel or a Leonard Cohen verse or an Atom Egoyan or Bruce Sweeney movie. Each envelope-pushing piece makes its contribution to this process and the filmmakers in Vancouver have done more than their share.

It comes down to creating a moment of truthfulness that an audience immediately recognizes. You could be switching channels and come upon an Astaire dance that you know is coming from his soul. That honesty is becoming increasingly rare in movies as the risk-free studio system, fawning film critics, and mega-mass marketing combine to dominate screens with cynical, exploitive product.

§

Like many Vancouver filmmakers, Ross Weber isn't one to dwell on being Canadian but it keeps coming up. "I don't even think about it. I'm just trying to make a good movie. I'm into truth in cinema, so I'm not going to try and make Vancouver look like something else. It's important that you know the stories that are indigenous to your place. You've got to do that. Otherwise, it's not going to be truthful in any way. But I don't have any special idea about being a Canadian filmmaker or anything. I mean, *whatever*. This is where I live, this is where I'm going to make movies. I'm not a nationalist in any sense of the word."

Still, there is a film community in this place where Weber lives and it's caused him to wonder about some things. "There hasn't really been a big world hit from Canada. There hasn't been a Canadian film that's basically just put this country on the map. I'm kind of waiting for that. What would be that movie? What would it be about? Who would do that? What is our identity? I don't think anybody's really found it. We're a whole pile of different little countries all kind of strung together. You got this kind of west coast scene, you got the Toronto scene, you got the Halifax thing – they make kind of different movies – you've got Quebec. What would break this country right out? I don't know what it is."

The service film industry can produce product but it can never have the instantly recognized honesty of a Dylan lyric or a Brando mumble because it is detached from the place of production. The Italian film industry is organic to Italy, as is France's or England's or India's. The American industry is organic to Hollywood. That's it's natural home, where its actors, crews, directors, and writers live. Fishing, logging, and Canadian filmmaking are natural to B.C. Just as Hollywood's great movies were mostly about Americans, the great movies that come from Canada will be about Canadians.

At the start of the twenty-first century, Vancouver is still watching itself reflected on screen. Only now, it isn't just watching itself through somebody else's lives in *The Grapes of Wrath* and *Rebel Without a Cause*. It is also watching itself in *Double Happiness* and *Last Wedding*.

INDEX

*Dreaming
in the Rain*

David Spaner is a film critic for *The Province* newspaper in Vancouver. A graduate of Simon Fraser University and Langara College, he has worked as a reporter, editor, and feature writer for numerous publications. Born in North York, Ontario, David grew up in Vancouver.